The Internet for the Older and Wiser

About U3A

Most of us, in our working lives, have spent plenty of time learning the things that our employers need us to know. Now we want to learn for its own sake; for the pleasure of finding things out. The autonomous Universities of the Third Age, run as educational co-operatives by third agers, exist throughout the UK to provide for older men and women the opportunity to share their knowledge of and an enthusiasm for a wide range of learning pursuits.

Third Age Trust, which is the national representative body for the U3A movement in the UK, underpins the work of U3As through the provision of comprehensive educational and administrative support.

The Internet for the Older and Wiser

Get Up and Running Safely on the Web

Adrian Arnold

A John Wiley and Sons, Ltd., Publication

British Library Cataloguing in Publication Data

A catalogue record for this book is available from the British Library

ISBN 978-0-470-74839-8

Typeset in 11/13 Zapf Humanist 601 BT by Laserwords Private Limited, Chennai, India
Printed in China by SNP Leefung Printers Ltd

Dedication

For Kimbo, Tallymora, Hame – and Pophles

Contents

Contents

Acknowledgements

This book would never have been published were it not for the stimulation, support and encouragement I have received from many people but three stand out in my mind.

The stimulation came from Stuart Bark who persuaded me to take up the teaching of computing in the first place. The support came in unlimited supply from Colleen Goldring and her team at Wiley's while my wife, Jen, kept me going with her unfailing encouragement throughout the difficult times. My sincere thanks go to you all.

About the Author

Adrian Arnold qualified as a veterinary surgeon from Cambridge University in 1964. Having served as an assistant in general practices in Dunstable and Woking he set up his own veterinary practice in Crawley in 1968. Having created a four-man, two-centre practice the family decided to move to Colchester in Essex where he set up another new practice in 1987. Throughout this time he became a freelance journalist writing for both the local and veterinary press. In 1989 he became one of the first vets in the country to computerise his veterinary records and computing has remained a hobby ever since.

His other hobbies included light aircraft flying, digital photography, reading and travelling to meet friends and relatives in Europe, America, Africa and Asia.

Adrian and his wife, Jen, who still sits as a magistrate, have three children and four grandchildren while they enjoy his retirement in a small village in the Stour Valley.

Publisher's Acknowledgements

Some of the people who helped bring this book to market include the following:

Editorial & Production
VP Consumer and Technology Publishing Director: Michelle Leete
Associate Director – Book Content Management: Martin Tribe
Associate Publisher: Chris Webb
Executive Commissioning Editor: Birgit Gruber
Assistant Editor: Colleen Goldring
Editorial Assistant: Ellie Scott
Content Editor: Claire Spinks
Copy Editor: Martin Noble

Marketing
Senior Marketing Manager: Louise Breinholt
Marketing Executive: Chloe Tunnicliffe

Composition Services
Compositor: Laserwords Private Limited
Proof Reader: Lynette James
Indexer: Geraldine Begley

Icons used in this Book

Throughout the book you will notice symbolic images. These have been introduced to help focus your attention on certain information and are summarised as follows:

Tip	Tips and suggestions to help make life easier.	
Note	Take note of these little extras to avoid confusion.	
Warning	Read carefully, a few things could go wrong at this point.	
Try It	Go on enjoy yourself, you won't break it.	
Trivia	A little bit of fun to bring a smile to your face.	
Summary	Recap at the end of each chapter with the short summary.	
Brain Training	Brain training, test out your memory.	

PRACTICE MAKES
PERFECT

To build upon the lessons learnt in this book, visit www.pcwisdom.co.uk

- **More training tutorials**

- **Links to resources**

- **Advice through frequently asked questions**

- **Social networking tips**

- **Videos and podcasts from the author**

- **Author blogs**

Introduction

Equipment needed: a computer; Internet Explorer program and a connection to the Internet.

Skills needed: some knowledge of the keyboard and mouse.

This book is for those people who have started their computing career but have become becalmed in the waters of the Internet. A certain amount of basic computing knowledge would be very useful if you are to get the full benefit of this book. The first book – *Computing for the Older and Wiser* – was targeted at beginners while this book tends to assume some previous knowledge, even if it is limited.

During my years of teaching people to use their home computers I have found that, after the first few lessons, they are quite happy to experiment with their new-found knowledge but come back to me after a few months with questions about more advanced topics. This book hopes to answer some of those questions. It is like letting a person into a field and allowing them to explore the wildlife but, after a while, they begin to look over the hedges and see further possibilities lying in adjacent fields but find that the gates are locked. This book provides the keys to some of those gates.

I have based all my teaching on the PC machine using either Windows XP or Windows Vista Home Edition and the basic Windows programs such as Internet Explorer, Windows Mail and Outlook Express. The reason for this is that these programs are available to every owner of a PC computer. That is not to say that they are necessarily the very best programs for the job; in fact, there are better programs mentioned in the book which will have to be installed on your computer. You will learn how to achieve such results in the earlier chapters. For instance, you may find that you enjoy surfing the Internet using an alternative web browser to Internet Explorer such as Firefox, Safari or Google's latest project, the Chrome browser. Apple Mac users may find some useful information within these pages, but the book is not really designed for those computer users.

The book follows a similar pattern to that of the first one in that the early chapters lead the reader through the complications of filling in registration forms and downloading programs in considerable detail. The later chapters assume that these lessons have been taken on board and therefore there is less need for detailed instruction. Most chapters also provide revision sections in the shape of brain-training for those subjects which are essential if you are to get the most out of your computer. There is little point in trying to set up an online banking account if you are unsure of how to search for your bank's website using a search engine.

> This is not to say that you have to follow the chapters one by one. If you see something later in the book that appeals to you, feel free to explore, but bear in mind that I will have assumed some previous knowledge gained from the earlier chapters.

Not all the chapters will appeal to everyone so just choose those that are of interest to you. You may have developed a burning desire to explore your family tree, in which case you will find valuable advice in Chapter 18 while the contents of Chapter 16 on Social Networking may hold no attraction for you whatsoever.

There are hints and tips littered throughout the book to make your computing experience more enjoyable and efficient, but there will be times when you find yourself completely stuck. Don't worry. I am always on the end of an email at **bu33kin@tiscali.co.uk**, or alternatively you can contact me through the 'Ask a Question' function on the website **www.pcwisdom.co.uk**.

> If I have one piece of advice that runs throughout the book it would be 'give it a go.' The sky will not fall in if you make a mess of creating a family video or listen to the wrong radio programme on your computer.

This book is about the acquisition of knowledge, but the margin notes of trivia need not be remembered. They are placed there to bring a smile to your face while you are working your way through the book. Computing should be fun and not a chore. Enjoy yourself!

PART I
Using your Internet tools

Colin takes the threat of computer viruses very seriously...

Getting started

Equipment needed: a computer; Internet Explorer program; connection to the Internet. (A guardian angel would be helpful too.)

Skills needed: some knowledge of the keyboard and mouse.

So you have been presented with this electronic box of wizardry, and you are wondering how on earth to get it to do something useful. Where do you start? Before we begin to make a computerised telephone call, free of charge, to your cousin in Azerbaijan or book a supermarket delivery to your home, it would seem to be a good idea to get the hang of the basic use of the Internet on your new computer.

The theory is quite simple. You connect the computer to the vast net of worldwide communications via the telephone. This is the Internet. The World Wide Web – or Web for short – is the information found at the end of these communication networks. To make this connection you need to start a program called an Internet browser which has been programmed to 'talk' on the telephone. Most of the Internet is free to use but there is no such thing as a free lunch and there are some payments to be made up front.

Internet Service Providers (ISPs)

Before you can connect to the Internet there are one or two things you will have to do to setup the connection between your computer and the outside world. The first of these is to subscribe to an Internet Service Provider known as an ISP.

This is like a telephone service for which you have to pay a line rental – although you can combine this fee with your normal telephone charges, mobile phone and even your television services.

There are hundreds if not thousands of ISPs vying for your custom. You may have seen some of their TV adverts, without understanding a word of what they are offering. Personally I would recommend using one of the national providers rather than a local company which, while providing you with better support (sometimes), often do not have the line capacity to cope with the demand of an increasing number of users. Some of the better known and more reliable national service providers include BT Internet, Pipex, Tiscali, Virgin Media, O2, Orange and TalkTalk, but there are many more.

These companies not only provide access to the Internet but telephone, mobile and cable television services so there is every chance of your being able to pick up a package deal that will reduce your communications budget even before you opted for an Internet service (see Chapter 11).

The real problem is how to choose between these companies' offerings. If you are just launching yourself into the world of Internet communication then I would suggest you have a chat with friends and neighbours who have already signed up for the revolution. This is where your 'guardian angel' will prove invaluable. Check out my notes on such people later in this chapter.

Make sure that you read the small print carefully. The cheaper subscription rates may impose a limit on the amount of material you can download each month and may commit you to a yearly contract. In your early web-surfing days you will probably not use a lot of your allotted download limit but once you start downloading large computer programs from the Web it can quickly mount up.

Connection types

The first – and slowest – form of computer communication is known as a 'dial-up' connection and, although this is still the only available means of communication in the wilder parts of the country, the most common, and much faster method is called broadband. To give you some sort of idea of the difference between the two we might say that the highest speed you are likely to get on dial-up is 40 mph whereas, with a broadband cable connection, you can accelerate to 8,000 mph! The advantages of such speed will become apparent as we progress through the book. A realistic figure should be around the equivalent of 2,000 mph. Unfortunately I live in a rural area and the best speed I can get is the equivalent of 600 mph but even that is far better than the 40 mph dial-up connection and I can live with that.

Connection to the telephone system also comes in two different flavours – wired and wireless. The latter has the advantage of reducing the size of the snake's nest of cables waiting to trip you up; you can use your computer in different parts of the house depending on your mood and the layout of your home or take it to a friend's house to show them your latest family snaps (ask for your guardian angel's help to connect to your friend's wireless connection). You can even connect wirelessly to a keyboard, printer or a mouse if you want to reduce the number of cables still further.

There are two basic types of wireless connection – WiFi and Bluetooth. WiFi is used to connect the computer to the router that receives the signals over the telephone system and transmits these signals in computer-friendly form to the computer itself. These are strong wireless signals and have a range of up to 100 metres unless there are a number of very thick brick walls in the way, in which case you will need a more powerful router and an aerial extension to overcome these obstacles.

Bluetooth emits a weaker signal and is used to connect compatible devices over a short distance such as keyboard to computer or mobile phone to headpiece.

Your guardian angel

If the family do not live locally there will be several friends and neighbours who are sufficiently computer-literate to wire up the machine, get you registered with an Internet Service Provider, set up your email system and get you logged on to the Internet. The whole process of unpacking the computer, connecting the various cables, calibrating the monitor, setting up the Internet Service Provider's system together with an email address of your choosing should take no longer than an hour and a half. While you are unlikely to understand exactly what your 'angel' is doing for most of this time, your presence will be needed when you have to decide on a memorable email address, username and password. You will also need to have your credit card handy when setting up your ISP account.

I introduced this concept of a guardian angel in my original book, *Computing for the Older and Wiser*, but it will bear repetition here. When you buy a car you would not expect to have to service the vehicle and prepare it for the road once you had handed over the money. In the same way I do not expect you to wire up your computer and test all the various connections. You are no more a computer engineer than a car mechanic but there are plenty of competent people out there who would be only too happy to do it for you. These are your 'guardian angels'. Some are professionals, like the shop you bought the computer from, but others are happy to get you going for the price of a couple of hours' babysitting or a modest bottle of wine. Your first port of call should be your family – daughters and sons-in-law are usually very keen to get the older members of the family into the computing way of life and are only too happy to set the computer up for you.

A gentle word of warning here. Once your kind angel has got the computer all set up, working and connected to the Internet, try to avoid calling them every other day to solve a minor problem. That is what this book is for.

Broadband and dial-up connections

Your angel will have set you up with a telephone connection – either dial-up or broadband – so that you can access the Internet as well as an email address. If you are in a rural area your only option for Internet access may be a dial-up connection for which you will be charged by the minute for the time you remain connected to the Internet. These charges can quickly mount up, so be sure to disconnect from your connection whenever you are not actively using the Internet facilities. Emails can be composed while 'offline' – or disconnected – and then sent in a few seconds once you have reconnected. This is all rather tedious compared to broadband where you remain connected the whole time without incurring any additional charges. You simply pay a monthly connection fee.

Broadband connections are infinitely faster than those using dial-up so, if you have the option, I would recommend that you always choose the broadband option.

You will have seen plenty of advertisements on TV and the papers offering broadband speeds of up to eight megabits per second but I would suggest that you take these with a large pinch of salt. The speed of your connection has far less to do with the company offering you the service than the length of copper wire than lies between your home and the local telephone exchange. If you live more than five kilometres away from the exchange, no amount of tweaking by the Internet Service Provider (ISP) will get you more than one megabit per second and often less than this. The quality of the wired connection will also have an impact on your reception speeds as well. The broadband signal is very sensitive to breaks in the line such as extension cables running from your telephone point to the computer.

The most important characteristic of your ISP is the quality of their support service. Many of these service providers will reply to any query you might have by email within 24 hours but others will leave you hanging on the phone for ages while the premium call number ratchets up your telephone bill. Take advice from computer users in your local area regarding the kind of support they get when they need it.

Rural areas are particularly prone to slow connection speeds while those city dwellers that have access to cable connections to their TV will enjoy blisteringly fast communications.

If you want to check your Internet connection speed go to **www.speedtest.net**. This is a free service that will test both the upload and download speeds of your own computer connection. Download speeds are always considerably faster than upload connections. But we are getting ahead of ourselves and we have to decide which type of computer is best for you.

Laptop or desktop computer

If you are only 'thinking of getting a computer' you might like to consider the advantages and disadvantages of the two basic types of computer – the desktop and the laptop. Put quite simply, the desktop machine takes up more space with its separate computer case, screen, keyboard and mouse, but is usually much cheaper than the laptop. The laptop is an integrated computer that you can easily move around the house, has a built-in keyboard and does not need a mouse. Unfortunately, any laptop with a screen larger than 16 inches will cost you a lot more than the equivalent desktop. Laptop batteries may well limit the length of time you can spend on the machine before it needs re-charging. On the other hand they can be used quite happily while connected to the mains supply.

I am often asked about the relative advantages of the two basic types of computer – desktop or laptop – so I will try and list these here.

Reproduced from Google™

Figure 2.1   **Figure 2.2**

Desktop

These are largely immobile units with separate screens, keyboards, mice and computer cases which take up more space than the equivalent laptop (see Figure 2.1). Downsizing our living accommodation as we get older often means that a desktop machine takes up a lot of valuable space which we can ill afford. There is also the problem of the number of cables connecting the various parts of the computer.

On the other hand you will get more value for your money by opting for a desktop computer with a large screen. A good second-hand machine will cost you very little and will fulfil all your computing needs for the next few years. You do not have to worry about continually recharging a battery which can be a nuisance when using a laptop.

Laptop

These are very often the obvious choice of the older computer user (see Figure 2.2), largely for the reasons of space mentioned above, but they are not the answer to every problem. Yes, you can lounge on your sofa and tap away on the keyboard to your heart's content, but sooner or later you are going to want to connect the machine to a large printer to get hard copy of Gordon Ramsey's latest recipe. Laptop batteries are improving every year but, at the moment, even the very best batteries only last about six hours before needing a recharge.

Most laptops are equipped with a 15.4 inch screen which makes reading the text something of a strain so I personally would recommend a 17 inch screen to spare the eyes. Finally there is the question of the mouse pointer control. On a laptop this is achieved by using a trackpad (or touchpad) integrated into the keyboard. By stroking a finger across this trackpad the pointer is made to move at your command. Many of these trackpads are very sensitive indeed, especially when they incorporate a scrolling facility, and the majority of my pupils find it easier to use a mouse with their laptop which detracts somewhat from their portability. These mice can be wireless which obviates the difficulties of a stray cable waiting to trip you up when you go to answer the door.

A byte, in computer terms, means eight bits. A nibble is half that: four bits. Two nibbles make a byte!

Battery life is a permanently contentious issue when using laptops. Battery technology is advancing rapidly year by year but the demands of the computer are increasing at a similar rate and, at the moment, the two tend to cancel each other out. Laptops can get very power hungry if you begin to push their limits so a few words of advice here will help you extend the life of your battery between charges.

- Playing CDs and DVDs will drain a laptop battery just like removing a plug from a bath.

- The brightness of the screen also makes high demands on the power supply so try turning it down a bit – but don't ruin your eyes.

- Programs running in the background like the wireless router, desktop search and music libraries can be switched off to conserve power.

- Switch the computer off if you are not going to use it for the next hour or so.

- Do not use the computer on mains power all the time. The battery needs exercise to keep fit.

- Learn to put the computer into Hibernate mode rather than Standby as this will use only minimal power. Many laptop keyboards have a Hibernate key.

- Multi-tasking or using many different programs at the same time will strain the battery resources.

- If you find that you need to use several programs at the same time, consider increasing the computer's memory by getting your supplier to install more RAM (Random Access Memory). This reduces the need to spin the hard disk to get the information required.

- Laptops operate much more efficiently when cool so keep the air vents clear of dust. Don't forget that the ventilation of most laptops is through the base of the machine so supporting the computer on a cushion on your lap will effectively seal off the air flow and, once the computer chip overheats, it will shut itself down. This can be very frustrating if you are halfway through searching for that tempting recipe featured on Nigella Lawson's latest television series.

All of this sounds as if laptops have limited use and this is certainly not the case. A small saloon car still has a multitude of uses but there are times when a larger vehicle is needed to carry bulky loads.

So what is my final word of advice? If you are limited by living space then opt for a laptop with a reasonable screen size – 15.4 inches at least – but if you have the luxury of a study or small unused bedroom then a desktop machine will go on performing all your present and future needs, day in, day out.

Now that we have got everything up and running, we can start to put the computer through its paces in the next chapter.

Computing courses

While your guardian angel may be kind enough to set up your computer, please do not try and take advantage of his or her generosity by asking for a full computing course. Many Age Concern branches offer free computing lessons so check out your local branch while you are getting advice on your home heating benefits. The University of the Third Age (U3A) has computing groups across the country that are designed to help computing beginners. Check out your local branch at **www.u3a.org.uk**.

Summary

- You will need an account with an Internet Service Provider
- You will benefit from a broadband connection
- A laptop takes up less room but needs a good battery
- A desktop machine needs more space but is generally cheaper
- Make friends with your guardian angel

Brain Training

There may be more than one correct answer to these questions.

1. What is an ISP?

☐ a) An Internal Service Port ☐ b) An Internet Service Provider

☐ c) An Idiots Page ☐ d) An Internet Subscription Plan

2. What does broadband mean?

☐ a) A wide elastic band ☐ b) A modem

☐ c) A fast Internet connection ☐ d) Another term for a dial-up connection

3. Why is a laptop better than a desktop machine?

☐ a) It takes up less space ☐ b) There are fewer wires to trip over

☐ c) It makes web surfing faster ☐ d) It is cheaper

4. What does 'being offline' mean?

☐ a) You are not connected to the Internet ☐ b) You don't understand the question

☐ c) Your mouse has come off its tracks ☐ d) Your credit card details have been rejected

5. Why is a desktop better than a laptop?

☐ a) It is a faster machine ☐ b) It is cheaper

☐ c) You can use it as a telephone ☐ d) It is less prone to overheating

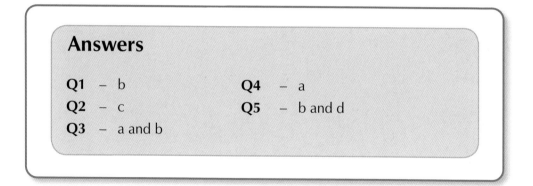

Answers

Q1 – b

Q2 – c

Q3 – a and b

Q4 – a

Q5 – b and d

Browsing the Internet

3

Equipment needed: a computer; Internet Explorer program; connection to the Internet and a printer.

Skills needed: some knowledge of the keyboard and mouse.

Now that we have got the computer set up it is time to start using it to surf the Web. This is a particularly apt cliché as there are times when you will feel as though you are riding a rollercoaster with all the thrills and anxieties of challenging a mountainous wave to carry you forward. As with all new skills, it takes practice before you gain the confidence to push your abilities to the next level – so let us start in the shallows before venturing into deeper water.

The first step is to get to know the Internet browser program. This is your connection to the Internet world and so it is worthwhile taking a little time getting to know the mechanics – rather like exploring the dashboard and controls of a car when you first learn to drive. Every PC computer fitted with a Windows operating system will have the Internet Explorer web browser installed automatically.

Figure 3.1

Find the Internet Explorer program by clicking on the Start button and then the Internet Explorer button or, if the Internet Explorer icon is shown on your desktop, double click on it. Now wait: it can take a number of seconds before the computer opens up the program and makes the necessary connection to the telephone network.

The latest version of the program is Version 8 but these instructions will work perfectly well with its older brother Internet Explorer 7.

The first page to be displayed when you open up Internet Explorer is known as the Home page. This has been set up by your Internet Service Provider (ISP) to display their own page in an attempt to persuade you to buy more of their products. Depending upon the ISP some of these pages are more useful than others but, for this exercise, I want you to ignore the page content and concentrate on the elements of the browser window.

Take a look at the following image and try to familiarise yourself with its structure which is very similar to other windows that you may have been using for word processing or sending an email message. In spite of its vague familiarity you will notice a number of facilities specific to Internet Explorer which we will deal with below.

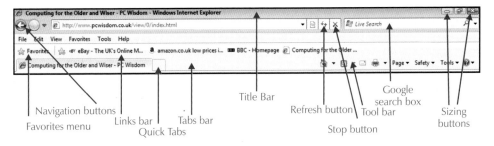

Figure 3.2

At the very top we find the Title bar which displays the name of the website. The sizing buttons lie at the right hand end of this bar. Below the title bar there are the Back and Forward navigating icons together with the Navigation History button, the Address bar and the Search Box. The next line contains the Menu bar and below this lies the Links bar which has been set up automatically by the Internet Explorer program. We will learn how to customise these links to your own requirements later in this chapter. The last line offers access to the Favorites menu, the open Tabs and Tool bar. Let us deal with these options individually.

If you do not see some of these toolbars then they have probably not been activated. Go to View on the Menu bar and choose Toolbars. Tick on the ones that are unselected and they will become available for use.

If these various toolbars and menus restrict your view of the main web page you can hide them by pressing the F11 key on the keyboard. This will remove most of the clutter leaving only the navigation buttons. To restore the view of the toolbars just press F11 again.

Title bar

This is the very top line of the browser window and displays the name of the web page being viewed. At the right hand end of this bar are the sizing buttons which allow you to minimise, maximise and close the window.

Navigation buttons

 These lie at the left hand end of the next line in front of the address box.

Figure 3.3

They allow you to move back and forth between your browsed pages of the Internet. To the right of these two buttons lies a small blue arrowhead – the Navigation History button. This will drop down a list of all the pages you have visited during your current session on this tab.

Address bar

This is where you type in the web address of the page you wish to visit. Having entered the address hit the Enter key or click on the Go button.

Refresh and Stop buttons

 Web pages are updated very frequently, especially news pages, and by selecting the Refresh icon (the two arrows) you will be certain of getting the very latest version of the page. Sometimes a page takes a very long time to load, by which time you may have decided that it isn't worth the effort. Just click on the Stop button to halt the process.

Figure 3.4

Search box

This is a shortcut to a search engine – in this case, Google – where you can start exploring the Web. The subject of searching the Internet is a large one and is fully discussed in Chapter 4. Do not use this box to search within the page on your screen. Use the Ctrl+F method described later in the chapter for this.

The Menu bar

Many of the menus offered by this bar will have become familiar to you from your earlier computing experience such as word processing and email programs. The only difference is that this one is specific to the web browser. Many of the commands available from the Menu bar are available as Tools or other icons on the various bars.

Click on a few of the menu options and see what happens when you activate them. The sky will not fall down if you make a mistake and, by practising, you will increase your knowledge enormously. If anything goes really badly wrong you can always shut the program down, make yourself a cup of tea and try again later. You are not going to bring down a Government website by clicking on these options.

The Links bar

This bar should not be confused with the *hyperlinks*, also known as 'links', found on a web page. These buttons on the Links bar are entries to web pages that you use on a regular basis and obviate the need to type in their address every time you want to visit them. To add a website to the Links bar click on the Add to Favorites bar icon

The Favorites icon

Once you begin browsing the Web in earnest you will find this gold star icon becoming more and more valuable. The Favorites menu is where you store the addresses of all your interesting websites. Some of these websites may have impossibly long web addresses such as this one:

http://maps.yahoo.com/py/maps.py?Pyt=Tmap&addr=2801+Ocean+Park+Blvd&cit
y=Santa+Monica&state=CA&csz=Santa+Monica,+CA+90 405-5200&slt=34.018220&s
ln=-118.457158&name=&zip=90405-5200 &country=us&&BFKey=&BFCat=&BFClient=
&mag=6&desc=&cs=9&ne wmag=8&poititle=&poi=&ds=n

Instead of trying to remember this list of characters – in the correct order – you just click on the Favorites icon and, from the dropdown menu, choose Add to Favorites. We will practise this later in the chapter.

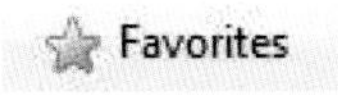

⭐ Favorites

The Tabs bar

This allows you to have several different pages open at the same time. There are a number of ways in which you can open a page in a new tab:

- Go the File menu and choose New Tab from the dropdown menu.
- Use Ctrl+T.
- Click the mouse wheel on a new link.
- Click on the blank tab at the end of the Tabs bar and enter a new web address.

⊞ ▾	🌐 Imagineus Computing	🅱🅱🅲 BBC SPORT	🎵 Apple - iTunes - The w... ✕

Figure 3.5

In Figure 3.5 there are three open tabs along the top offering immediate access to the BBC Sport page and a movie download site as well as the Imagineus page.

Tool bar

Using these icons you can navigate to your home page, send an email, print the web page, alter the appearance of your browser, set a different home page, alter the text size as well as activate many more functions. The RSS feed icon allows you to get the latest news from websites of your choice. You can find out more about RSS feeds on the website **www.pcwisdom.co.uk**.

Figure 3.6

Some of the icons may seem strange but you can always find out what they do by hovering the mouse pointer over the icon to show an information box. Try the Page, Safety and Tools dropdown menus by clicking on the small arrows beside them to get an idea of what you can do. Faint heart never won fair lady and you will not break the thing by having a go!

The Status bar

Figure 3.7

This lies at the very bottom of the browser window. If your mouse pointer is lying over a link on the page, the address of that page is displayed at the left hand end of this bar. When a page is loading you will see a box filling with a green thermometer as the page is collected. This appears in the middle of the status bar.

Protected Mode provides the safety of an efficient Internet browsing experience while helping to keep hackers from taking over your browser, damaging your system and installing software. Internet Explorer Protected Mode helps protect users and their systems from malicious downloads by restricting those files that can be saved without the users consent.

Sometimes a web page seems too big to fit the width of your screen so you can vary the size of the page to obviate the need to keep scrolling back and forth to read the full content. Reducing the size to 75 per cent will often allow the page to fill the screen properly. Unfortunately it also reduces the size of the text, making it a little more difficult to read, so it is a matter of balancing your priorities.

In 1993, several new top-level Internet domains were added, so that those logging on from other planets could have Internet access. These domains included .ea (Earth), .ha (Hades), .ju (Jupiter), and .og (Outer Galaxy).

Domains

No, these are not your personal kingdoms but methods of bringing some form of order to the millions of web addresses (URLs) available on the Internet. Let me explain them by analysing a simple web address like **www.pcwisdom.co.uk**.

When you enter this address into the Address bar you may notice that the computer inserts the letters **http://** in front of the address line. This is a code that tells your ISP's computer that it wants to communicate in a special language called Hypertext Transfer Protocol – something else you need to know nothing about. If the computer enters the characters **https://** then it means that the page is encrypted and therefore safe for you to enter personal details. The **www.** tells the receiving computer that it is looking for a web page and not an email address or file transfer. In recent years websites have been appearing that dispense with **www.** altogether so that the BBC News website is simply **news.bbc.co.uk**. The latest web browsers recognise these web addresses but, to be certain of connection, I would advise that you type in the characters **http://** before such addresses.

Now look at the end of the address line where we have the characters '.co.uk'.

Look at the following list and you will begin to get some idea of how to interpret web addresses:

.com	commercial site both US and international
.co	commercial site outside the US
.edu	educational US
.ac	educational outside the US
.net	a network provider
.gov	government department
.mil	military
.nhs	hospital UK
.org	non-commercial organisation

The last letters normally denote the country of origin with the exception of the United States which does not have a geographic annotation. Examples of these country codes are:

.au	Australia	.co	Colombia
.fr	France	.de	Germany
.ie	Ireland	.it	Italy
.tv	Tuvalu	.ca	Canada
.fi	Finland	.do	Dominican Republic
.hk	Hong Kong	.in	India
.jp	Japan	.uk	United Kingdom

This is the domain and, in this case, **.co.uk** means that the website is probably based in the UK. The use of geographic domains does not guarantee its location. Several enterprising companies have registered Italian domains such as **.get.it** or **.buy.it** to encourage visitors to their sites. Tuvalu is a very small island nation that has found a useful source of revenue by offering the **.tv** domain to television companies. There is no such domain as **.co.us**. The United States always sticks with **.com**.

> You may also find web page addresses that end in .asp or .php. These are pages that are generated by the website's computer usually when creating a form for the visitor to complete.

Finally, we come to more complicated addresses such as **www.epicurious.com/ recipes/food/views/Stilton-Potato-Gratin-1269**. What on earth does all this mean? It is actually a recipe for a Stilton, onion and potato pie. The name of the page is Stilton-Potato-Gratin-1269 which is found in the views folder within the food folder within the recipes folder of the Epicurious website. You do not have to remember all this let alone type it in perfectly accurately because you normally find such web pages by selecting a series of links from the home page of the site. There are ways of remembering, or storing, such complicated addresses which I will explain later in this chapter under the heading of Favorites.

Home pages

The term Home page can be a little confusing because it has different meanings in different situations. When you type in an address such as **www.silversurfers.net** you will be taken to the home page of the Silver Surfers website where it acts rather like an index to the other pages on the website. The other home page we will be talking about is that of your own personal computer. This is the page that always appears when you first open your Internet browser. You can set this to any page on the World Wide Web as we shall see in the next section.

Setting your home page

As I mentioned above, the first page to be displayed when you activate the browser program, your home page, will be that of your ISP. At this point I want to take the opportunity to reset this home page to one that may be of more relevance to you. In this case we are going to change your home page from that of your ISP to that of the well-known search engine, Google.

We will be covering the use of Google and other searching facilities in Chapter 4 but, for this exercise, I want you to type Google's web address (also known as a URL or Uniform Resource Locator – but then you don't really need to know that) into the address box. Left click once on the address in the box and it should become highlighted in blue and will be replaced by any entry you make by the keyboard – so type in **www.google.co.uk**, or **www.google.com** if you're in the US, hit the Enter key or click on the Go arrow.

If this initial click does not highlight the current address (URL) in the Address bar then hold down the left mouse button drag the pointer across the text to achieve the same effect.

Reproduced from Google™

Figure 3.8

Bingo! Congratulations, you have just arrived at the first web page of your own choice. We are going to set this page as your home page so that it appears every time you open Internet Explorer.

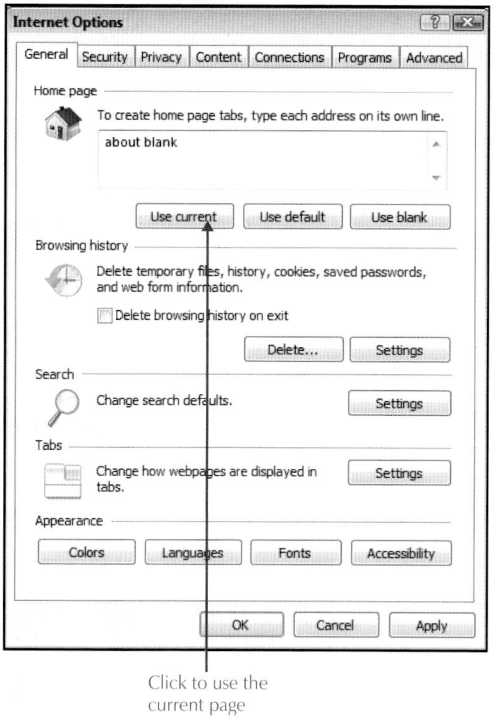

Click on Tools – either in the Tool bar or from the Menu bar and click on Internet Options. This will bring up the menu displayed on the left. As you may notice this menu offers a wide range of commands and customisations but the one we are interested in at the moment is the Home page option. You should have the Google page open so click on Use current and then click on Apply and, finally, OK.

It is as easy as that. The next time you open Explorer or click on the Home icon the Google page will be displayed. Later on you may find a page that is better suited to your own particular needs, in which case you simply repeat the process to change your home page again.

Click to use the current page

Figure 3.9

Using Favorites

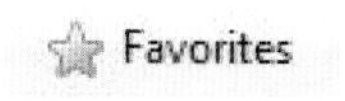

Having set up your home page we are now going to take a practical look at using the Favorites icon. For this exercise I want you to type in the address **www.pcwisdom.co.uk** into the Address box, hit Enter or click on the Go icon. This will bring up the website that supports both this book and the earlier *Computing for the Older and Wiser*. I sincerely hope that you will find the information offered on this website in the forms of tutorials and question and answer sessions both informative and entertaining. This is the sort of website to which you may want to return in the future so, with the initial page being displayed, click on the Favorites icon ⭐ Favorites and choose Add to Favorites, alter the description of the page if you wish, and click on Add. You could achieve the same result by clicking on Favorites on the Menu bar.

When you want to revisit one of your Favorites sites, simply drop down the Favorites menu and click on the site in question and you will instantly be transported to the page.

After a while you will have collected so many favourite sites that the list becomes unwieldy. I would suggest that you carry out a spring clean of this folder about once every six months. First of all, be ruthless and remove any sites that seemed like a good idea at the time but are now past their sell-by date. The way to delete any unwanted Favorites addresses simply right click on the entry and then left click on the Delete option.

To organise your Favorites, click on Favorites on the Menu bar and choose Organize Favorites.

Figure 3.10

This will present you with a list of your stored websites and the option to create New Folders (see Figure 3.11).

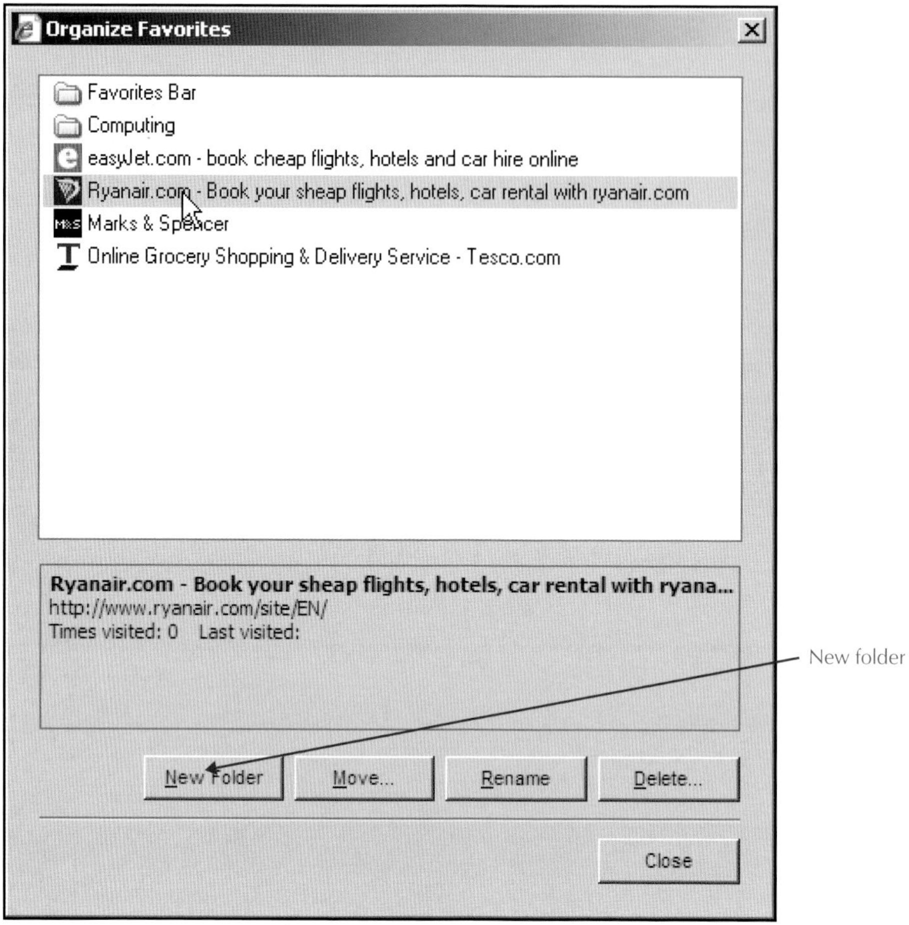

Figure 3.11

Create a number of sub-folders within the Favorites folder and move the entries to the appropriate folder by dragging the entries over the folder and releasing the mouse button. Commonly useful folders might include Travel, Computing, Shopping, Reference, Hobbies and Cooking.

This can be a tedious task but it is worth the time spent on the organisation. Internet Explorer provides a very basic organising system. Mozilla's Firefox browser provides a much better system of organising Favorites and you can import your Explorer favourites into the program at the touch of a button.

Online bookmarks

If you are likely to spend time using other people's computers but still want access to your personal favourites you could employ one of the many online bookmarking tools such as Google, Firefox's Foxmarks and the combined recommendation and bookmarks site, Delicious at **www.delicious.com**.

Browsing history

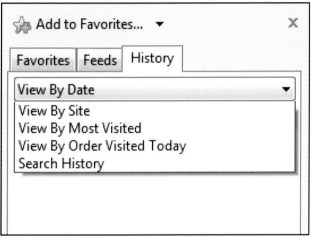

Figure 3.12

You may find that you forget to add a useful site to your Favorites and you have forgotten the necessary web address. No problem! Drop down the Favorites menu and click on the History tab. The browser keeps a record of all the websites you have visited over the recent period – usually three weeks. Click on the History tab on the menu and navigate your way back to the day when you visited the forgotten site and you can raise it again by clicking on the site name.

You can organise the History sites by clicking on the small black arrow to reveal a dropdown menu that allows you to view the sites by Date, Most Visited and alphabetically. Once selected you can now add the site by choosing Add to Favorites from the Favorites tab or the Favorites dropdown menu.

Add to Favorites (Links) bar

If you think that a certain page is one that you are going to refer to on a frequent basis you could add the page to your Links bar by clicking on the Add to Favorites icon. This makes an even shorter shortcut to your favourite web pages.

Navigating a website

Now we can start to browse the Web. For added practice we are going to raise a different web page – **www.imagineus.co.uk** – which is my own personal site. Type the address into the Address bar and you should see something similar to the screenshot below. Take a look at the web page and you will notice various words in a different colour to the normal text. These are links – also known as hyperlinks – to other pages on the website or even other sites on the World Wide Web.

You should bear in mind that these hyperlinks, or links for short, are slightly different to those on the Links bar on your browser. Your Links bar is attached to your browser while hyperlinks are embedded in web pages.

To establish whether some text or an image forms a link, move your mouse pointer over the possible point on the page where, if it is does form a link, it will change from an arrow to a hand pointer. See Selected Links in the screenshot below.

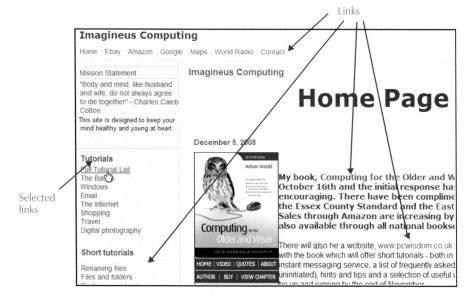

Figure 3.13

We have already noted the navigation buttons earlier in the chapter but, in that case, you will have noticed that both buttons were greyed-out. This was because the page displayed was the original home page – the first one loaded into the browser – and there are no pages to go forward or back to. Now that we have moved away from the home page there is the opportunity to go Back to that page. The Forward button is still unavailable until we have gone Back. I hope you are beginning to get the idea but, if not, try clicking on a few of the links on the Imagineus page which will take you to other pages on the Imagineus site or another page completely. No matter where you eventually navigate yourself to you can always retrace your steps by using the Back navigation button. Give it a try.

A word of warning here. The navigation buttons refer only to the tabbed page you are working on. If you open a page in a new tab your Navigation History will be different to that of any previous page. Try and remember which tab you were working with when you try to find your way back to a previous page.

After that slight detour, let us get back to using the links on the web page. If you click on the Full Tutorial List link – shown in the screenshot – you will be taken to the list of tutorials featured on the Imagineus site whereas if you click on the Computing for the Older and Wiser link you will arrive at the Amazon book store page featuring the book.

While you are on the Amazon page, try clicking on the various links offered on that page. Don't worry you won't get lost. You can always click repeatedly on the Back button to return to more friendly waters.

Copying and pasting

You can always copy part of a web page by highlighting it – known as selecting – by dragging the mouse pointer across part of the page while holding down the left mouse button. Copy the selected area either by going to Edit on the menu bar and choosing Copy or by right-clicking on the selected text and opting for the Copy option. You can then paste this selection into an email or word processor document by opening the new program and 'pasting' it into the new site using the Edit menu or the right mouse button. Once inserted into the new program you can change the size and appearance of the text by selecting it again and altering the font, size or colour. See the section on printing a web page later in this chapter.

Finding a word

Sometimes web pages get very long and it can take hours searching for the word you are looking for. There is a very useful shortcut to get round this problem. Simply press Ctrl+F on the keyboard and the following box will appear on the screen:

X Find:		Previous Next	🖉 Options ▾

Figure 3.14

Simply enter the word you are searching for in the box provided and select Next. The first incidence of the word in question will quickly be highlighted within its context. You can proceed to search for further entries of the word by using the Next button.

Navigation History

Repeated clicking on the Back button might lead to Repetitive Strain Injury so there is an alternative navigation aid provided. Look back at the original image in this chapter and you will see the small blue Navigation History arrow. Click on this and you will be shown a road map of where you have been in your recent browsing adventure and you can click on any of the pages to jump back to that point.

Downloading from the Internet

There will come a time when you may want to 'download' something from the Internet on to your own computer. This may be something as simple as an image or as complicated as a computer program. Once you have grasped the principles you should have no worries on this score.

Just old age?
full story ...

Right click on the picture

The Ins and Outs of Dog Training
Full story ...

Figure 3.15

Let us see how to download a picture. We are going to collect a picture from my own veterinary practice's website at **www.bergholtroadvets. co.uk**. As before, type this address into the Address bar – you should be getting used to this by now – and hit the Enter key. In the right hand column you will see links to four articles together with a couple of pictures. I want to download the one of the dog and child in a cat flap (see the image on the right). *Right* click on the picture and you will create a menu which, among many other options, offers the opportunity to 'Save Picture As…' Left click on this option and the Save Picture menu will be shown. The suggested file name looks rather strange because it has been extracted from a web page. So you can give it a different name before navigating your way to any particular folder you may want to store the image in and then click on Save.

Save Picture

Adrian ▸ Pictures | Search

File name: Cat%20flap%20friends

Save as type: JPEG (*.jpg)

Browse Folders

Save   Cancel

Navigate to folders

Figure 3.16

And that's it! All you have to do now is to open up the folder in which you saved the image, double click on it and it will be opened up in your image viewer program. This is a tiny image and any attempts to enlarge it will distort the image out of recognition. We will deal with photography and the Internet in much more detail in Chapter 12. The idea at the moment is to build your confidence in downloading stuff from the Web.

This first example was dead easy so let us try something a little more challenging. As I said we will be discussing digital photography in Chapter 12 but we could use this opportunity to download a very useful image cataloguing and manipulating program that we will be using in that chapter called Picasa 3. So go to **http://picasa.google.com/** and click on the Download Picasa 3 banner.

Thank you for downloading Picasa 3

(Your download should start automatically. If it doesn't, click here.)

Reproduced from Google™

Figure 3.17

If nothing seems to happen, like a window asking where you wish to save your file, then click on the 'click here' link to kickstart the process. Once everything is in order you will be asked whether you wish to Run or Save the file. At this stage in your browsing career I would suggest that you choose Save. This will save the setup program to your desktop for use at any future time. Choosing Run is safe enough but it does mean that you have less control over the whole process. After choosing Save, the browser will give you the opportunity to save the file somewhere other than the Desktop but I would leave it at its original setting and then start the process going by clicking on OK. Soon enough you will see a window showing how the download is progressing. You can minimise this window while you get on with other projects if you so wish, but eventually the process will finish and you will be asked again if you want to Run the installation program. A Picasa icon will also have been placed on your desktop. Downloading a program is one thing while installing it is another and both need to be completed for the program to work on your computer.

Installing a program

Once the program has been downloaded it must be installed. You can do this by either clicking on Run or closing that window, going to the desktop and double clicking on the Picasa icon.

picasa3-setup

Reproduced from Google™

Figure 3.18

Sometimes the Setup icon does not work, in which case you have to find the installation file. Internet Explorer either saves these files on your desktop or in your Documents folder so look for it there if you have any problems. You could also download it again and choose Run at the end of the download process. Whichever way you do it you will be asked by Vista whether you wish to continue installing the file. The obvious and necessary answer is yes. Following this you will see a number of small windows to which the obvious answers should be given. If in doubt accept the suggested options. See the screenshots below.

> ⚠ It is good computing practice to close all open programs before you choose to install a new one. This prevents any nasty computer clashes between active programs. They don't happen very often but when they do life can get rather complicated.

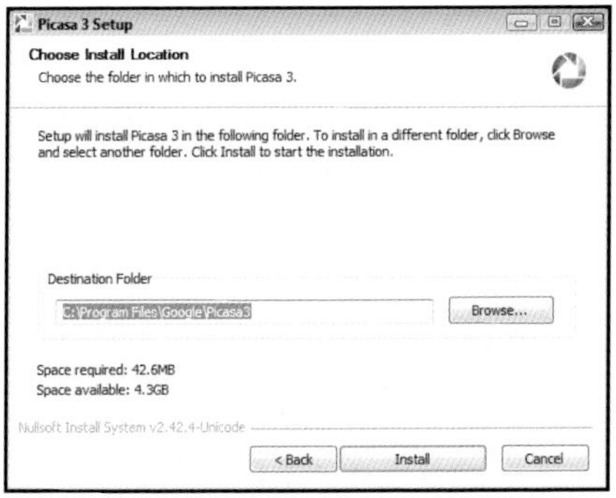

Reproduced from Google™

Figure 3.19

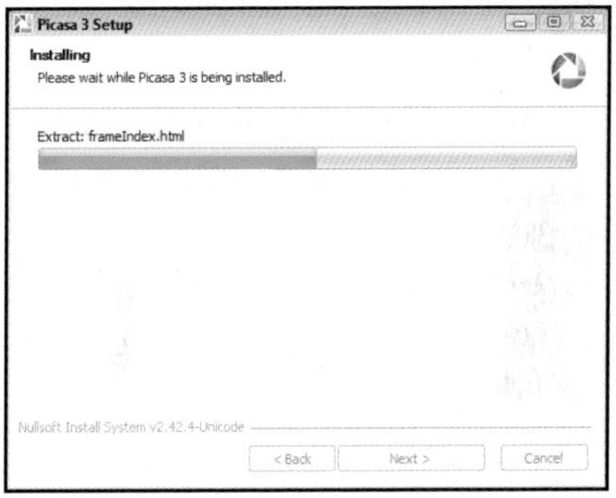

Reproduced from Google™

Figure 3.20

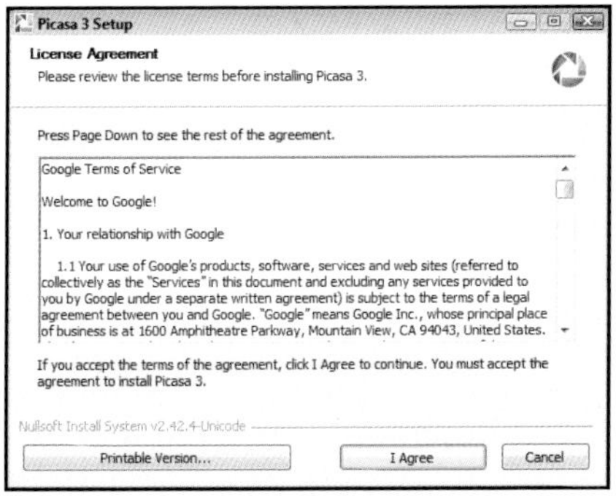

Reproduced from Google™

Figure 3.21

Reproduced from Google™

Deselect this

Figure 3.22

> ⚠ I would strongly suggest that, in the final window, you deselect the Run Picasa 3 option. The reason for this is that, once started, the program will begin to catalogue all the images on your computer and that is really a subject for Chapter 12.

All this downloading and installing may have left you short of mental oxygen, in which case take a break and congratulate yourself on your progress so far. The whole process of downloading and installing is covered again in the next chapter when we shall be downloading an anti-virus program for your email. It will give you a chance to try the process again to gain confidence.

Printing a web page

It is all very well looking up a recipe for duck à l'orange, but it is of little use on your computer screen. You need to take the recipe to the kitchen where it can take the heat, the steam and the boiling fat. We are talking about printing web pages.

Some web pages are carefully thought out and offer a printable version of the text omitting the glut of advertising material that surrounds the original page but in most cases you are going to have to create a printable page yourself.

Let's deal with the simplest scenario first. If you simply wish to print out the page shown on the screen in front of you, you only have to go to File on the Menu bar, choose Print, select your printer and click on OK. (There is an even shorter method of typing Ctrl+P which does the same job.) This may be all you need but all too often the web page is cluttered with links to unwanted sites, search boxes, promotional banners and other advertising material that you can happily do without. If you use the File>Print method you will have the option to preview the printed page which might change your ideas about printing the page.

In most cases you will only want to print out part of a page so we need to select the section of the web page that we want to print. Selection of text and objects on a web page is done in a very similar manner to that which we use in word processing – drag the mouse pointer across the required content as shown below. Release the mouse button when you have made your selection.

also available through all national booksellers.

There will also be a website, www.pcwisdom.co.uk ,designed to run in conjunction with the book which will offer short tutorials - both in text and video versions, an instant messaging service, a list of frequently asked questions (FAQs for the

Figure 3.23

Having selected the part of the page you want to print, go to File then Print and choose Selection. Don't forget to click on the final Print command to set the process going! Unfortunately this may result in the printing of the selection in tiny type that is barely readable, like this:

> There will also be a website, **www.pcwisdom.co.uk**, designed to run in conjunction with the book which will offer short tutorials - both in text and video versions, an instant messaging service, a list of frequently asked questions (FAQs for the uninitiated), hints and...

As in most cases there is a better way of doing this. If you find yourself in the situation where you need a magnifying glass to read your printed page try this method:

● Select the text.

● Go to the Edit menu and choose Copy or simply press Ctrl+C.

● Now open your word processor in a New Page.

● Go to Edit and choose Paste or use Ctrl+V.

● Select the text again if necessary and enlarge the font size before printing it out in a readable form.

Alternative web browsers

Internet Explorer is by no means the only – and certainly not the best – web browser available but it is the one available on all PC computers. For many years I used Mozilla's Firefox browser at **http://www.mozilla-europe.org/en/firefox/** which is faster, more stable and more secure than Internet Explorer. Recently I have been using the new browser developed by Google called Chrome at **www.google.com/chrome**. This is even faster than Firefox and offers a much cleaner interface although it takes a little time to get used to. Finally, there is Safari which used to be restricted to Apple Mac computers but a lot of PC users are now being attracted to it.

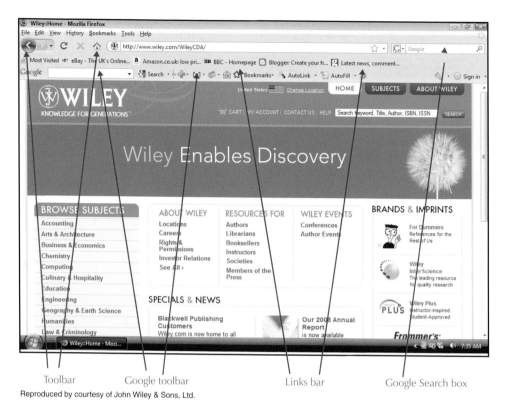

Toolbar   Google toolbar   Links bar   Google Search box

Reproduced by courtesy of John Wiley & Sons, Ltd.

Figure 3.24 Firefox toolbars

By all means continue to use Internet Explorer – after all it is already installed on your computer – but try one of the others to see if you get along with it. The toolbars and menus are slightly different but, with a bit of trial and error, you will soon get the hang of them. You can have as many web browsers on your computer as you like but only one that is the default browser – that is the one that always opens if access to a web page is needed.

There may be times when a program will only work if used with Internet Explorer but these occasions are getting rarer. Never forget that it is your computer and it does not belong to Microsoft or any other computing organisation.

Updating your browser

Whatever browser you settle upon you will be offered the opportunity to update the program as more and more functions are added and security loopholes are closed. These updates are published on an irregular basis but you will be notified by a pop-up screen if there is a new update available. I would strongly advise you to install these updates – they download and install themselves automatically once you have granted permission – so that you maintain the security of your system.

Summary

- Get to know your menus and toolbars
- Play around with webpage links
- Set a useful home page
- Store useful pages in Favorites
- Print out a web page
- Practise downloading
- Try alternative browsers

Brain Training

There may be more than one correct answer to these questions.

1. What are Links on the Links bar?

☐ a) They are other programs on your computer

☐ b) They activate chain reactions

☐ c) They are email addresses to your closest friends

☐ d) They are shortcuts to favourite websites

2. What is a URL?

☐ a) A Uniform Resource Locator – whatever that means

☐ b) A University Research Link

☐ c) A World Wide Web address

☐ d) An email address

3. Where do I type in a web address?

☐ a) In the Tool bar

☐ b) In the Menu bar

☐ c) In the Title bar

☐ d) In the Address bar

4. What goes into the Favorites list?

☐ a) Links to my favourite web pages

☐ b) Web addresses to useful websites

☐ c) Photos of your grandchildren

☐ d) A list of reminders of things to do

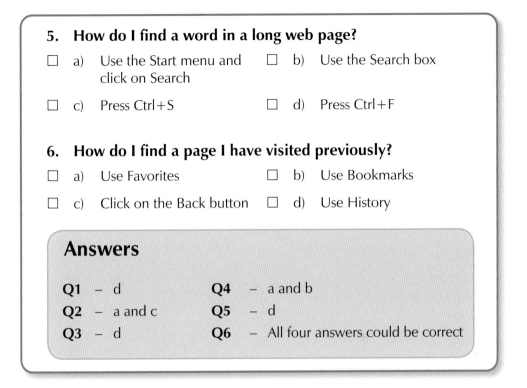

5. How do I find a word in a long web page?

☐ a) Use the Start menu and click on Search   ☐ b) Use the Search box

☐ c) Press Ctrl+S   ☐ d) Press Ctrl+F

6. How do I find a page I have visited previously?

☐ a) Use Favorites   ☐ b) Use Bookmarks

☐ c) Click on the Back button   ☐ d) Use History

Answers

Q1 – d   **Q4** – a and b
Q2 – a and c   **Q5** – d
Q3 – d   **Q6** – All four answers could be correct

Searching the Internet

4

Equipment needed: a computer; Internet Explorer program; and connection to the Internet.

Skills needed: some knowledge of the keyboard and mouse; ability to enter a web address.

To be able to use the Internet in the most productive way you are going to have to be able to search it. Personally, I cannot begin to remember all the web addresses – often called URLs (Uniform Resource Locators), but you don't have to know that – and even when I am fairly confident of an address I will usually check it on a search engine. For instance, for some reason or other I can never remember whether Tesco's finishes with .co.uk or .com and if the *Private Eye* magazine is **www.p.eye.com**, **www.privateye.co.uk** or just **priveye.com**. It isn't any of these: it is actually **www.private-eye.co.uk**.

Searching for known website addresses is only one small function of search engines and their human counterpart, directories. So what is the difference between a search engine, a directory or even a meta search engine?

Directories

Directories take a slightly different approach in that, having found websites using a 'spider', they are classified by members of the human race. They decide the classification headings and sub-sections and where the individual sites should be stored. One would have thought that human intervention of this kind would result in better searching experiences but this is not necessarily so. Let us take an example in which you are looking for a replacement pair of secateurs to prune your roses. If you access a directory such as the Open Directory or Yahoo you will be confronted by a long list of headings such as Recreation, Shopping and Home. Each of these classifications has sub-headings – Shopping relates to General Merchandise, Home & Garden and even Wholesale – any of which may contain information about secateurs.

In the case of the Open Directory there is actually one entry for the UK relating to secateurs classified under – wait for it – **Regional: Europe: United Kingdom: Business and Economy: Shopping: Recreation and Sports: Outdoors**. The Yahoo directory found 12 'secateur' sites in the UK but these were spread across sections such as **United Kingdom > Lawn and Garden > Business Directories** or **United Kingdom > Shopping > Outdoor Gear > Knives.** Now I must admit that I have complicated things rather too much in this case because both directories offer a search facility within their sites so that I can search directly for secateurs.

Searching for 'secateurs' in the UK in a search engine produced 103,000 results so you can see the difference. This does not mean to say that directories do not have their place. They are particularly useful in finding local suppliers of goods and services. One great advantage of directories is that each site has been recommended and checked by human intelligence rather than relying on the automation of computer searches.

Google came from the term 'Googol' which literally means 1 followed by 100 zeros.

Search engines

There must be very few people in the world – and none in the computing community – that have not heard of Google, in my opinion the Internet's premier search engine, but there are many more that will search the Web for information. Yahoo, AlltheWeb, AltaVista, Netscape, AOL and Ripple are just a few of the search engines operating on the Web. Most of these search engines are free to use but there are also specialist engines that require a subscription fee. These tend towards searches of financial and academic data. I am going to concentrate on both Google and Yahoo in this chapter.

Google

We all tend to think of Google as a search engine whereas it is very much more than this. Take a look at the list shown below.

Search		Explore and innovate	
Alerts	Receive news and search results via email	**Code**	Download APIs and open source code
Blog Search	Find blogs on your favorite topics	**Labs**	Try out new Google products
Book Search	Search the full text of books	**Communicate, show & share**	
Checkout	Complete online purchases more quickly and securely	**Blogger**	Express yourself online
Google Chrome^{New!}	A browser built for speed, stability and security	**Calendar**	Organise your schedule and share events with friends
Desktop	Search your own computer	**Docs**	Create and share your online documents, presentations, and spreadsheets
Directory	Browse the web by topic	**Google Mail**	Fast, searchable email with less spam
Earth	Explore the world from your PC	**Groups**	Create mailing lists and discussion groups
Finance	Business info, news, and interactive charts	**Orkut**	Meet new people and stay in touch with friends
Product Search	Search for stuff to buy	**Picasa**	Find, edit and share your photos
Images	Search for images on the web	**Reader**	Get all your blogs and news feeds fast
Maps	View maps and directions	**Talk**	IM and call your friends through your computer

Reproduced from Google^{TM}

Figure 4.1

Google offers mailing facilities, a directory, desktop searches, special interest groups, photographic programs as well as the video search site, YouTube, but more on some of these in later chapters. In this chapter we are simply dealing with the search engine capabilities of Google.

In the last chapter we established Google as the home page of our computer so you may have it immediately available on your browser.

A Googlewhack is when you get only ONE result from a minimum of two recognisable words. They are very rare and highly prized by the searching community.

Reproduced from Google™

Figure 4.2

One of the great beauties of Google is its simplicity. You simply click inside the search box to place the typing cursor, type in your search terms and click on Google Search. Depending upon the specificity of your search criteria you will be presented with a few hundred to over 3 million results. Sounds simple and it is – in many instances – but there will be times when your search only results in increasing confusion and frustration.

Try to be reasonably specific in your search terms. Typing in 'gardening' or 'bridge' will result in millions of results and it will be nigh on impossible to get the specific information you actually need. Don't forget that Google has links to more than 8 billion web pages.

Imagine the following scenario. You have just bought a football from a friend for your young grandson but the ball is a little flat and you find that you need a special valve to re-inflate it to its correct pressure. None of the local shops can help but you notice that the name of the manufacturers is printed on the ball – Manchester Football and Basketball Company. You type 'Manchester football company' into the Google search box. I did this as an exercise and came up with nearly 5 million 'hits', the vast majority of which related to the Manchester professional football clubs – United and City. Not what I was actually looking for! This is where we need to refine our search and use a bit of lateral thinking, so let us consider a few basic rules of searching:

1. If you are looking for a British site don't forget to click in the 'Pages from the UK' button. This will narrow your search down considerably as America contributes massively to the World Wide Web.

2. It does not matter whether you use upper or lower case in typing your search terms. 'Winston Churchill', 'winston churchill' and 'wINstON ChURChill' will all search for same man.

3. Refine your search by enclosing phrases within quotation marks. If you search for 'Edinburgh royal mile' you will get something like 5½ million responses but if you search for 'Edinburgh "royal mile"' that figure comes down to 572,000. Still a lot of pages but it demonstrates the point I am trying to get across.

4. Referring back to the Manchester football problem listed above you can eliminate reference to the two football clubs by using the minus sign to get Google to ignore the United and City pages. In this case your search terms should look something like 'manchester football company –united –city' which eliminates references to the two clubs. In this particular instance I would use the previous rule to look for '"Manchester football and basketball company"' as a phrase. This company is simply a figment of my imagination so the search for this phrase did not produce any results whatsoever!

5. As well as using the minus sign (-) you can equally profitably use the plus (+) sign. Let us imagine that you are trying to establish a certain fact about something that happened in the film *Rocky 3*. Google, and many other search engines, ignore certain common words like 'the', 'I' and 'and' as well as numbers and certain other characters such as @, ? and !. Therefore a search for 'Rocky 3 film' would ignore the number 3 completely unless you specified the end for the number by searching for 'rocky +3 film'. There are many instances when the plus (+) and minus (-) signs will focus your search on what you are really looking for.

6. Use the Advanced Search facility when you are trying to make your search results more specific. This option lies just to the right of the main search box.

As an example of tip 3, let us try and find the words of the song 'Windmills of Your Mind'. You may have forgotten the title of the song or poem but, in this case, you remember that the song contains the phrase 'the circles that you find'. To get the full text of the song type in '"circles that you find" lyric' in the search box and instantly you will get a long list of web pages that feature the full lyric.

Don't forget that Google can search for images, news, special interest groups, maps and even shopping on the Web.

Advanced searching

The Advanced Search link lies just to the right of the main Google search box.

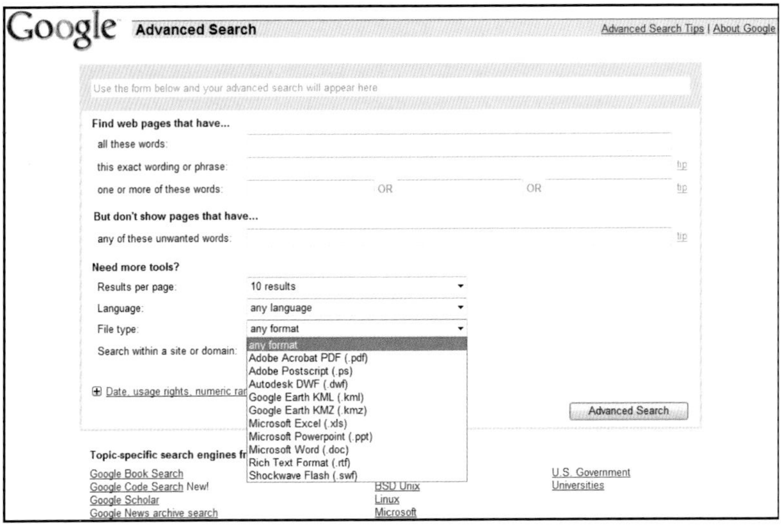

Reproduced from Google™

Figure 4.3

As you can see this allows you to set multiple parameters for your search – even to the language in which the page is written. Using the language parameter will often result in more useful search results, especially for those for whom English is not their first language. The Internet is truly international.

Other Google functions

Click on more at the top of your screen for further options including:

Maps
Blog searches
Google Alerts
Images
And many more…

Yahoo

This search engine works in a similar manner to Google.

Like Google, Yahoo offers the facility to search for those pages located in the UK. Here is a curious fact – searching for 'news builth wells' on the Web resulted in 768,000 hits while restricting the search to the UK lowered this figure to 550,000. This suggests that there are some 200,000 sites offering information about news in Builth Wells in other parts of the globe! The mind starts to boggle at this point.

If you wish to know more about searching tips for Yahoo try going to http://help.yahoo.com/l/us/yahoo/search/basics/basics-05.html. I know it is a long address but it would give you practice in entering web addresses correctly and appreciating the importance of absolute accuracy. A screenshot of the shortcuts available on Yahoo is shown below.

As you can see you can search for hundreds of pieces of information on Yahoo even to the extent of establishing the manufacturer, age, model and owner of aircraft registration numbers. Simply enter the number of the American registered aircraft – the one you see on the wings and tail of the aircraft – such as N223WH, and you will discover that it is the registration of a small Cessna light aircraft.

• Airport Information	• Images	• Sports Scores
• Airline Registration Information	• ISBN Numbers	• Stock Quotes
• Area Codes	• Local Search	• Synonym Finder
• Calculator	• Maps	• Time Zones
• Dictionary Definitions	• Movie Showtimes	• Traffic Reports
• Encyclopedia Lookup	• Movie Trailers	• UPC Codes
• Exchange Rates	• News	• Videos
• Flight Comparison	• Package Tracking	• VIN Number
• Gas Prices	• Patents	• Weather
• Hotel Comparison		• Weights, Measures, and Temperatures
		• ZIP Codes

Shortcuts Cheat Sheet

Airport Information	For the latest airport conditions as well as maps, directions, local weather, and airport terminal maps, where available, search on the airport name or airport code and the term "airport."	Example: ohare airport Yahoo! Search
Aircraft Registration Information	To find detailed information, such as manufacturer, model, and owner, about aircraft registered in the U.S., search on the FAA Registration number, or "N-number" that can be found on the tail of an airplane.	Example: N2451F Yahoo! Search

Reproduced with permission of Yahoo! Inc. ©2009 Yahoo! Inc

Figure 4.4

Yahoo as well as other search engines also helps with your searching by using its Search Assist function. This analyses the text you have typed into the search box and makes a number of suggestions to help you arrive at your preferred destination. Search Assist is normally activated by default but, if not, click on the Options link to the right of the Yahoo search box and select Preferences. Now click Edit in the Search Assist section and make any changes you the settings you wish to use.

US-centric Web

This last search raises an interesting point. In spite of the global spread of the World Wide Web it is still concentrated firmly in the USA. You can only search Yahoo in this manner for US registered aircraft. Searching for area codes, airport information and utility prices using these shortcuts in Yahoo will only elicit American information. You will have to use standard searching methods to access information about such information in Europe and throughout the rest of the world.

This is one of the reasons why I recommend that you restrict your searches to the UK or Europe by using the appropriate boxes or by adding 'uk' to your search terms to get information more specific to this country.

Leaning so far towards the United States you may improve your search results by including the American spelling, as well as the English one, when searching for words like 'colour', 'honour' and 'authorise'. Try adding 'color', 'tumor' and 'authorize' to your search words.

Search for help with your computer problems

There may be times when something has gone wrong with your computer and you are tempted to send out an SOS to your guardian angel or take it back to the computer shop. Why not see if other people have encountered this problem and put a simple answer on the Web?

You may find that your printer has suddenly stopped working for no apparent reason. There may well be a simple solution that you can apply yourself. Obviously you will have checked that the printer is both plugged in and switched on but it may be that you have not used the printer for several weeks and the ink cartridges have dried out like an unused ballpoint pen. On the other hand you may have a 'corrupted' or bad file waiting in a queue to be printed. Not only is the printer unable to print this file but the file itself is blocking all the other documents you have sent to the machine. Try searching for 'printing problems' on the Internet.

Metasearch engines

Metasearch engines are slightly different. These are programs that *combine* search engine results – programs such as Google, Yahoo, Live Search, About.com, MIVA and LookSmart. Metasearch engines trawl through search engine findings to give an amalgamated result.

Let us take the use of the metasearch engine, Copernic, as an example. Personally I prefer to call these programs 'accumulators' in that they collect and collate information from many different search engines. This enables your searching 'net' to be cast much wider than the individual searching tools such as Google and Yahoo.

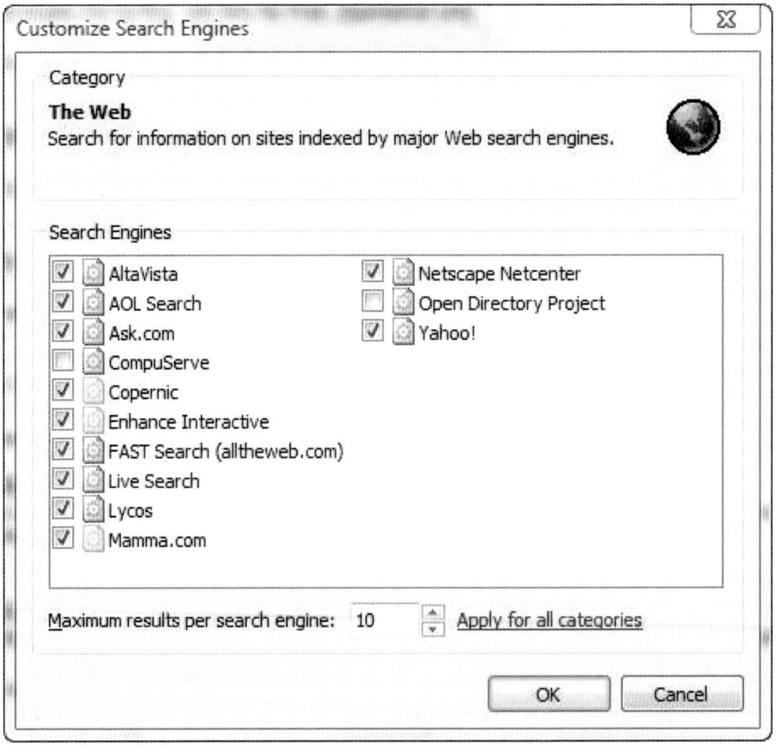

Figure 4.5

Copernic also offers a number of themed searches as seen in the left hand column of the search results screenshot as well as the facility to retain previous search results for future reference. The program offers a number of options, many of which have to be paid for, but the basic program can be downloaded free from **www.copernic.com/en/products/agent/index.html**. (Remember to choose the free Basic program. There are two further commercial options that have to be paid for but the Basic version will provide invaluable results.)

> The point I am trying to get across is that there is more than one way to achieve an end or find what you are really looking for.

Use tabs for easier searching in Internet Explorer

Searching for information online can be rather time-consuming. Unless you're lucky enough to stumble upon what you want straight away, it involves looking at a good few of the web pages suggested by a search engine. Even then, you may not find all the information on a single page: one website may give you a few details, another may provide some extra tips and a third may fill in the blanks, and you have to put this lot together in your mind.

This means that you not only have to keep track of those few useful pages as you find them, but you have to keep finding your way back to the page containing the search engine's results in order to try one of the other web pages it found.

> This is where the tabs feature of Internet Explorer really comes into its own. Let's say you've just done a search at Google (or some other search engine) and the list of results has appeared in front of you. As you look down it, you find a link that looks as though it may be worth visiting. Don't just click it in the ordinary way: instead, hold down the Ctrl key on your keyboard as you click the link.

Does this page give you any useful information? If it doesn't, you might as well get rid of it. Move the mouse up to its tab again and click the little 'x' button that appears in it and the tab will close.

You can also open a page in a new tab by clicking on the link with the mouse wheel or by right-clicking on a link and choosing Open Link in a New Tab.

When you do this, Internet Explorer will add a new tab (which you'll see near the top of the window, to the right of the tab for your page of search results) and will use that tab to open the link you clicked. Move the mouse up to this newly arrived tab and click it to see the page that has just opened.

If the page does contain useful details, you'd probably like to keep it open. In that case, just click the tab containing your original page of search results to continue looking through them. In the same way, each time you find a potentially useful link, hold Ctrl when clicking it to make it open in a new tab (or click with the mouse wheel), switch to that tab to read the page, and then decide whether or not it's worth keeping that tab open to refer to later.

By making use of tabs in this way, your search results pages are easy to return to just by clicking the relevant tab, and all the useful pages you found along the way can be kept open too, so that you can compare and collate the information they contain.

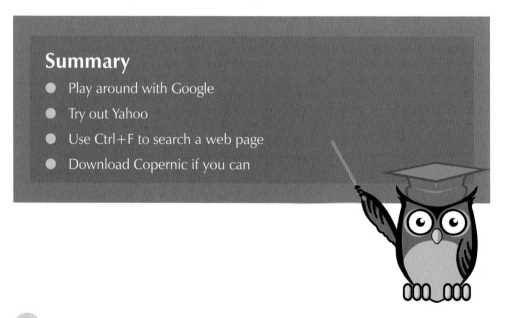

Summary
- Play around with Google
- Try out Yahoo
- Use Ctrl+F to search a web page
- Download Copernic if you can

Brain Training

There may be more than one correct answer to these questions.

1. What are Internet directories?

☐ a) Lists of telephone numbers that can be dialled by the computer

☐ b) American Yellow Pages

☐ c) Tools to assist your searching of the Web

☐ d) Searchable lists of websites assembled by humans

2. How do I search for a phrase when using a search engine?

☐ a) Capitalise the words

☐ b) Enclose the phrase in single quotes

☐ c) Enclose the phrase in double quotation marks

☐ d) Just type in the phrase

3. What can Google search for?

☐ a) Maps

☐ b) Photos

☐ c) Newsgroups

☐ d) Appointments

4. What can Yahoo search for?

☐ a) Flight arrival times

☐ b) Video clips

☐ c) Maps

☐ d) Weather forecasts

5. Which web address will take you to the Google page?

☐ a) www.google.com

☐ b) www.google.co.uk

☐ c) www.google.net

☐ d) www.google.org.us

6. What are browser tabs?

☐ a) Separate web pages on the same browser   ☐ b) Nasty programs put on your computer by your ISP

☐ c) Links to other web pages   ☐ d) Ear tags for sheep

Answers

Q1	–	c and d		
Q2	–	c		
Q3	–	All four		

Q4	–	All four
Q5	–	a and b
Q6	–	a and c

Staying safe online

5

Equipment needed: a computer; Internet Explorer program; connection to the Internet; an anti-virus program from the Internet; a firewall and a record of usernames and passwords.

Skills needed: some knowledge of the keyboard and mouse plus some confidence; knowledge of downloading a program.

Many people are justifiably anxious about the prospect of Internet fraud and the loss of their financial identities. To avoid such difficulties I suggest following these guidelines:

- Never include personal security or financial details in an email message.
- Delete all unknown email messages.
- *Never* reply to unrecognised messages.
- Never activate a web link in a message from an unknown source.
- Use passwords of eight characters using upper and lower case characters, numbers and symbols. Write them down and secure in a safe place.
- Keep your operating system up to date.
- Keep your anti-virus and anti-spyware programs up to date.
- Set parental controls when adding another user profile on your computer.
- Use Windows Content Advisor.

Viruses and other nasties

While we are on the subject of staying safe online, let us look at the problem of computer viruses. Whenever you are connected to the Internet you are potentially vulnerable to a variety of unpleasant intrusions that come under the common classification of 'viruses'. In medical terms a virus is an infection and that is what computer viruses do to your computer – they infect it.

So what do computer viruses do? Some are relatively harmless and simply display an irritating message while others can wipe the contents of your hard disk – not something I would like to contemplate. The latter are fortunately very rare.

Trojans

A Trojan refers to a program that appears innocuous, but hidden inside is usually something harmful, probably a worm or a virus. The lure of Trojans is that you may download a game or a picture, thinking it's harmless, but once you run the program, the worm or virus gets to work. Sometimes they will only do things to annoy you, but usually the worm or virus will cause damage to your system.

Viruses

Viruses are computer programs with the sole purpose of destroying data on our computers. The virus may only destroy unimportant files, or it may decide to erase all of your document files. A virus can cause an infected computer to do funny things on certain dates, such as April Fool's Day, as well as issue serious commands such as removing parts of the operating system, thus disabling the operation and the starting up of the computer.

Viruses are spread through messages we get from friends, download off the net, or install through a floppy disk, CD or DVD of dubious provenance. A virus will often come disguised under the cloak of a Trojan, which is the carrier for the virus.

Worms

Worms operate differently. They multiply within the computer system. They generally come through email messages, but computers can also become infected if they download a Trojan file which has a worm inserted. If you receive a worm program through your email and then run it, this program sends the worm file out to everyone listed in your email address book. If you work in a major corporation, this could means hundreds of people, and so the multiplying continues.

A worm is similar to a virus, except that it doesn't usually aim to damage your computer or files. Indeed, it doesn't want to do anything to draw attention to itself, because if you were aware of it you'd obviously try to remove it. The worm in question does nothing at all until called into action by its creator, who is then able to take control of your computer – and the many other infected computers – to form a giant network known as a 'botnet'. These computers, all working together, can be used to launch attacks on other computers and networks, steal personal information from all infected computers in large quantities, and install yet more malicious software.

Phishing

This may sound like catching a trout but you are the one who is likely to land up on the dinner table. Have a look at the email I received recently, shown below.

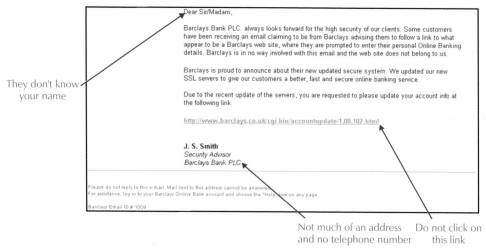

Figure 5.1

It has an 'official' look to it but there are a number of questionable points to it. First of all you can compare the logo on the email to their real logo which can be viewed on their website. Check to see if they are the same.

Then there are the facts that they are unable to address you by name or offer a full address or telephone number. It is a recognised scam which was correctly intercepted by my anti-virus program and sent to the Spam folder immediately.

Very often these messages sound very convincing, assuring you that they have your best interests at heart whereas, in fact, they have the very opposite intention. A similar scam reads as follows:

Dear Valued Customer,

> Our new security system will help you to avoid frequently fraud transactions and to keep your investments in safety.

> Due to technical update we recommend you to reactivate your account. Click on the link below to login and begin using your updated Barclays account.

> To log into your account, please visit the NetBank website at *http://www.barclays.co.uk*

> If you have questions about your online statement, please send us a Bank Mail or call us at 0846 600 2323 (outside the UK dial +44 247 686 2063).

> We appreciate your business. It's truly our pleasure to serve you.

> Barclays Customer Care

> This email is for notification only. To contact us,

> please log into your account and send a Bank Mail.

How kind. How considerate. How fraudulent!

> Your bank will never email you with such requests. They will always contact you by ordinary letter – often recorded delivery. Even if they ring you it is a wise precaution to thank them for their call and ring them back on the telephone number listed on your bank account to make sure that they are genuine representatives of your bank.

The very last thing you should *ever* do is to activate any link included in the message.

Anti-virus programs

Something you will need very early on in your computing career is an effective anti-virus program. Many anti-virus programs can be bought off the shelf on CD from any computer store, such as Norton Anti-Virus and McAfee, but you can also get a very powerful anti-virus program called AVG Anti-Virus – for free – by downloading it from the Web. We are going to collect it from a highly-respected source of free programs (freeware) called Tucows at **www.tucows.com**. Once you have the Tucows page on your screen, type the words 'avg anti virus' (without the quotes) into the Tucows search box and click on Go.

Reproduced by courtesy of Tucows Inc.

Figure 5.2

At the top of the resulting list you will see some sponsored links to AVG Anti-virus but I am not interested in these, we need to scroll down the page using the mouse wheel or the scroll bar on the left side of the window to get to the AVG Anti-Virus Free Edition. The notes confirm that it is a freeware program and that it works on all recent Windows operating systems. Notice also that the file size is more than 56MB. Now you may not know a lot about Internet file sizes yet so take my word for it, this is a very big file and you will need a broadband connection to download it. A simple dialup connection would take more than two hours to download the program even if it had the capability.

I am assuming that you have a broadband connection so click on the underlined link.

This brings up the next page where you are invited to Download Now. Click on this banner and you get a standard security warning inviting you either to Run or Save the program. At this stage in your browsing career I would suggest that you choose Save. This will save the setup program to your desktop for use at any future time. Choosing Run is safe enough but it does mean that you have less control over the whole process.

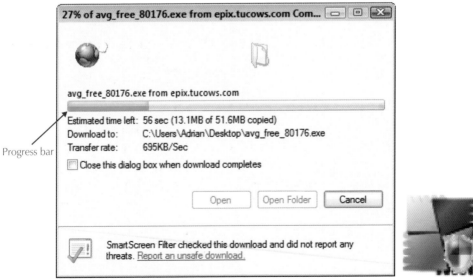

Reproduced by courtesy of Tucows Inc.

Figure 5.3

After choosing Save, the browser will give you the opportunity to save the file somewhere other than the Desktop but I would leave it at its original setting and then start the process going by clicking on OK. The download progress is shown by the green bar inching its way across the bar and the increasing percentage

Reproduced by courtesy of Tucows Inc.

Figure 5.4   **Figure 5.5**

figure at the top of the window. You can minimise this window to be getting on with other computing jobs if you wish but eventually the download will complete and you will find an icon on your desktop looking like the icon in Figure 5.5. Double click on this icon to install the program. The completed progress window will also give you an opportunity to Run the downloaded file. Choose either option to install the program on your computer.

Keep your operating system up to date

If you use Windows Vista or XP, You will have come across the feature named Automatic Updates. At regular intervals, when you're connected to the Internet, this feature contacts Microsoft's servers to check whether there are any updates for Windows needed by your computer. If there are, it downloads them and installs them on your system.

The question is – are these updates really necessary? Some of you may have heard that these updates cause more trouble than they are worth. Some of these programs can be very large but they only take a few minutes to install. The actual download takes place behind the scenes while you are working on other things – if you have a broadband connection, that is. Microsoft usually issues new updates on the second Tuesday of every month. Some people have even got into the habit of turning this feature off, but I would not recommend this.

There's a very good reason why these updates are absolutely vital, and a recent news story highlights it quite well. There is a new computer worm known variously as 'Conficker' and 'Downandup' spreading around the Internet and wreaking havoc with personal computers.

The thing about this Conficker worm is that it's very easily avoided. Back in October 2007, Microsoft discovered a security flaw in Windows and released a fix for it via the Automatic Updates system. As always, the world's hackers immediately analysed this update to find out what flaw it was fixing, and they created this Conficker worm to target computers which didn't have the fix installed.

Automatic Updates are very necessary indeed. Just as it is important to keep your anti-virus and anti-spyware software updated, you must also allow Automatic Updates to do its job. If you don't, it's like locking the doors and leaving all the windows open when you go out.

As long as you haven't switched off Automatic Updates, this fix will have been installed on your PC in October 2007, and your computer will be protected. However, the hackers know that a fair percentage of Windows users turn off Automatic Updates, and that percentage could add up to millions of PCs, all vulnerable to attack and well worth targeting. It is reckoned that 30 million PCs have already been silently infected with the Conficker worm simply because their owners prevented Windows from installing updates.

Avoiding inappropriate websites

A number of my pupils are naturally anxious to avoid unsuitable or pornographic websites appearing on their browser.

Content Advisor

This rarely happens but let me help you avoid any future embarrassment. Do you remember the Internet Options facility on the Tools menu? We used it to reset our home page. Go to Tools, choose Internet Options but, this time, click on the Content advisor tab and choose Enable.

This offers you the opportunity to set the security levels that will operate if and when you open web pages that include content such as violence, sexual content, drug use and other adult subjects, or content that might, for instance, constitute a risk to your computer. Click on the subject and adjust the slider to suit your own tastes.

There is one drawback to using Content Advisor in that it relies upon a globally recognised rating system that relies on website developers rating their own websites and completing a brief questionnaire. These results are added to the coding of the site which the Content Advisor checks against your chosen settings and blocks them if they offend the rules.

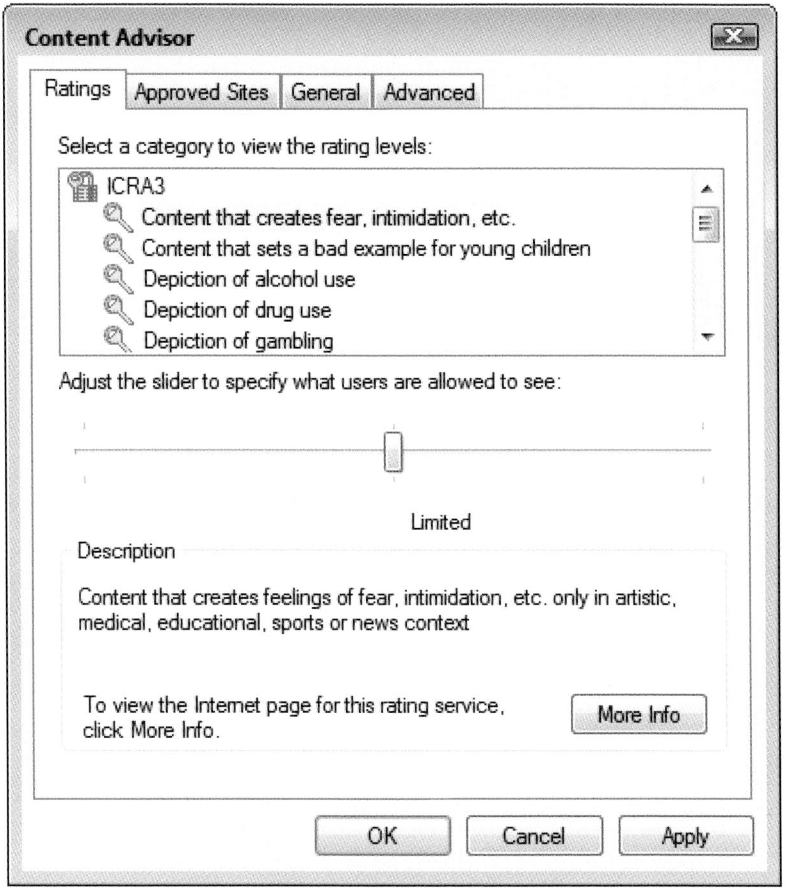

Figure 5.6

It is wishful thinking to imagine that every website author will fill in the questionnaire and therefore any site without such coding will be automatically blocked. If you are certain that a particular site is appropriate, you can accept it by using your supervisor password and it will be added to the list of approved sites.

You can set different levels of protection for each and every user of your computer.

Parental Controls

If your computer is likely to be used by children or grandchildren you can set several parameters that govern what kind of material they can view on the Web as well as the times when they can use the Internet. You will need to set up a User Account for such users by going to Start then Control Panel and choose User Accounts. Make sure that your own account and any used by other adults in the household are protected by passwords before setting up a new account for the younger members of the household.

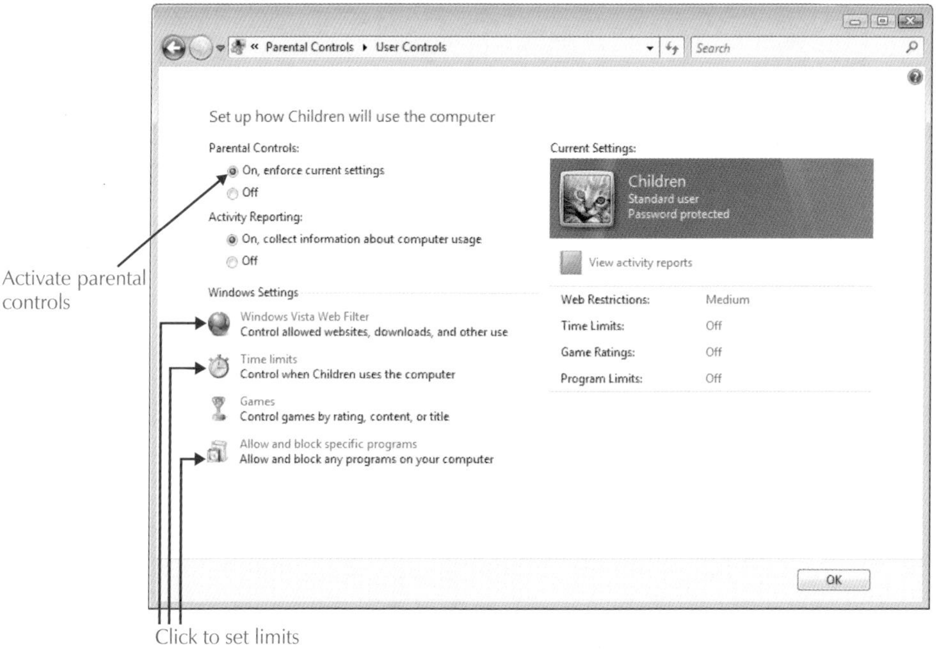

Figure 5.7

There are four restriction levels that are designed to identify content you want to block:

● High. Children's sites include content that is understandable and usable by children, and that is appropriate for them. The language of a children's site is typically aimed at 8 to 12 year-olds, and the concepts presented are accessible to younger minds. When you choose this level, you permit your child to see children's sites, as well as any website that you add to the list of allowed websites.

● Medium. With this level, websites are filtered based on web content categories. This lets your child explore the wide range of information on the Internet, but not see content that is inappropriate. You can review the online activity report to see what sites your child visited or tried to visit.

● None. No web content is automatically blocked.

● Custom. This level also uses content categories to filter websites, but allows you to filter more content categories.

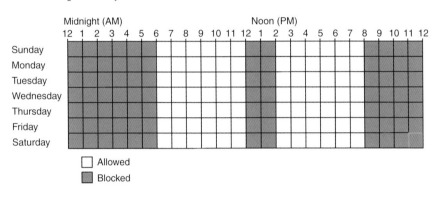

Control when Children will use the computer

Click and drag the hours you want to block or allow.

Figure 5.8

Regardless of which restriction level you choose, you can always allow or block specific websites by adding them to the Allow and block list. You can also block or allow the use of the various programs installed on your computer. Click on the 'Allow and block specific programs' link and the computer will list all the programs available on the hard disk which you can mark as allowed or denied. Be patient because it will take several minutes for the computer to list all the available programs installed on your machine.

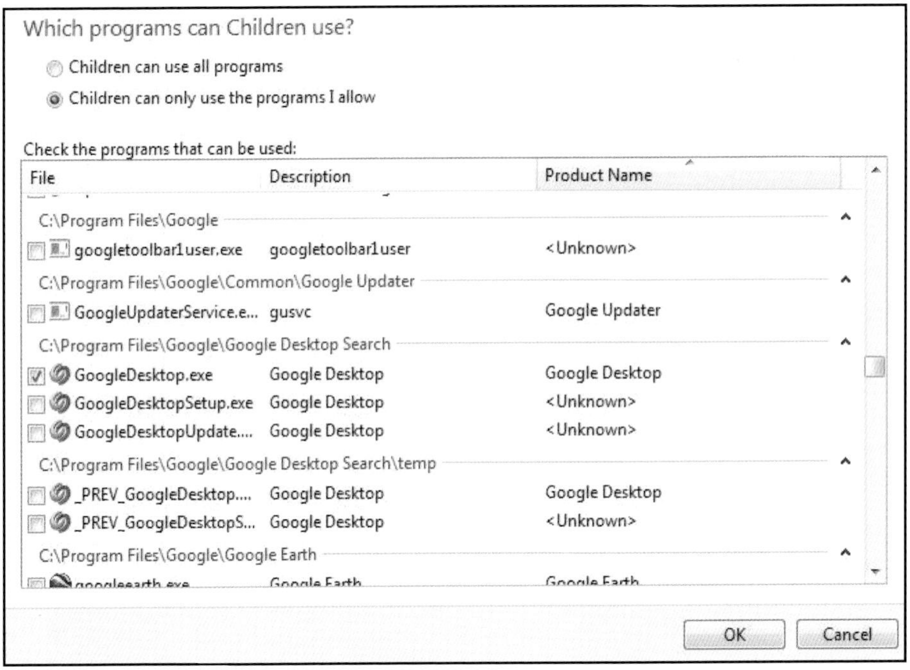

Which programs can Children use?

⊙ Children can use all programs
⦿ Children can only use the programs I allow

Check the programs that can be used:

File	Description	Product Name
C:\Program Files\Google		
☐ 🔲 googletoolbar1user.exe	googletoolbar1user	<Unknown>
C:\Program Files\Google\Common\Google Updater		
☐ 🔲 GoogleUpdaterService.e...	gusvc	Google Updater
C:\Program Files\Google\Google Desktop Search		
☑ 🟢 GoogleDesktop.exe	Google Desktop	Google Desktop
☐ 🟢 GoogleDesktopSetup.exe	Google Desktop	<Unknown>
☐ 🟢 GoogleDesktopUpdate....	Google Desktop	<Unknown>
C:\Program Files\Google\Google Desktop Search\temp		
☐ 🟢 _PREV_GoogleDesktop....	Google Desktop	Google Desktop
☐ 🟢 _PREV_GoogleDesktopS...	Google Desktop	<Unknown>
C:\Program Files\Google\Google Earth		
☐ 🟢 googleearth.exe	Google Earth	Google Earth

[OK] [Cancel]

Figure 5.9

Tick the boxes that you deem appropriate for your younger users. If they express a wish to use other programs you will have the opportunity to discuss it with them before activating the program by using your own password. Communication rather than condemnation is the best way forward.

Preventing outside intrusion

When your computer is connected to the Internet you are potentially vulnerable to invasion from the criminally minded. The risk of such an invasion should not be exaggerated, as in many Hollywood blockbusters, but a few simple precautions will help to set your mind at rest.

The weakest link in your armoury will be any wireless connection or router you use to maintain your Internet connection. Make sure that when your 'guardian angel' first sets up your system that he or she secures the wireless router with a strong password. Routers are often supplied with no password at all or a very weak one such as 'password'. Similarly the user name is usually set to 'admin'. The 'unclean' of the computing world simply have to open up their laptop within range of your router – often several hundred metres – pick up your router signal and they have potential access to your machine. Choose a password that is memorable to you but unlikely to be guessed by outsiders. You will not have to use this password very often so make sure you write it down and store it in a safe place.

For the benefit of your guardian angel I would recommend WPA (WiFi Protection Access) rather than WEP (Wired Equivalency Protection) as the latter is very much more difficult to circumnavigate.

Firewalls

A firewall is designed to prevent unauthorised access to or from a private network. They can be activated by using both hardware and software, or a combination of both. Firewalls are frequently used to prevent unauthorised Internet users from accessing private networks connected to the Internet, especially intranets (see the Glossary). All messages entering or leaving the intranet pass through the firewall, which examines each message and blocks those that do not meet the specified security criteria.

Both WindowsXP and Vista come supplied with inbuilt firewalls but increased protection can be gained by using commercial products such as Norton, McAfee and the 'paid for' version of AVG. This offers, in addition to all the features in the free version, protection against hidden threats when downloading files; an anti-spam program against email threats and its own firewall to stop hackers from getting into your PC. The paid version also offers free round-the-clock support. The firewall capabilities of the Windows programs are continually being updated which is another reason to keep your system up to date.

Online backup

You may be under the impression that your files are perfectly safe stored on your computer's hard disk but a catastrophic fire or a visit by a thief may result in the loss of your machine with all its contents. To avoid such disasters many people opt to store their files online using a commercial company to keep their files safe.

One such company is Carbonite at **www.carbonite.com**. Go to the website, enter your email address, create a password and the program will download itself. Once installed you can use the program to backup those essential files such as your documents, photos and music collection. By default, Carbonite offers to backup your Windows system settings and all the files in your Documents folder but you can make your own selection and add files and folders at a later date.

The main problem with online backup systems is the reduced speed of uploading such files. It is amazing how many files you will accumulate over a year and uploading the files for the first time will take hours if not days on a slow connection. You may have to leave your computer on all night to complete the necessary upload. The upside of all this is that once you have completed the initial upload the program only needs to upload those files that have changed since the previous uploading session. You can even set the program to perform automatic backups at times when you are less likely to be using the computer.

The cost of such a service varies and the prices can be found online. The advantage of such a system is the security that it offers by means of your own unique password and the fact that any disaster at home will not affect your computer files. Restoring these files to a new computer is a simple procedure whereby you select the files that you want to download and set the system going.

Usernames and passwords

Quite soon you will begin to realise that as you register yourself on different websites you are going to accumulate a large number of usernames and passwords.

I would strongly suggest that you keep a file of these details preferably stored away in a filing cabinet away from your computer.

You may be tempted to use the same username and password for each separate site. There are two reasons for avoiding this. The first is the obvious one that, if someone gains access to your details they can use them on most of your visited sites so that your shopping details and login information, including passwords, are readily accessible to the intruder. The second is that many sites have very specific rules regarding these entries. Some require numbers as well as letters; some ask for at least eight letters and others will not allow you to use your common usernames because they have been previously registered to someone else. To give you some idea of the number of names and passwords that you will need I would point out that your computer, your email program and any other sites you sign up to will all require the submission of usernames and passwords. This is not to say that you have to have completely different details for every site that requires registration but even if you stick to three or four names and passwords it can be difficult to remember which ones went with which company. Keep a list and keep it safe.

Summary

- Get to know the implications of viruses, etc.
- Keep your operating system up to date
- Set parental controls if you feel the need
- Set up Content Advisor
- Make sure your guardian angel has set up a firewall
- Make a record of your usernames and passwords

Brain Training

There may be more than one correct answer to these questions.

1. What is phishing?

☐ a) Angling for phlat phish ☐ b) Searching the Internet

☐ c) An attempt to access your security details ☐ d) A banking scam

2. What do viruses do to a computer?

☐ a) Not a lot ☐ b) Wipe out all your memory

☐ c) Create silly messages on certain dates ☐ d) Cause computer havoc

3. What are updates?

☐ a) Important improvements to your computer programs ☐ b) Meetings with the opposite sex on the way to work

☐ c) They maintain the security of your computer ☐ d) Improved versions of old programs

4. What are inappropriate websites?

☐ a) You decide ☐ b) Sites depicting pornography and violence

☐ c) Computer viruses ☐ d) Pages that do not answer your questions

5. What is a firewall?

☐ a) A means of preventing access to your computer

☐ b) A security system that maintains the security of your system

☐ c) A tool that prevents access to inappropriate web pages

☐ d) A small sprinkler inside the computer case

Answers

Q1 – c and d

Q2 – All four answers could be correct

Q3 – a and c

Q4 – a, b and presumably d

Q5 – a and b

Getting help

6

Equipment needed: a computer; Internet Explorer program; connection to the Internet.

Skills needed: some knowledge of the keyboard and mouse.

The guardian angel who set up your computer will usually respond favourably to most of your initial questions but please do not extend their patience by ringing them every other day with questions that you can answer yourself by going to the Web.

Offline help

Most computer programs come equipped with a Help facility. Some are about as useful as a slap in the belly with a wet fish but the majority can answer quite complex questions about the use of the program in question. The Help function will always be found at the right hand end of the Menu bar or it can be activated by pressing the F1 key.

For example, you may want to spread the words out in a document by double spacing the lines of type but you have no idea how to do this. With the word processing program open, click on Help and type in the words 'double spacing' in the search bar. The program will take a few seconds before presenting you with various alternative suggestions. Click on the most likely entry and you will find the following advice:

1. Select the text that you want to change, or click **Select All** on the **Edit** menu.

2. On the **Formatting** toolbar, point to **Line Spacing** .

   If the **Formatting** toolbar is not visible, on the **View** menu, point to **Toolbars**, and then click **Formatting**.

3. Click the arrow next to **Line Spacing** , and then click **2.0**.

You will find a Help function in all programs including Internet Explorer, photographic programs, music playing programs and even the Windows operating system, although this last option is accessed from the Start menu under Help and Support. You may want to look up the keyboard shortcut which brings up the Task Manager. You will find this in the Help and Support function. (The answer, incidentally, is a combination of Ctrl+Alt+Delete.)

> The international distress call of Mayday comes from the French 'm'aidez' meaning 'help me'.

Task Manager

> There may be times when a particular program stops working for no apparent reason. The program is said to have 'hung' and often prevents the use of other programs. If all attempts to close the program down fail then it is time to use the Task Manager. By using the key combination of Ctrl+Alt+Del a window will appear showing all the active programs. Select the hung program and choose End Task.

Most of these help facilities are available offline but since the subject of this book is the use of the Internet let us explore the possibilities of getting help from the Web. As we have seen in the Searching chapter you can find out almost anything on the Web which includes advice on how to use your computer.

Online help

Suppose, you needed to connect a microphone to your computer and were

Figure 6.1

baffled by the number of sockets that could be the right one. The sockets themselves are often identified by impressed logos but these are of little use at your present stage of computing knowledge. Simply search for 'microphone socket' on a search engine such as Google. It will help direct you to the right socket.

Troubleshooting

A number of my pupils have had problems with their printers – varying from a complete inability to do their job or grabbing the paper at ridiculous angles. In the majority of cases the cost of having a printer repaired outweighs that of a new machine. Fortunately a number of these problems can be solved by some investigation on the Web. It may be that a corrupted document is jamming up the queue of other documents waiting to be printed; your printer heads may have become blocked after drying out through lack of use or your print cartridges may just have run out of ink. All these situations can be resolved at home without recourse to an expensive professional.

'Troubleshoot' is a very useful word to include in your search terms when looking for a solution to a technical problem. In the case of the sort of problem I have described above, searching for 'troubleshoot printer problem' or 'troubleshoot paper feed printer' will offer a multitude of useful websites offering you the necessary advice entirely free of charge.

Printers are not the only bits of computer equipment to suffer solvable glitches. Imperfect scanning results will be explained following a search for 'troubleshoot scanner'; 'troubleshoot monitor setting' will help you to correct any viewing problems you might encounter – the list is endless.

Note that I have suggested using the singular form of the words 'printer', 'scanner' and 'problem' when entering your search terms. This encourages the search engine to find both the singular and plural forms of the word.

Forums and newsgroups

In addition to the millions of websites available to help you solve your problems there are also a similar number of forums and newsgroups devoted to specialist subjects from an interest in archaeology to discussions about the finer points of stump work. If you don't know what stump work is then check it out on your search engine – it has got nothing to do with forestry! I will deal with news groups in Chapter 7 as they form part of your email program but forums are slightly different. They are usually found on websites such as 50Connect at **http://forums.50connect.co.uk/**, Sagazone at **www.sagazone.co.uk** or Computer Forum at **www.computerforum.com**. You will often find the answer to your query from previously asked questions but there is nothing to prevent you from posting your own query to a relevant forum. The only requisite is that you register with the forum by entering your name and email address.

Registering is almost always free of charge but I would suggest that you use one of your secondary email addresses (see Chapter 7) when registering so that your main Inbox does not get cluttered with unwanted messages. You can always unsubscribe to these forums if you find that they don't suit you.

Newsgroups are slightly different. (You can set up your email program – Outlook Express or Windows Mail – to receive newsgroup postings and I will cover that in Chapter 7.) There is another more effective way of getting information from these newsgroups and you can use Google for this. Whereas the ordinary Google search engine finds web pages, Google Groups is a massive index of 'newsgroups', an area of the Internet where people discuss topics by writing email-like messages.

If you have a problem, it's a safe bet that someone somewhere has had the same problem, has asked for a solution in one of these newsgroups, and has been given an answer. If so, Google Groups should have copies of all the related messages.

You can reach Google Groups by typing **http://groups.google.com** into your browser's Address box and pressing Enter. When you arrive, you'll see the usual search box at the top where you type the words you want to search for. The only difference is that you'll be searching the newsgroups rather than web pages, but you don't do anything differently yourself. The results look much the same as those you'd see when searching for web pages, but each result leads to a conversation that has taken place in the newsgroups: if you click one of the results, you'll reach a page containing all the messages in the conversation, in the order they were written. Many of the answers will have a plus sign beside them, indicating that there are several entries on the subject. These multiple entries and replies are known as 'threads' and are well worth following.

Google Groups is not just useful for finding answers to computing questions, incidentally. There are tens of thousands of different newsgroups covering every topic under the sun (I remember years ago there was even a newsgroup devoted to tomato ketchup!), and Google indexes almost all of them, so it's a good place to search for any type of information.

The great thing about newsgroups is that all these messages are written by ordinary individuals rather than companies with a product to sell. They can be blunt or even rude at times, and sometimes the conversation in these messages can veer off on to a completely different issue from the one it began with, but there are times when I find it a much better source of information than the World Wide Web and the standard search engines such as Google search.

PCWisdom website

Finally you can always ask me for help by going to the website that accompanies this book – **www.pcwisdom.co.uk**. Simply click on the Have a Question link and type in your request for help. I will try and get back to you within a couple of days. You will also find various tutorials and a Question and Answer page which may solve your problem immediately.

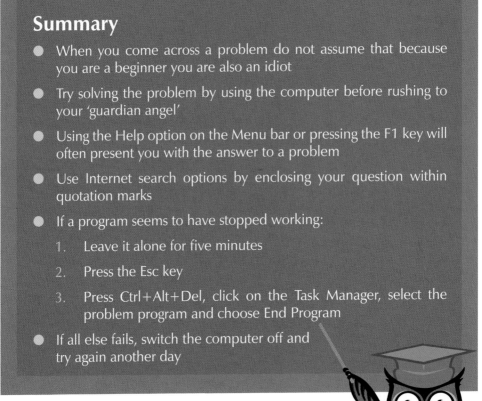

Summary

- When you come across a problem do not assume that because you are a beginner you are also an idiot

- Try solving the problem by using the computer before rushing to your 'guardian angel'

- Using the Help option on the Menu bar or pressing the F1 key will often present you with the answer to a problem

- Use Internet search options by enclosing your question within quotation marks

- If a program seems to have stopped working:

    1. Leave it alone for five minutes

    2. Press the Esc key

    3. Press Ctrl+Alt+Del, click on the Task Manager, select the problem program and choose End Program

- If all else fails, switch the computer off and try again another day

Brain Training

There may be more than one correct answer to these questions.

1. **Which key always brings up a Help menu?**

   ☐ a) Ctrl+H   ☐ b) F12

   ☐ c) F1   ☐ d) The Help key

2. **What might be wrong if you cannot hear audio from your computer?**

   ☐ a) You are using a laptop   ☐ b) You have got the speakers on mute

   ☐ c) The speaker jack is plugged into the pink socket   ☐ d) The speakers are turned off

3. **What might be wrong if your printer fails to work?**

   ☐ a) It is not plugged in   ☐ b) The ink has run out

   ☐ c) You did not press Alt+P   ☐ d) There is a corrupted file in the printer queue

4. **Which of the following applies to newsgroups?**

   ☐ a) You need to pay a small subscription fee   ☐ b) They can be accessed by your email program

   ☐ c) They can be searched by Google   ☐ d) You will need to set one up

5. What is a scanner?

☐ a) A computer program that maps speed cameras

☐ b) A photocopier

☐ c) An alternative to a fax machine

☐ d) A speech recognition program

Answers

Q1 – c	**Q4** – b and c
Q2 – b, c and d	**Q5** – b and c
Q3 – a, b and d	

Email

Equipment needed: a computer;Internet Explorer program; connection to the Internet; an anti-virus program; a firewall and a record of usernames and passwords.

Skills needed: some knowledge of the keyboard and mouse plus some confidence; knowledge of downloading a program.

Most people mention email as their main use of the Internet so we had better sort this potential problem area out now. Many of you may be au fait with the process of sending an email but, for those who are still having a few problems, here is a recap of the procedure.

Open up your email program – in this case Windows Mail, but the process is almost identical in Outlook Express and other email programmes. Study the toolbar below. Most of the toolbar icons are obvious in their action and those that are not labelled can be identified by pointing at the icon when a descriptive box will appear.

Figure 7.1

Reply and Forward icons

To use these functions select the message to which you wish to reply or that which you want to forward on to another contact and click on the appropriate icon.

Reply All

This icon allows you to reply to all the recipients of the selected message.

Folder icon

This displays or hides the folders in the left pane of the window.

Find and Search

These two options can lead to some confusion. The Find icon allows you to search for messages according to the sender, subject, date within different folders. The Search box looks in the body of the messages to find the desired text.

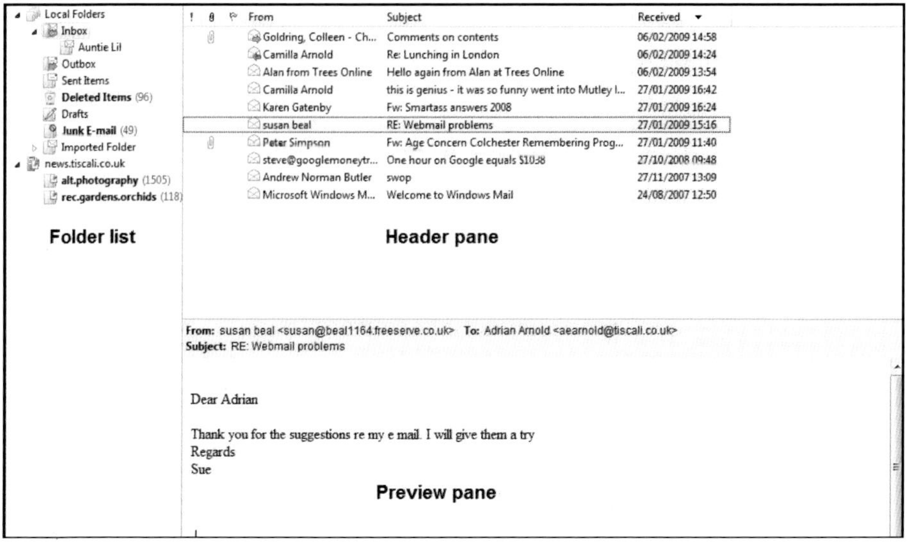

Figure 7.2

Windows Mail layout

Below these Menu and Tool bars you will find the rest of the window occupied by various panes showing the folders, headers and previews. To open a message in its own window double click anywhere along its header line.

Add a contact to the Address book

Every time you send an email you will need to insert the address of the recipient. Of course you can type it in to the Address box every time but that becomes tedious after a while. If you enter your contacts details in the Address book they will remain there for instant access so let us see how this can be done.

> John Paul II was the first pope to send an email message while the Queen sent her first email in 1976.

Windows Mail

Click on the Contacts/Address book box and choose New Contact.

New contact   New contact group

Figure 7.3

The next window allows you to enter not only the name and email address but also many other details such as telephone numbers, addresses, birthdays reminders and even an image of the person.

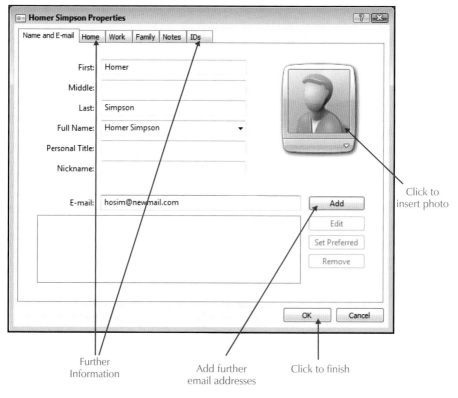

Figure 7.4

Once you have filled in the necessary boxes, click on OK to complete the entry – you can always add details to the contact information at a later date.

Outlook Express

Outlook Express does things slightly differently so we will look at this now.

Select the Address book from its icon, choose New from the File menu and click on New Contact. The resulting window will look very similar to the Windows Mail address details but without some of the latest options such as a photograph.

Note that the Add button is there to add a second email address for this person – *not* to add it to the Address book. Do this by clicking on OK.

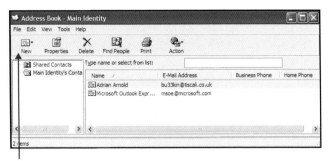

Click to add
new contact

Figure 7.5

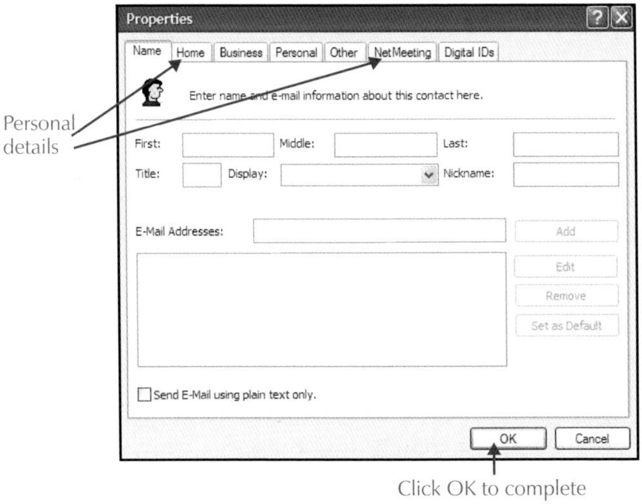

Personal
details

Click OK to complete

Figure 7.6

Send an email message

The technique is almost identical for both programs. Click on the Create Mail icon in Windows Mail (or New in Outlook Express) and the message window will appear.

1. Enter the address in the Address bar by typing the address or click on the To: book icon and select from the address book and click on the To: button.

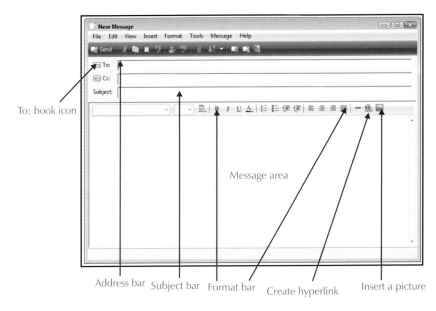

To: book icon

Message area

Address bar Subject bar Format bar Create hyperlink Insert a picture

Figure 7.7

2. Add any further addresses in the Cc: box to send copies of the message to other people.

3. Enter the subject in the Subject box.

4. Type your message in the Message area after clicking within that area to place the flashing cursor.

5. Click on Send. This will despatch the message immediately if you are connected to a broadband connection but will go to the Outbox folder if you are using dial-up. In this case you will then have to select the Send/Receive button to send it on its way.

35 billion emails are sent each day throughout the world.

Netiquette

There are a number of accepted practices when sending messages by email, to forums or newsgroups which, if followed, will elicit more helpful replies. DON'T USE CAPITALS THE WHOLE TIME. It is the messaging equivalent of shouting and anyway the text is more difficult to read. You can get your feelings across by using curious keyboard characters known as emoticons. These create images when turned through 90 degrees create the image of a facial expression.

:)   smiling

;)   winking

:=(sad

: 0   surprised

: /   concerned or baffled

Various texting abbreviations are acceptable in these situations such as LOL meaning laughing out loud or IMHO, in my humble opinion. There are thousands of these acronyms in use today and your grandchildren will be able to keep you up to date with the latest developments. You will find a comprehensive list of texting abbreviations at **www.webopedia.com/quick_ref/textmessageabbreviations.asp**

Try to avoid fancy fonts. They can be difficult to read and some computers will not recognise the less common typefaces.

A computer engineer called Ray Tomlinson was the first person to send an email message in 1971.

Attachments and insertions

These two actions perform very similar tasks. Using the Attach icon allows you to send a computer file, which may be a report, minutes of a meeting or a photograph, with the message. Insert puts the contents of that file within the body of the message.

If you 'attached' a photo your recipient would have to click on the attached file and open it in a suitable program, but if you 'inserted' it, it would appear within the message itself. It is usually a matter of personal choice.

To attach a file simply select the Attach icon (the paperclip), navigate your way to the file in question, select it by left clicking then choose Insert or Open.

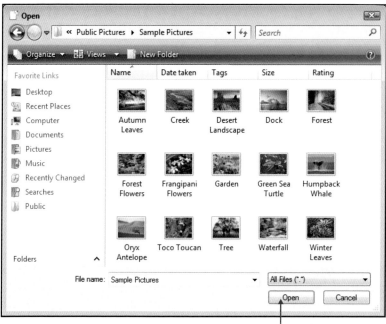

Click here to attach file

Figure 7.8

This action adds another box to the message containing details of the attached file.

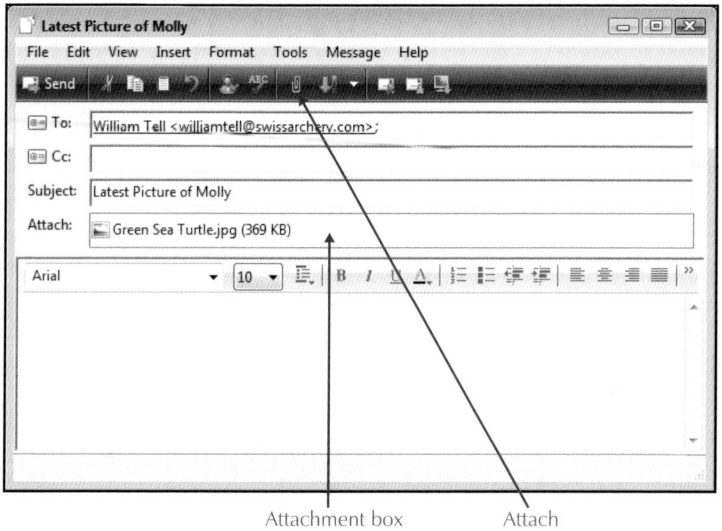

Attachment box   Attach

Figure 7.9

Some image and sound files can be very large – and video files are even larger – so be aware that these are going to take some time to transfer and enough of them will clog up your recipient's mailbox.

Inserting a picture into an email

There is another way of sending a picture with an email. Isn't there always? Instead of sending the picture as an image file you could select Insert then select Picture, select the file and choose Insert. Using this method the picture will be placed within the message text so that your addressee will see the picture immediately without having to open it as a separate file.

Hyperlinks

When you enter a web address or email address into the message area it is converted to a hyperlink – or 'link' as it is more usually known. This means that the recipient simply has to click on the link to open up the relevant program and display the information. Some web addresses (URLs) can be very long and clumsy which might spoil the layout of your message so there is another method of attaching a link – by using the Hyperlink icon.

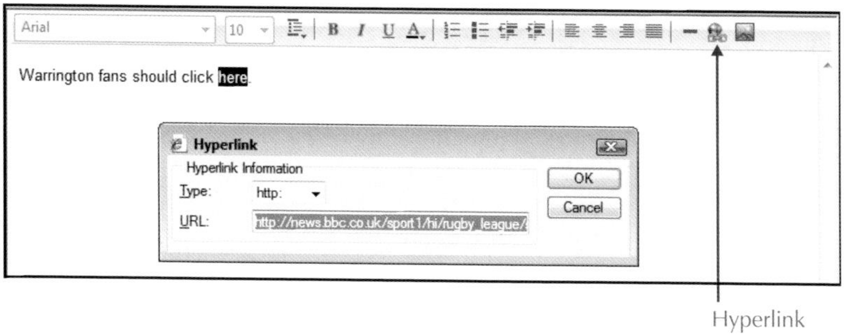

Hyperlink

Figure 7.10

http://picasaweb.google.co.uk/adrian.vetman/Venice# is the web page that shows one of my web photo albums but it will look clumsy and ugly within an email. To tidy it up, you simply say that family and friends should click Here. Highlight the word 'Here' and select the hyperlink icon.

Copy the link address from the web page and paste it into the URL box. Click on OK and the word 'Here' will be coloured blue and underlined like any other link.

Get a second email address

The time spent deleting SPAM costs United States businesses $21.6 billion annually.

Why, when I only have a single address for my letter post? The main reason is to reduce the amount of junk email or 'spam' that you will begin to accumulate. Once you have started to shop or subscribe to various organisations on the Internet you will begin to receive unsolicited email from across the globe and it will soon begin to drive you to distraction. I will discuss spam filters later in this chapter but, for the time being, take my word for it.

Each time you buy a book, book a flight, check into a hotel or subscribe to a newsletter you are going to have to provide an email address. Almost all companies try to reassure us that they do not release details of email addresses but they get out there somehow and there are people who will give their eye teeth for lists of active email addresses so that they can bombard you with unnecessary, irritating and frankly, fraudulent messages offering anything from instant fortune to fake Rolex watches with more unpleasantries in between.

You will not be able to avoid it but you can reduce the amount of junk email you receive by observing a few simple rules:

- Only give out your main email address to your nearest and dearest.
- Use a second address for your Internet buying and subscribing.
- Use even a third or fourth email address for registering on sites that you are slightly unsure of.
- Use an effective anti-spam filter. We will discuss these later in this chapter.

Where can you get another address from? For starters your ISP will certainly allow you to have at least five email addresses but what if you want to swap your Internet Service Provider? You will lose all these addresses in favour of those created by your new provider. In spite of this I maintain three email addresses with my ISP – one for friends and family, another for correspondence about my books and a third for those web registrations that I make with forums and newsgroups.

In addition to your ISP email addresses you can obtain further email accounts from web based companies such as Hotmail, Google and Mail.com. The latter offers free email addresses, a spam filter and the options to choose from 250 address options. You can check it out at **www.mail.com**. You can even create your own web page which will have its own email contact facilities (see Chapter 17).

Setting up an email account

Your guardian angel will have set up your initial address but you would be wise to know how it is done. When you are signing up to an ISP you will need to establish an email account whereby you can send and receive messages from across the world. The signing up procedure installs the email details on your email program which is almost certainly Outlook Express in Windows XP or Windows Mail in Vista. However there will be occasions when you need to look up details of your account or alter some of the settings, so let us go through the procedure of setting up an email account on your personal program.

Windows
Mail

Figure 7.11

I will be dealing with Windows Mail but the steps are almost identical when using Outlook Express. First of all, open the Windows Mail program by clicking on its icon or go to the Start menu then Programs and select Windows Mail.

Now click on Tools on the menu bar and select Accounts. Choose Add and select Email account. This will activate a wizard which is not someone related to Harry Potter but a series of actions that you follow to establish a new account.

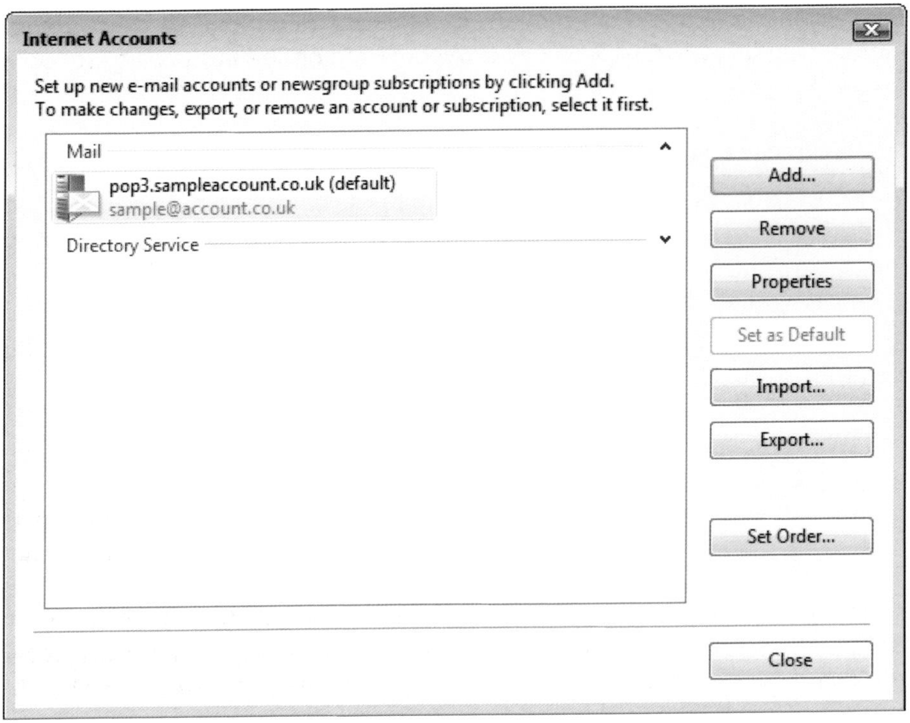

Figure 7.12

The first entry required is your name which is how your correspondents will identify any message you send them. On the next page, enter the new email address. The following page needs some information from your email provider which you will have been given when you set up the new email account. These are the email servers for both incoming and outgoing messages. The former is normally something like pop.btinternet.com and the latter may be smtp.btinternet.com. These server addresses *never* have a space in them and the words are separated by dots (full stops).

Each company will have their own way of addressing the servers. Some, for instance, may substitute the word 'mail' for both 'pop' and 'smtp'. Check out the email account confirmation you got when setting up the account.

We are nearly there now so please bear with me. The penultimate page asks for the username and password you were given by your provider. The username may or may not be your full email address. Tick the box to remember your password, click OK and, if everything is in order select Finish on the last page to set up the account.

If you have managed to achieve all this in one go, award yourself a gold star and a well-earned cup of coffee. Congratulations.

Setting up a mail account

Owning a Google mail account not only gives you a useful second email address if, for some reason, your main address becomes corrupted but also gives you entry to a huge world of web facilities within one structure. However, there are many other sites which offer you free email accounts, in this instance I will use Google to demonstrate how to set up a Internet mail account. You will be able to store your documents, save your pictures as albums on the Web, write your own blog (a kind of web diary – See Chapter 15) and even receive email on your mobile phone.

Google mail is a free web based email program that can be accessed from any Internet connected computer in the world as well as forwarding any mail received to your usual email program such as Outlook Express or Windows Mail. Setting up a Google account is very simple if you follow the steps listed below.

1. Go to the website **http://mail.google.com** and you will be presented with the window displayed below.

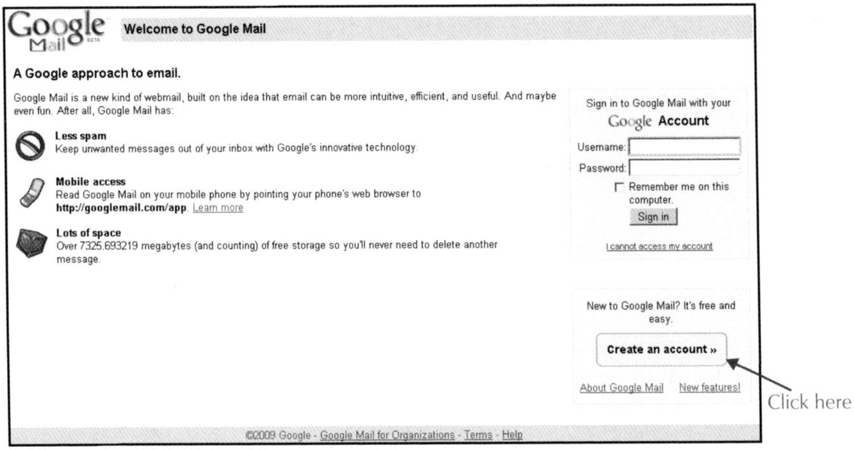

Reproduced from Google™

Figure 7.13

2. Click on 'Sign up for Google Mail'.

3. Fill in the appropriate boxes. Choose a login name – in this case I have chosen the name 'thebard' – then click on 'Check availability'. You may have to play around with a number of alternatives before you get an acceptable name. Try putting a full stop between two words such as 'the.bard'. This often results in an acceptable name.

4. Choose a password using both letters and numbers but make sure it is something you will be able to remember.

5. Choose a security question either from the dropdown list or make up your own question. This is to identify yourself if you forget your username or password.

6. Select your location from the dropdown list.

7. Copy the 'warped' letters into the box below. This is to prevent automatic computer-generated applications.

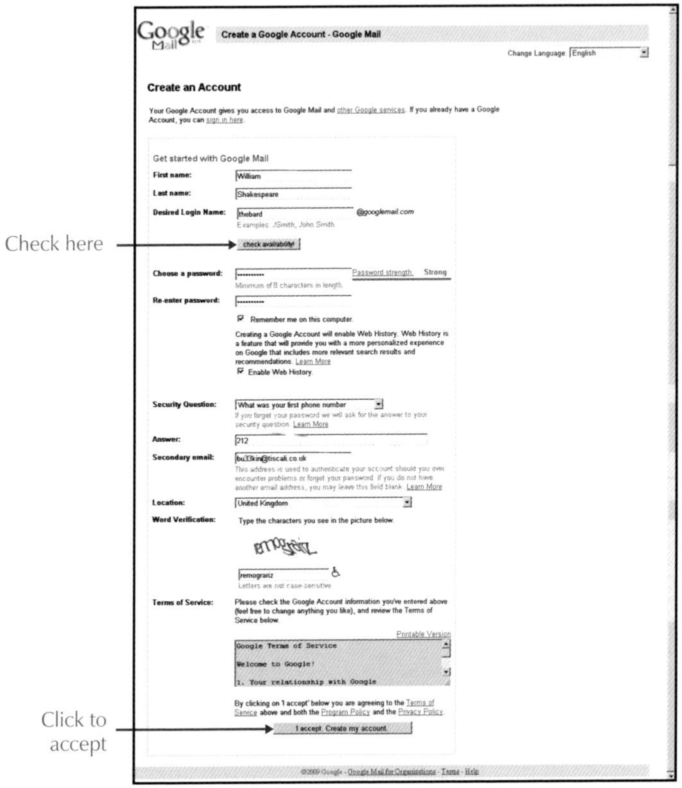

Reproduced from Google™

Figure 7.14

8. Finally click the Accept button to activate your account.

9. Go to Contacts and start entering the email addresses from your old address book. You can do this quite quickly by going to your Address Book in Outlook Express or Windows Mail then choose Export from the File dropdown menu. Select the CSV format, give the file a name such as Outlook contacts and save it in the Documents folder.

10. The go back to your Google mail page, choose Contacts and click on Import. Navigate your way to the 'Outlook Contacts CSV' file and follow the importing instructions.

Reproduced from Google™   Import CSV file

Figure 7.15

11. To get Google mail to forward your mail to your usual email program click on Settings and then the Forwarding and POP/IMAP settings and follow the instructions. There are good tutorial instructions for almost all email programs – just follow the instructions for your particular program.

Settings

General   Accounts   Labels   Filters   **Forwarding and POP/IMAP**   Chat   Web Clips   Labs   Themes

Forwarding: ○ Disable forwarding
  ● Forward a copy of incoming mail to [   ] and
  [delete Google Mail's copy   ▼]

  Tip: You can also forward only some of your mail by creating a filter!

POP Download: **1. Status:** POP is enabled for all mail that has arrived since Jan 17
Learn more   ○ Enable POP for **all mail** (even mail that's already been downloaded)
  ○ Enable POP for **mail that arrives from now on**
  ○ **Disable** POP

  2. When messages are accessed with POP [keep Google Mail's copy in the Inbox   ▼]

  3. Configure your email client (e.g. Outlook, Eudora, Netscape Mail)
  Configuration instructions

IMAP Access: **1. Status:** IMAP is disabled
(access Google Mail from   ○ Enable IMAP
other clients using IMAP)   ● Disable IMAP
Learn more

  2. Configure your email client (e.g. Outlook, Thunderbird, iPhone)
  Configuration instructions

  [Save Changes]   [Cancel]

Reproduced from Google™

Figure 7.16

12. You're done. Congratulations.

There are other examples of subscribing to various websites later in the book so you will have plenty of opportunities to practice filling in these application forms.

Newsgroups

I have discussed the advantages of newsgroups in the previous chapter. In this chapter I want to show you how to setup and subscribe to newsgroups from your email program. Your ISP will almost certainly offer a list of newsgroups to which you can subscribe but first of all you have to set up your mail program to view them.

Open up your Windows Mail program (or Outlook Express – the procedure is almost identical in both programs). Select Accounts from the Menu bar and choose Add.

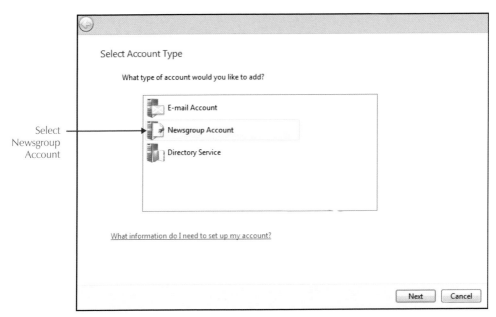

Figure 7.17

Select Newsgroup account and click on Next. You will then be asked for a user name.

I suggest that you use a nickname rather than your own name for security reasons.

Click on Next and you will need to enter the News server address. You will have been provided with this information when you first signed up to your ISP but if you have mislaid the information or put it in one of those irretrievable 'safe places' you can make an educated guess by entering 'news'. In front of your ISP's domain name as I have done below.

Internet News Server Name

Type the name of the Internet news (NNTP) server your Internet service provider has given you.

News (NNTP) server:

news.tiscali.co.uk

If your Internet service provider has informed you that you must log on to your news (NNTP) server and has provided you with an NNTP account name and password, then select the check box below.

☐ My news server requires me to log on

[Next] [Cancel]

Do not select this box

Figure 7.18

Do not tick the 'log on' box as very few news servers require this and it can become something of a pain. The last page summarises your newsgroup settings and so click on Finish. This will add a new folder to the Mail side panel. Now we need to populate your newsgroup with a list of available groups so click on the Newsgroups icon and wait for the list of groups to be downloaded. This can take a few minutes as there may be more than 75,000 groups to be downloaded. The vast majority of these will be of no interest whatsoever so you need to enter a subject that you are interested in when a much shorter list of alternatives will be displayed.

Try subscribing to a few newsgroups and posting the odd question. You will probably receive an answer within a day or two from an active group.

Anti-spam filters

While most free email providers offer a degree of spam filtering some are a lot better than others. The average ones will filter out messages with words like sex, Viagra and other salacious terms in the subject box but we tend to get what we pay for in this world and the commercial anti-spam programs are much more artful and selective. There are hundreds of such programs available and it would be pointless to list even a few dozen but there are two I can recommend.

The first, Mailwasher at **www.mailwasher.net**, has a free option which is very effective but requires a little more effort on your part and the other is Cloudmark which is the one I have been using for the past five years. You will find it at **www.cloudmark.com**. Look them up on the Web and see if either one of them appeals to you but whatever you do make sure that you have got some sort of anti-spam protection in place because as sure as eggs are potential chickens you are going to get spam in the not-too-distant future. To give you some idea of the amount of spam out there, I would estimate that of every 100 email messages that try to get to my inbox at least 80 are unsolicited rubbish and Cloudmark sorts them out automatically within seconds.

Email rules

No, this is not a graffiti slogan. Email rules are means by which you can classify and catalogue your email messages. Once you start to gather email messages in your inbox you will find it increasingly difficult to retrieve that message from Auntie Betsy reminding you of her holiday dates or that useful website recommended by your pal, Philip.

Most of your mail can be left in your inbox for future reference but there are advantages in collating all the messages from Philip and Auntie Betsy into their individual mail folders within your main Inbox folder.

New Mail Rule ⊟ ✕

Select your Conditions and Actions first, then specify the values in the Description.

1. Select the Conditions for your rule:

☑ Where the From line contains people
☐ Where the Subject line contains specific words
☐ Where the message body contains specific words
☐ Where the To line contains people

2. Select the Actions for your rule:

☑ Move it to the specified folder
☐ Copy it to the specified folder
☐ Delete it
☐ Forward it to people

3. Rule Description (click on an underlined value to edit it):

Apply this rule after the message arrives
Where the From line contains people
Move it to the specified folder

4. Name of the rule:

New Mail Rule #1

OK   Cancel

Click to specify folder   Click to specify people

Figure 7.19

Saving your messages

Many beginners tend to delete email messages as soon as they have read them and I would advise against this unless the messages are obviously of no value. Your daughter may have emailed you with the details of the grandchildren's half-term dates. You may have put them in your diary or marked them on a calendar but diaries and calendars go missing and you may forget the dates. By retaining the message in your Inbox you will always have a copy to refer to should the need arise. Your brother may have sent you an interesting web reference in an email but, if you delete it, you will not be able to remember it to show to the neighbour who pops in for a cup of tea three weeks later. You never know when this kind of information is going to be useful. I keep all my messages for nine months just in case. Email messages take up such a tiny portion of your hard disk memory that it seems pointless not to use it.

Accessing your email from the Web

Both email and the World Wide Web use the Internet but they operate using different programs. The Web is accessed using an Internet browser such as Internet Explorer or Firefox while email uses something like Windows Mail or Outlook Express. Having said that it is possible, in many instances, to use your Internet browser to access your email account via the Web using the webmail facility offered by most Internet Service Providers. This can be very useful if you are away from your home computer when on holiday or just visiting friends with Internet access. It is a rather convoluted way of dealing with your email but can be very useful at times.

To read your messages on the Web you must first login to your ISP's website and then login in with your username and password

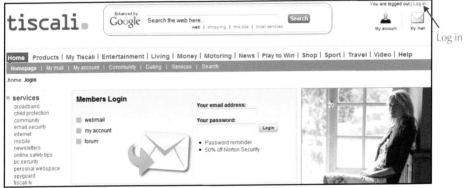

Reproduced by courtesy of Tiscali

Figure 7.20

Once you are logged in you can access your mailbox and read those messages that have not yet been downloaded to your email program on your home computer. You can reply to these messages and even create new messages but you may find that you do not have an address book on the Web and have to rely upon your memory for the recipient's email address. This does not apply to the Reply function as the sender's email address is plainly visible.

If you delete a message in your webmail Inbox it will not be downloaded and stored on to your home computer when you return so that you have a copy of the email for reference later. Once you have deleted it from your web mail inbox it is gone forever unless the sender re-sends the message at your request.

Setting up mailing groups

There may be times, if you are an officer of a club or simply someone who has groups of friends, when you want to send the same message to a group of people. You could spend a long time entering all the individual addresses into the To: or Cc: boxes but there is a simpler way of doing it – by using Group addresses.

You may have an address list of a hundred people but only 20 of those are likely to be amused by some of the humour you find on the Web. In this case you could set up a mailing group consisting of these specific addresses and label it something like Humour.

Here is how you set about creating such a group:

1. Open your mail program – either Windows Mail or Outlook Express and open your Address or Contacts file.

 If you do not see the New Contacts option in Windows Mail Contacts, open the Contacts window and right click in a blank space within the window and choose Customize This Folder from the dropdown menu.

Under 'What kind of folder do you want' choose Contacts from the dropdown menu and click on Apply. This will restore the Contact Group option.

2. Select the New Contact Group.

3. Name the group and then start to add the members. You can add members to the group either from your Contacts list or manually.

4. Click on OK to add the group to your contacts list. You only have to set up a group once and you can edit the member details whenever you wish by selecting it from the Contacts list and adding or removing members.

5. To send a single message with any attachments to all members of this group select the Group name from your address book as the recipient of the email and all the relevant addresses will be entered automatically.

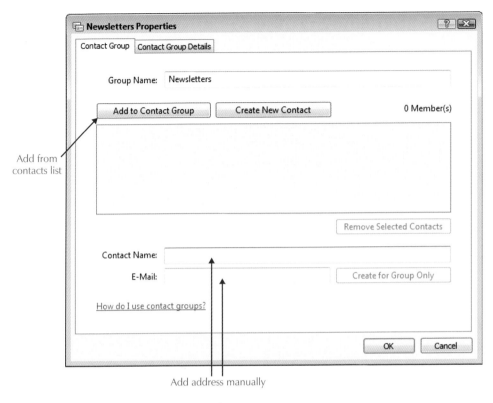

Add from
contacts list

Add address manually

Figure 7.21

Email viruses

Please make sure that you have installed an effective anti-virus program on your computer and that it is regularly updated with the latest information. New viruses are finding their way onto the Internet every week. See Chapter 5 about viruses and other nasties lurking on the Web.

One last word of warning. Do not open any attachments in an email from someone you do not know. The name of the file may tempt your interest but most viruses are spread within attachment files and become activated when the attachment is opened.

Summary

- How to add email contacts
- How to send emails
- Email attachments
- Inserting hyperlinks
- Setting up a Google mail account
- Subscribing to newsgroups
- Accessing your mail from the Internet
- Email viruses

Brain Training

There may be more than one correct answer to these questions.

1. **What happens when you include an email address in an email?**

   ☐ a) The address is highlighted in red

   ☐ b) Nothing

   ☐ c) The address is highlighted in blue and underlined

   ☐ d) It establishes a link to an email program

2. **What does the emoticon (;-) indicate?**

   ☐ a) A smile

   ☐ b) A winking smile

   ☐ c) A dental appointment

   ☐ d) I'm baffled

3. **How many email addresses can be allocated to a private individual?**

   ☐ a) two

   ☐ b) five

   ☐ c) 100

   ☐ d) As many as you like

4. **What happens if you change your Internet Service Provider?**

   ☐ a) You lose access to your ISP email account

   ☐ b) Nothing much

   ☐ c) You will need to use a different web browser

   ☐ d) You will be offered a different email address

5. Which of the following statements apply to spam?

☐ a) You will not get spam if you don't buy on the Internet

☐ b) You ought to get a spam filter

☐ c) You only get spam if you use Internet Explorer

☐ d) You should never reply to spam messages

6. What can you attach to an email?

☐ a) A first-class stamp

☐ b) A photo of Fido with his ball

☐ c) A voice recording

☐ d) A spreadsheet

Answers

Q1 – c and d   **Q4** – a and d
Q2 – b   **Q5** – b and d
Q3 – d   **Q6** – b, c and d

Entertainment on the Web

8

Equipment needed: a computer; Internet Explorer program; a broadband connection to the Internet; an active computer speaker system; a firewall and a record of usernames and passwords.

Skills needed: some knowledge of the keyboard and mouse; knowledge of downloading a program (Chapters 3 and 5) and the knowledge of how to use Favorites (Chapter 3).

Computer speakers

To get full advantages of the entertainment possibilities afforded by the Web you will need to have your speaker system up and running. Many of the queries that are put to me involve the lack of sound and I find that, in many instances the speakers have been set to 'mute'. This is shown by the small icon at the right hand end of the task bar at the bottom of the window having a No Entry sign alongside it. To activate your sound system double click on the icon to reveal the menu. Click on the mute button to restore the sound and drag the slider to adjust the sound levels.

Many modern keyboards have sound adjustment buttons lying across the top of the keyboard included an On/Off mute button and volume controls.

While you have the mute function turned off you will also find volume controls available on screen lying at the bottom of the video windows of many programs such as YouTube and the BBC's iPlayer (see Figure 8.2).

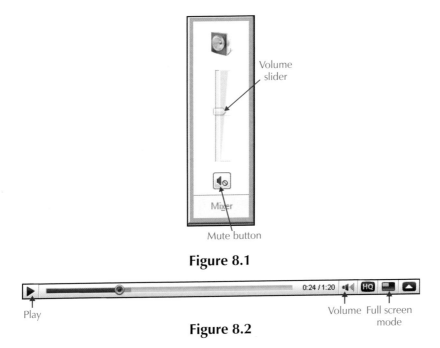

Figure 8.1

Figure 8.2

These screen controls offer further controls over and above the volume settings. Clicking on the Play button starts the recording and changes the button icon to double vertical lines which denotes the Pause function. The Pop Out button plays the video in a separate window. Playing programs in full screen mode makes for easier viewing but the quality is not as good as that seen on a television set. We will be discussing videos on the Web later in this chapter.

Broadband speed

Sound and video transmissions require a fairly decent speed of connection – dial-up connections are too slow to make video watching a worthwhile experience. I live in a rural area and I can only get about 500 kilobytes per second whereas urban areas will get up to 8,000 kilobytes per second. This means that sometimes the audio or video download has to 'catch up' with the recording resulting in breaks in the transmitted program. This can be a little frustrating at times but, once the program has downloaded completely, you can run it again without interruption. If you live more than five kilometres from the telephone exchange there is little you can do about this in spite of what various ISP adverts say – unless you want to move house, that is.

Radio on the Web

Having set up your sound controls we can now start to explore the possibilities of listening to the radio while you work. Throughout the world there are thousands of websites that broadcast radio transmissions from Radio USA at **www.irnusaradio.com**, through the BBC at **www.bbc.co.uk/radio** to Radio Melbourne at **www.abc.net.au/melbourne**. You are not restricted to current broadcasts as many popular programs are retained on the various sites for several weeks.

The controls for such radio websites use are largely generic with the forward arrow (>) issuing the Play command, two vertical lines (| |) pausing the broadcast and a crossed out speaker symbol muting the sound.

Worldwide radio

Using the Internet you are not confined to radio broadcasts from your own country. You can tune in to almost any radio station under the sun by going to **www.liveworldradio.com** where you will find links to radio broadcasts classified by country, genre, language and even foreign TV stations. You can even brush up your language skills by playing a foreign news broadcast while you catalogue your digital photographs.

Other sources of worldwide radio can be found at:

- **www.live-radio.net/info.shtml**
- **http://www.wrn.org/** (Click on Listeners)
- **www.bbc.co.uk/worldservice/**
- **www.internet-radio.org.uk/**
- **www.reciva.com/**

Television on the Web

If you wish to view BBC programmes on the computer you will need to download the BBC.iPlayer. You will find all the details of this useful option at **http://iplayerhelp.external.bbc.co.uk**. Commercial television is also available in the UK using different 'players' from ITV at **www.itv.com** and Sky at **http://tv.sky.com**.

In the same way as you can catch up on your favourite radio programmes you can do the same with television transmissions. However, if you have a new computer you may find that you need to download a couple of programs to be able to view television programmes on the screen. These are Adobe Flash Player and Adobe Media Player. Don't worry about searching for them on the Web because, if you need them, the TV website will recognise their absence, direct your browser to the necessary website and lead you through the downloading processes.

TV programmes are available throughout the world but they are sometimes restricted to computers resident in the country of origin therefore only computer users in the USA can receive TV programmes from the ABC network at **www.abc.com**; NBC at **www.nbc.com** and CBS at **www.cbs.com**. There are many European television stations that broadcast over the Internet and can be received across the continent. There are too many such stations to mention by name but a Google search for Web TV and the desired country of origin will offer the thousands of websites offering TV broadcasts. Homesick Australians can get similar TV broadcasts from stations such as ABC Australia at **www.abc.net.au**. To the best of my knowledge all these Web TV programmes are free-to-air on your computer.

Gone With the Wind is the only Civil War epic ever filmed without a single battle scene.

If you have applied Internet Explorer's Content Advisor (see Chapter 5) you may find that you have to enter your password – several times – before it allows you to view the web page. Personally I found the persistent intrusion of this window rather frustrating so I have reset the Content Advisor to its default setting. Go to Tools then Internet Options and click on the Content tab and choose Disable to turn this option off.

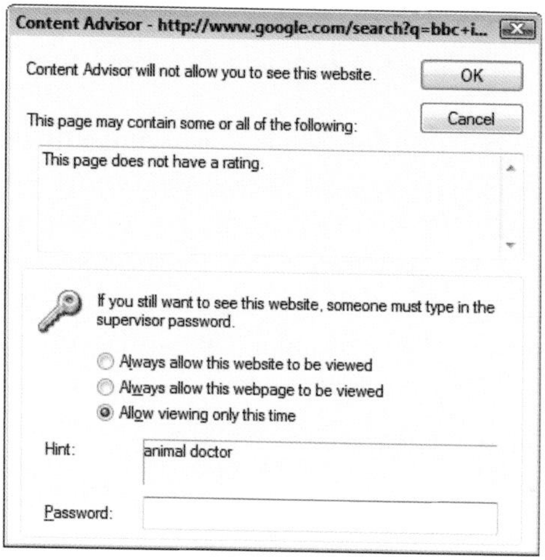

Figure 8.3

YouTube recordings

YouTube at **www.youtube.com** is a fascinating site. These are short video clips on more subjects than you could ever imagine – news, comedy, tutorials and personal recordings are there for the asking. If you want to see something life-enhancing have a look at **http://uk.youtube.com/watch?v=VQ3d3KigPQM** or, if you want a good giggle, try **http://uk.youtube.com/watch?v=4OT_kw48rl4**.

Alright these addresses are rather complicated so I will make it a bit easier for you – the first video can be found at **http://tinyurl.com/9f35fp** and the second at **http://tinyurl.com/d4waqv**.

Apart from making you smile you can learn a great deal from the video tutorials posted on YouTube. Simply enter the subject you are interested in into the search box and add the word 'tutorial'. You can get visual information about how to crochet or make a mitre joint for your woodwork project. You can play the clips over and over again. Don't forget that the Internet is multilingual so you may get a number of commentaries in a foreign language. Just scroll down the list of search results and you are bound to find something in your mother tongue.

To make full use of the YouTube offerings you will need to sign up. It costs nothing to subscribe and you only have to complete the form once.

You will be signing up to a number of sites as you go through the book so now is a good time to practice filling in subscription forms. Most of the boxes are self-explanatory but the Word Verification may cause you a few headaches. This entry is to prevent hackers and other members of the criminal fraternity from automatically creating thousands of accounts for nefarious purposes. Only a human eye can decipher the swirling letters and even then it can be difficult to read it accurately. If you are having problems click on New Image which you may find easier to read. Click on the box to agree to the terms of use and privacy policy and then click on Create my account and you are ready to enjoy the YouTube experience.

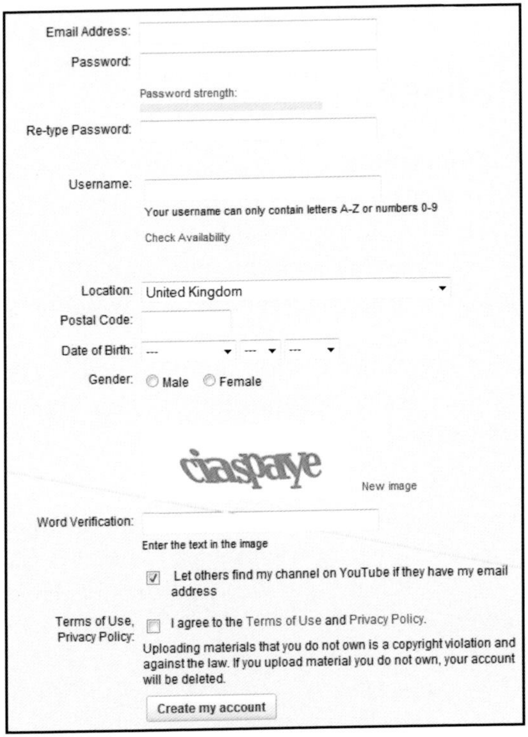

Figure 8.4

You can also upload your own short videos.

To upload your video to YouTube you must bear in mind that you must be a subscriber to YouTube (which is free) and that the maximum file size allowed is 1 gigabyte. Full details of how to upload your movies to YouTube will be found at www.webvideozone.com/public/308.cfm, www.youtube.com/watch?v=9w-gQAwS2uc or use the YouTube Help facility at http://help.youtube.com/support/youtube/.

Windows Media Player

This program comes installed with your Windows operating system but it is being continually updated with more and more features so it is always best to check that you have the latest version. Updating the program is free. The latest version for Windows XP is 11 while Vista has progressed to version 12. To update the latest version use your search engine to find 'Windows Media Player update' and follow the links.

Figure 8.5

So what is Windows Media Player? Basically it does what it says on the tin – it will play movies, music, home videos, slide shows of your best pictures and even recorded TV programmes. Using this program you can create playlists of your favourite music, download your favourite numbers, transfer your CDs to the computer (known as 'ripping') and even create new CDs of your music library (use the Burn option). The capabilities of this program are such that it would take a whole book to explain so I would suggest that you play around with it and explore its functions.

One of the great advantages of Media Player is that you can copy music from your CD collection straight into your computer so that you do not have to search for that elusive CD every time. For users of laptops this is the best way of listening to your music because playing tracks from a CD puts quite a drain on the battery.

Apple Quicktime

This used to be the Apple Macintosh version of Windows Media Player but it is now available for Windows systems. It is very similar to the Windows program and performs the same functions. Some websites prefer to use Quicktime in preference to Media Player but they are becoming less demanding and usually play on either program. You can download the program from **www.apple.com/quicktime/download/** where you will be offered the option of the free player or an enhanced version for a fee – look up prices on the website. As I suggested before, if you have difficulty in typing in the exact address, you can always search for 'quicktime downloads' in a search engine and click directly on the relevant link.

25 per cent of an apple's volume is air. That is why they float.

Newspapers

If you want to save yourself some money, why not cancel your newspaper subscription and read the news online? Most newspaper sites have a search facility so that you can find that elusive article without having to spread the pages across the kitchen floor. Reading the news online also offers the option of reading news from previous editions.

A selection of newspaper websites:

- *Daily Telegraph* – **www.telegraph.co.uk**
- *The Times* – **www.timesonline.co.uk**
- *The Boston Globe* – **www.boston.com/bostonglobe**
- *Daily Mail* – **www.dailymail.co.uk**
- *Allgemeine Zeitung* – **http://osc.westline.de/azonline/**
- *Evening Standard* – **www.thisislondon.co.uk/standard/**
- *The Guardian* – **www.guardian.co.uk**
- *Le Figaro* – **www.lefigaro.fr**

Once again you can find the website of your own daily rag by entering its name into a search engine and following the links.

eBooks

While on the subject of reading matter you may be interested to know that you can download thousands of books in both printed and audio format. For many you will have to pay a small fee but others, especially the classics, are available free. Such books are known as eBooks.

The partial list shown in Figure 8.8 gives some idea of the breadth and depth of one eBook library. This particular site – **www.ebooks.com** – offers more than 130,000 volumes and the prices are available online.

If you want to try out the experience of reading a book from your computer then visit Project Gutenberg at **www.gutenberg.org** where thousands of volunteers have made over 27,000 books available free. This project is one of the best examples of altruism on the Internet.

Most online booksellers like Amazon or Waterstones offer eBooks in their catalogues. There are handheld eBook readers being developed for this market so that you can even take an eBook to bed with you. At the moment there are a number of competing formats as there were in the early days of video recording when VHS and Betamax were vying for dominance in the market. These readers have had a mixed press so far and, personally, I prefer turning the pages and using bookmarkers with traditionally bound volumes. The current market leaders seem to be Kindle, sold by Amazon, and the Sony Reader, promoted by Waterstones.

You can also download these books for reading on your own personal organisers, such as the Dell Axiom, Blackberries and Hewlett Packard's iPAQ, while you are travelling to work by train.

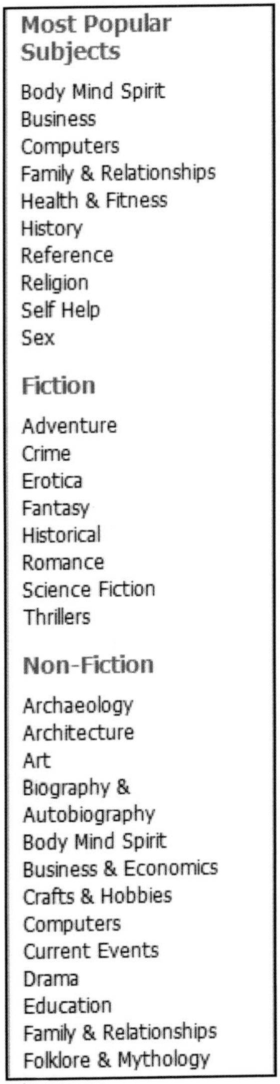

Most Popular Subjects

Body Mind Spirit
Business
Computers
Family & Relationships
Health & Fitness
History
Reference
Religion
Self Help
Sex

Fiction

Adventure
Crime
Erotica
Fantasy
Historical
Romance
Science Fiction
Thrillers

Non-Fiction

Archaeology
Architecture
Art
Biography & Autobiography
Body Mind Spirit
Business & Economics
Crafts & Hobbies
Computers
Current Events
Drama
Education
Family & Relationships
Folklore & Mythology

Reproduced by permission of ebooks.com

Figure 8.6

An alternative to eBooks are the audio books which are read by actors, other broadcasters and the authors themselves. You can buy or rent these books from **www.audiobooksonline.co.uk** in the same way as you do with movie DVDs and music CDs. Connect a pair of headphones to the computer, settle down in a comfortable chair and lose yourself in another world.

Music

Talking about losing yourself in another world we now come to the question of music on the Internet but, before we enter this subject, don't forget that you can easily slip a CD into your computer and listen to your chosen tracks while working away at your home accounts.

Spotify

A curious name for a great site. Go to **www.spotify.com**, install the small program and you are ready to listen to all your favourite music free of charge if you are prepared to put up with the occasional advert. These adverts do not interrupt the music but appear between numbers. However, if you get irritated by them, you can opt for a paid subscription a month which removes the interruptions, there is a charge for this subscription and prices are available online

I have tried to find an artist or composer that the program does not list with a singular lack of success. There is everybody here – from Harry Lauder, Caruso and Beethoven to Duffy and the Pet Shop Boys. I even have Beethoven's Eroica symphony playing in the background as I type this.

iTunes

There are hundreds of sites offering music tracks for download but I am going to concentrate on one of the biggest players – iTunes. Like Apple Quicktime this was originally developed for users of Macintosh computers but it is now available for PC users. Download it from **www.apple.com/itunes/download**. iTunes works in a similar way to Windows Media Player but it offers an enormous range of music for download as well as affording the opportunities for storing and cataloguing your own music, creating playlists and downloading album covers. Again charges apply but details are available online.

iTunes 8

The entertainment capital of your world.

Free for Mac + PC

Download ⊗ 64 MB

About iTunes

iTunes is a free application for Mac and PC. It plays all your digital music and video. It syncs content to your iPod, iPhone, and Apple TV. And it's an entertainment superstore that stays open 24/7.

Figure 8.7

Having installed the program, open it by clicking on the desktop icon – and wait. The first thing that iTunes does when it is opened for the first time is to search through your computer's hard disk to find all your stored music files and puts them into your personal library. This will include any music tracks you have transferred to your hard disk from CDs using the Windows Media Player described above.

Figure 8.8

When it has finished cataloguing these files you can play any one of them by clicking on the Music link in the Library section and then selecting the tune you want to play.

To buy a music track or album, click on Store on the Menu bar and then select Search from the dropdown menu. Enter the name of the song and/or the artist and you will see a long list of available songs. In the screenshot below you will see that the store offers 150 songs by Neil Diamond together with a number of full albums. If you are uncertain whether it is the right song, you can play a short excerpt of the number by using the controls that lie just below the Menu bar of the iTunes window.

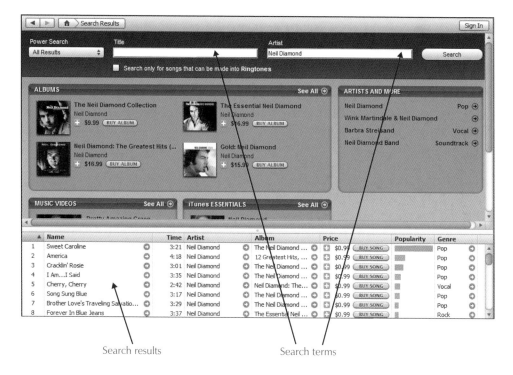

Search results   Search terms

Figure 8.9

You will also notice that you can buy films or television shows online, iTunes does not restrict itself to music so play around with the program.

There are endless possibilities, so much so that if you want to learn more about its capabilities I would suggest buying a book such as *iPod and iTunes for Dummies* by Tony Bove, published with an accompanying DVD by John Wiley & Sons, Ltd.

The longest film ever released was **** by Andy Warhol, which lasted 24 hours. It proved, not surprisingly, an utter failure commercially.

File sharing

This is an interesting development on the Web which did not find initial favour with the music publishers. Often known as P2P (standing for peer-to-peer or person-to-person), the idea is that you can download music tracks from the libraries of other members of the public who have the program running on their own computers.

Years ago the original Napster was forced to shut down their site because they lost a major court battle against the Recording Industry Association of America (*RIAA*). But, in 2003, a federal judge in Los Angeles ruled that Streamcast and Grokster were not liable for breaking copyright infringement laws.

Basically, the judge ruled that although file sharing can be used for illegal practices, that file sharing itself was not considered illegal. So, as of now, file sharing networks in the US are legal. However the RIAA is very serious about finding, and suing, people who are breaking copyright infringement laws. Therefore, you should take the lawsuit risks very seriously *before* using a P2P application.

Moroever, if a file sharer downloads or shares copyrighted material, then the file sharer is breaking copyright infringement laws. Therefore, the file sharer breaking such laws could possibly become targeted, and sued, by the RIAA.

There are still many websites that offer free file sharing but I would suggest that you stick with a company like the new Napster that complies with current law.

Download the Napster program from **www.napster.co.uk** and enjoy the seven-day free trial period to see if it is the sort of thing you might be interested in. After the trial period you will need to pay a subscription and payment details can be found online.

Summary

- To benefit from sound and video broadcasts from the Web you will need a broadband connection

- Some TV broadcasts are restricted to the country of origin

- You will find many valuable tutorials broadcast by YouTube

- You must restrict any contribution to YouTube to a file size of one gigabyte or less

- Newspaper websites often offer greater depth to the current headlines

- Listen to the music of your choice – legally and free of charge – by using Spotify

- The Internet allows you to sample music tracks before committing yourself to a purchase

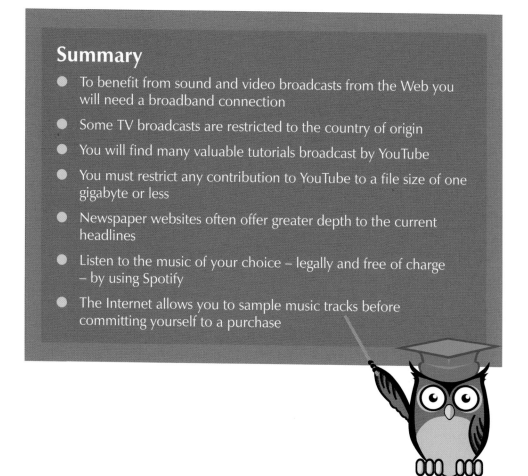

Brain Training

There may be more than one correct answer to these questions.

1. What do you need to watch video on the Internet?

☐ a) A dial-up telephone connection

☐ b) A downloadable program

☐ c) A broadband connection

☐ d) A very fast video card on your computer

2. What does Apple Quicktime do?

☐ a) Plays videos

☐ b) Teaches you to dance

☐ c) Allows you to edit photographs

☐ d) Accesses the Internet on an Apple computer

3. Which of the following applies to a Google mail account?

☐ a) It must be your main email account

☐ b) It is free

☐ c) It must be your only email account

☐ d) It is useful to have an alternative email address

4. What will you need to watch BBC TV programmes on the computer?

☐ a) A TV licence

☐ b) A broadband connection

☐ c) An Internet browser

☐ d) A paid-up subscription

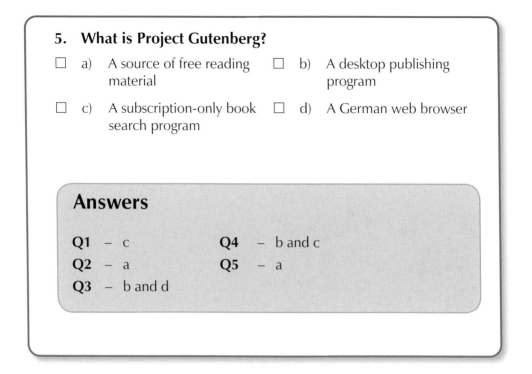

5. What is Project Gutenberg?

☐ a) A source of free reading material

☐ b) A desktop publishing program

☐ c) A subscription-only book search program

☐ d) A German web browser

Answers

Q1 – c   **Q4** – b and c

Q2 – a   **Q5** – a

Q3 – b and d

PART II
Shopping

You could try getting a few quid for him on eBay.

Shopping

9

Equipment needed: a computer; a printer; Internet Explorer program; an email address; connection to the Internet; a credit or debit card; a firewall and a record of usernames and passwords.

Skills needed: knowledge of the keyboard and mouse plus knowledge of downloading a program (Chapters 3 and 5).

Shopping on the Internet is one of the most rewarding computing activities available to the new computer user. There is very little that is not available to the modern internet surfer – from the latest blockbuster movie and its best selling book through the smallest engineering widget to supersonic jet aircraft. You will find a number of shopping tutorials on the website accompanying this book at **www.pcwisdom.co.uk.**

Online shopping also reduces your carbon footprint to a fraction of that incurred by the daily trips to the local high street. Instead of spraining your back and shoulder muscles in carrying bulk purchases home, you can have them delivered to your door – and even stored in your fridge if you speak nicely to the delivery man while offering him a cup of tea.

I will give you a couple of examples based on shopping in the UK but the facts remain whether you are shopping in London, Marseilles or New York.

A couple of years ago, my wife and I spoiled ourselves by buying an American-style fridge/freezer that offered instant chilled water and an ice dispenser. We were delighted with our purchase until the time arrived when we needed to replace the water filter. I returned to the shop that sold us the fridge and asked for a replacement filter. 'Certainly, sir. That will be £28.57,' came the enthusiastic reply. £28.57! That is almost 10 per cent of the cost of the original fridge and needed replacing every six months. I'm sorry but no way, Jose. There must be a cheaper way of keeping the water palatable and, of course, there is. The Internet. A quick search soon found a wealth of suppliers happy to sell me the identical model for less than £12.50 and even cheaper if I was prepared to buy a couple of filters at the same time.

This Christmas two of our children asked for identical glass tumblers to add to their glass collections. These were not garage forecourt glasses but expensive designer creations for sale in our local county town showrooms for £70 a pop. We are enormously proud of our children and love them very dearly but at £140 a pair they were going to stretch our retirement budget to breaking point. Cue the Internet! You guessed it. We finally got the four tumblers for £49.50 each – not 'seconds' but brand new items.

So how come prices can be so much lower on the Web? There are a number of reasons but the main one is the cost of overheads.

There are still hundreds of bargains to be had in your local area so beware of knowing the price of everything and the value of nothing. Secondly, remember that if something seems to be too good to be true then it probably is.

Payment over the Internet

So now that you have found your bargain, how do you pay for it? The obvious answer is by debit or credit card but obvious answers do not necessarily offer the full picture. I would normally recommend payment by credit card because these companies offer considerable protection against fraud and poor service.

Credit cards

Section 75 of the Consumer Credit Act, 1974 (equal liability) only applies to credit transactions, therefore, the finance company does not have any liability for purchases that have been paid for by charge cards as these are debit cards not credit cards. Some American Express and Diners Cards are examples of debit cards. For more details about the relative advantages of the two types of cards throughout the world I suggest that you visit **www.onlyfinance.com/Credit-Cards/ Credit-vs-Debit-cards.aspx**.

Under the provisions of Section 75 of the Consumer Credit Act 1974, if you buy goods or services costing in excess of £100 using a credit card, should the goods or services prove to be defective, you will have an equal claim for compensation against both the seller of the goods or service and the finance company.

The use of credit can be traced back to Assyria, Babylon and Egypt 3,000 years ago. According to the *Encyclopaedia Britannica* the use of credit card started in the US in the 1920s.

I am sure you have read or heard of horrendous stories in the media in which details of unsuspecting individuals credit cards being 'cloned' or otherwise stolen and misappropriated. You will not often hear of the good news offered to buyers of goods who made their purchase using their credit cards since they are almost always covered by their credit card agreement. But what happens if the same fate should happen to you? First of all, don't panic. From the very outset of your Internet buying career try to develop some good habits.

1. Keep all documentation relating to online sales in a folder so that you have the evidence to put before your credit card company.

2. Check your statements regularly.

3. Photograph any damage to the goods or packaging.

4. Contact your credit card company as soon as possible if you have any doubts about the purchase.

5. Make sure that there is a valid telephone number and address to which future queries can be addressed should anything go wrong. A PO box is not a valid address in this respect.

Bear in mind that you almost need a degree in computing technology to 'hack' or gain access to an online transaction that you have not initiated yourself. Don't forget that, until you have entered your name, address, telephone number and credit card details onto your screen you are in no danger of making an unwanted purchase. With this in mind I would strongly recommend practising making purchases of goods and services – without going to the final step of placing the order – before committing yourself to your first online transaction.

Because of the increased costs of insuring against fraud and defective goods you may find that companies make a small additional charge to cover these credit card costs. It is a small price to pay for peace of mind.

Debit cards

You can also use your debit cards online but they do not carry the same protection should anything go wrong with the transaction. Anyone with a bank account can obtain a debit card but, if you exceed your agreed overdraft limit, the bank charges can be high. Retailers will not charge you extra for the use of a debit card as they do not have to cover the higher protection costs involved.

Cheques

It is a sign of the times that cheques are welcomed less and less frequently both on the high street and on the Internet – in fact very few online retailers will accept cheques as a method of payment.

PayPal

With the increasing demise of the cheque a number of alternate methods are becoming available on the Internet. One of the first and most reliable is the service offered by the PayPal company. The principle behind the system is payment to email addresses but, first of all, you must set up your PayPal account.

Details of how to set up a PayPal account are described in Chapter 11 under the eBay section. You will need a PayPal account if you are going to make much use of the eBay auction site.

There is another method of paying for goods and services over the Internet called Google Checkout. This seems to be gaining in popularity and some people find it easier to use than PayPal. You can find it starting at **https://www.google.com/ accounts**.

I hope that the preceding information will have gone a long way to reassuring you about paying for goods and services over the Internet so let us have a look at a few examples of using this new-found confidence.

Buying a book on the Web

One of the earliest and most successful online shopping outlets is the Amazon website. The company started off in 1995 by simply selling new books at extremely worthwhile discounts and since that time has extended its operations to include, videos, DVDs, music CDs, computer hardware and software, toys, jewellery, furniture and DIY equipment. It also sells secondhand books and equipment through its associate stores as well as running an auction site.

Amazon's original name was Cadabra.

This being our first venture into buying on the Internet we shall concentrate on a simple book purchase. Let us imagine that a nephew of yours has been recommended a particular book by friends of his and he would like to have it as a birthday present. Unfortunately he has forgotten the name of the author and only thinks that the title of the book is something like 'Trip Watch'. All he can remember is that it features a character named Jack Reacher which, let's face it, is not really very helpful but let us see if Amazon can find the book he is looking for.

Open up the Amazon page at **www.amazon.co.uk** or **www.amazon. com**. As you are a new customer you should begin the sign-in procedure by entering your email address and your chosen password. You are not committing yourself to any payment by doing this.

Reproduced by courtesy of Amazon.com Inc.

Figure 9.1

1. Click on 'Sign in using our secure server'. You will notice that both this page and the following one have web addresses than start with '**https://**' which means that the information is being sent over a secure connection.

The first book to be sold by Amazon was on artificial intelligence by Douglas Hofstadter.

Registration

New to Amazon.co.uk? Register Below.

My name is:

My e-mail address:

Type it again:

Birthday: Month ▾ Day ▾ (optional)

Protect your information with a password
This will be your only Amazon.co.uk password

Enter a new password:

Type it again:

Continue ▶

Reproduced by courtesy of Amazon.com Inc.

Figure 9.2

2. Once we have completed the registration process we can get on with our search for that elusive book so click on Continue and you will be presented with a very simple search page. Select Books from the dropdown menu and type the words 'Jack Reacher' (upper or lower case – it does not matter) into the search bar and click on the Go button.

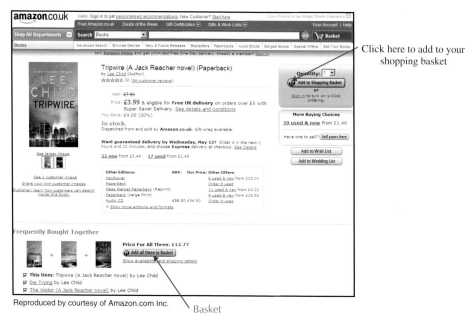

Reproduced by courtesy of Amazon.com Inc.

Go button

Figure 9.3

3. Almost immediately a list of more than 80 books will be displayed showing us that the author of these books is Lee Child and that one of the books is called *Tripwire* so it sounds as if we have found the right one.

4. Click on the title of the *Tripwire* book and full details of the publication will be displayed including any customer reviews and similar books that other people have bought when buying this book.

Click here to add to your shopping basket

Reproduced by courtesy of Amazon.com Inc.

Basket

Figure 9.4

5. Once you have decided to buy the book click on Add to Shopping Basket. You are not committed to this purchase by doing this as you can always remove it from the shopping basket at a later stage. You might like to use the Back navigation button to return to the Tripwire page and choose one of the other recommended books – if you are feeling generous – and add that one to the basket.

6. Now that you have chosen the items you want to send, click on the Basket icon which you will find to the right of the Go icon at the right hand end of the search bar.

Reproduced by courtesy of Amazon.com Inc.

Figure 9.5

This will display those items you have placed in the basket ready for ordering, together with details of post and packing costs; the option to have the items gift wrapped and the likely delivery date.

7. At this stage you are going to have to register your credit card's details with Amazon to complete your purchase. Fill in the requested information together with your card details, billing address as well as the name and address to which you want the items sent. Once again you will see that the web address has the '**https://**' prefix assuring you of the safety of the information you are about to give.

8. Only now that you have submitted your payment details are you in danger of actually committing yourself to ordering the book but this will not happen until you click on the Place Your Order button. You can stop your order at any time up to the point of placing your order. You will still be able to cancel your order after it has been made but only if you do so within about an hour of placing the order.

9. Once you have actually placed your order you will receive an email confirming your order within a few minutes so it is a good idea to check your email inbox to make sure that the order is correct.

10. Depending upon stock levels and the class of postage you have chosen you will get a further email message informing you when the book has been dispatched.

Not all books have to be bought in pristine condition and many old favourites may have gone out of print so why not consider buying second-hand? I have found many long-lost books for pupils and friends by going to AbeBooks at **www.abebooks.com**. This is a loose association of thousands of booksellers across the world who put their collections up for sale on the Web. The site is easily searched by title, author or keyword and the prices are staggeringly cheap even when you take postage and packing into account.

Amazon offers free post and packing for all orders over a certain amount sent to the same address, but this delivery option may take two or three days longer to arrive. The company has stores in the UK, USA, France, Germany, Canada, China and Japan so that, if you have relatives in these areas to whom you wish to send a present, you can order through the local store and take advantage of their local postage rates.

You will gain a lot of confidence if you conduct a few practice runs through various ordering processes right up to the point of committing yourself to placing the order and then deleting the items from your shopping basket.

Buying a car

No, I am not suggesting that you rush out and buy a new car now that you are becoming more familiar with your computer but rather using the concept as an example of what the Internet can do for you. Let us say, for the sake of argument, that in these times of economic hardship you have decided that your large 4x4 saloon is costing too much to run, you are feeling guilty about its dirty carbon footprint and would like to trade it in for a more economical mode of transport. What sort of price can you expect to get for your gas guzzler? How much money are you likely to save if you changed to one of the modern hybrid cars like a Toyota Prius? The local car salesman will quote you enough facts and figures to make your head spin so why not do a bit of research on your own behalf.

We could use a comparison website but these prices are for retail sales and there are better sites available with trade-in values. There are many secondhand car valuation sites on the Internet. Doing a Google search for 'secondhand car prices UK' results in over 270,000 sites but the most useful sites are likely to be found in the first few pages of search results. Many of these sites are more interested in selling you a secondhand car than informing you of general price trends so you will have to winnow your way through this lengthy list – checking out the site summaries as you go. On the other hand you could try a different Google search such as 'valuation car UK'. This eliminates a lot of the secondhand car dealer sites and gives better valuation results.

Always think of changing your Google search terms if you do not find what you are looking for on your first attempt – a bit of lateral thinking is often required in these situations.

One or two of these valuation sites, such as the industry standard, Glass's Guide, may charge you a small fee for each valuation but since we are only after guidelines rather than definitive prices I would recommend you first visit the What Car website at **www.whatcar.com/valuations.aspx**. To get a fair valuation of your Range Rover simply enter the make, model, year and mileage from the dropdown menus and click on Calculate.

It is always a good idea to get a second opinion in these cases so I would suggest checking the initial valuations against another site such as Parkers Guides at **www.parkers.co.uk/cars/used-prices/#**.

Immediately you will see details of the dealer's price, trade-in, private and trade prices for the model specified by you. Not only this but it also lists further useful information about the vehicle such as fuel consumption, insurance group and reliability issues. Armed with this information you will know that if a salesman starts by offering you a value of £1,000 as part exchange for another vehicle when you know that a fairer price would be in the region of £2,500 he is not going to be offering you any favours and this might be the time to walk away from the deal.

So now we have some idea of the money we have to play with when buying the smaller car and all we have to do is find the perfect replacement. You could trawl through the local and national papers checking out the cars available or visit all the car showrooms in your area but you will save yourself a lot of time, petrol and hassle by making an initial search of the Internet. The Auto Trader website is a very good example of the search site you are looking for. Type in **www.autotrader.co.uk** to your Internet browser address bar and you will find more than 350,000 vehicles for sale by both commercial dealers and private sellers.

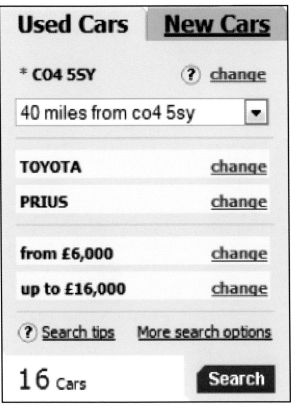

Reproduced by permission of Trader Media Group

Figure 9.6

Let us take a look at the current prices of a secondhand Honda Prius.

In the top left corner of the Auto Trader home page are various boxes that need to be filled in with your search details. In the example on the left you will see that I have stipulated a Toyota Prius no more than 40 miles from my chosen location and within the price range of £6–16,000. These criteria match up with 16 cars so I simply click on Search to show the specific details of these vehicles.

Most cars are photographed from various angles to give you an impression of their condition and, if the car is being sold by a dealer, there will be a link to the showroom's website where you may find several other models listed and described. In this case there is one car being offered by a specialist Toyota dealer who has three other cars on offer. The website gives details of the address and telephone number so that you can contact the company to confirm that the cars are still available for sale and that you are not going to have a wasted journey.

The forecourt salesman is interested in just one thing – getting the best deal he possibly can from you as a customer and he has the advantage of having the latest figures at his fingertips.

Finally, you can return to the car valuation websites – What Car and Parkers Guides – to check that the prices being asked for the Prius are reasonable. You still need to check the car over and take it for a test drive but you have only spent about half an hour on the computer as opposed to hours of trade magazine browsing and miles of unnecessary driving. I hope you get the picture.

Buying groceries

Many people enjoy the shopping experience but, to others, it is one of life's tedious chores. If you are one of the latter and the prospect of dragging large boxes of special offer soap powder, bargain packs of toilet paper and heavy crates of beer fills you with despair then shopping for your daily needs on a supermarket website may be the answer.

I don't want to pretend that using these sites is without its drawbacks but, with a little planning, they can save you a lot of driving, parking and backache. My experience of using a number of supermarket delivery services raises a few particular problems. The first of these is that you have to stipulate a time when you are going to be at home to receive the goods. This is less of a problem for the older generation who can organise their days around these delivery times. It is more difficult for those in full-time employment to ensure that their boss will allow them to leave on time to meet the home delivery.

Secondly, you do not get the opportunity to view and handle the goods on offer and decide on alternatives if your original shopping choice happens to be out of stock. Supermarkets will sometimes try and deliver alternative goods but they may not satisfy your personal needs. When you need granary flour for a home baking recipe the self-raising alternative will rarely do.

Finally, do not forget two other factors that apply to your shopping habits. Shopping gets you out of the house – the computer can turn you into an isolated recluse if you are not careful – and often results in happy meetings with friends you have been meaning to invite round for a cup of coffee. There is also a small delivery fee.

Tesco, Sainsbury's, Waitrose and Asda in the UK are among the many supermarkets offering online ordering and delivery so let us toss a coin and check out one of these websites. The coin came down in favour of Sainsbury's which is interesting because that is one site I have not dealt with in the past so this will be just as much of a learning curve for me as it is for you. I am pretty sure that the web address is something like **www.sainsburys.com** but I cannot be certain so I will do a Google search for Sainsbury's. There, you see, I was wrong. The correct address is **www.sainsburys.co.uk** so I click on the Google link and further click on the Groceries section.

Reproduced by permission of J Sainsbury Plc

Figure 9.7

Before I go any further I consider that this site may be one I will want to return to in the future so I add the Sainsbury's Groceries page to my Favourites in my browser. (The method of doing this is described in Chapter 3.) Now I know that even if I forget the web address for this site it is safely tucked away in my Favorites list and it is only a simple mouse click away.

The next task is to register on the site. You will find that most websites require registration which pre-empts the need to fill in your details every time you visit and, except in very rare cases, is free.

Back at the Groceries page we have to make sure that the company will deliver to our address so we enter our home postcode and click the Check Postcode icon. The chances are pretty good that you will be within their delivery network but if you live on the Isle of Mull in the Inner Hebrides you may be out of luck. Best to check before you start creating a long shopping list only to find that your address is not yet covered by the supermarket's delivery network.

Reproduced by permission of J Sainsbury Plc

Figure 9.8

In my example case we are in luck, they do deliver to my area and so I have to fill in the registration form. This is quite a long form but you only have to complete it once and you are registered until you choose to delete your registration. Don't forget to tick the box that states that you have read their Terms and Conditions and when you are finished click on Register. If you have omitted any details you will be returned to the registration page with instructions as to where you went wrong but eventually your registration will be accepted and you will be invited to continue shopping. So let's buy a few groceries.

The groceries section is further sub-divided into smaller groups such as fresh food, food cupboard, frozen, drinks and newsagents among others. Select your chosen items and they will be added to your basket.

There will be times when you cannot find the specific item you are looking for because you cannot guess which section contains the goods. No worries, simply enter the name of the product in the search box and you will be shown a list of everything that corresponds to your search request.

Throughout this journey of ordering you will be tempted by special offers than can be added to your order.

Finally you complete your order and you must pay for the goods by clicking on the Checkout button or you could save your trolley for later additions.

You will now be asked to book a delivery time so click on an appropriate time slot and click again on Continue.

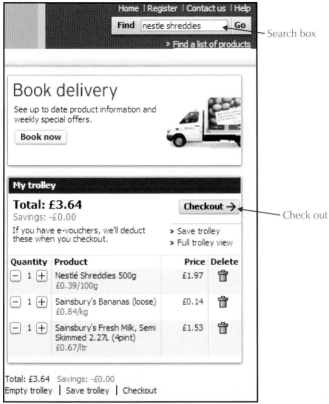

Search box

Check out

Reproduced by permission of J Sainsbury Plc

Figure 9.9

I have deliberately gone through this shopping exercise in some detail because all future buying exercises are likely to follow the same pattern.

Entering your first order is going to take a long time as you search for each individual item and then decide which pack you need. Fortunately these supermarket sites keep a record of your shopping habits and will maintain a personal shopping list for you once you have completed the first few orders. It is then a simple matter to access this list and tick off the usual items while adding extra items as and when they are needed.

Buying specialist items

So far we have been dealing with routine shopping enquiries – with the exception of buying a new car. Now I want to stretch the mind a little further and consider the opportunities of buying more esoteric items.

Perhaps you are an enthusiastic gardener and, after visiting a National Trust garden, you have had the desire to plant a particular tree in your own back garden. You have already established with the head gardener that the tree in question is *Betula papyrifera* or the White Birch. (This tree grows to a height of 30 to 40 feet so I hope you have got a large garden.) How do we find a supplier of such a plant? A further Google search for 'Betula papyrifera UK' – the 'UK' is inserted to limit the search to British tree nurseries (if you are based in the UK you will want to limit your search to this country) – soon brings up The Tree Shop website in the Forest of Dean in Gloucestershire. Various plants of differing sizes are available for sale by direct mail order together with advice on how to care for the tree, together with a contact telephone number.

I have never dealt with this company before but, with the reassurance of a valid address and telephone number and the fact that they have been trading since 1937, I am happy to deal with them. Using a credit card as payment gives me extra security should anything go wrong with the transaction. These specialist plants do not come cheap so do not expect to get a fantastic bargain – not all prices on the Internet are the lowest of the low.

For a final, completely different, item I have chosen to search for a more economical supplier of tungsten light bulbs which seem to cost the earth at local electrical suppliers and prove to have a short lifespan in our household. Another Google search locates The Light Bulb Company with an address and telephone number in Oxford. They offer light bulbs of every description from standard incandescent through halogen units to energy saving lamps. Checking out the prices, I find that their prices, including postage, are at least two-thirds of those on the High Street and even better savings can be achieved if the item you are looking for happens to fall into one of their Sales categories. More money saved!

Yellow Pages

The large part of this chapter has been concerned with the purchase of goods but do not forget that 'services' are also available on the Internet. One of the most comprehensive sources of information for such services is the Internet version of Yellow Pages found at **www.yell.com**. Using this site you can find an acupuncturist in Aberystwyth or a yacht maker in the Yeovil area. With over 2 million business listings, the computerised search facility is so much faster than leafing your way through the heavy book and it covers the whole country rather than simply your local area.

Internet auctions

There are plenty of bargains to be had on Internet auction sites and these are dealt with in Chapter 11.

The Internet is not just a vast shopping centre but it is an encyclopaedia, a dictionary, thesaurus and library of reference manuals all rolled into one.

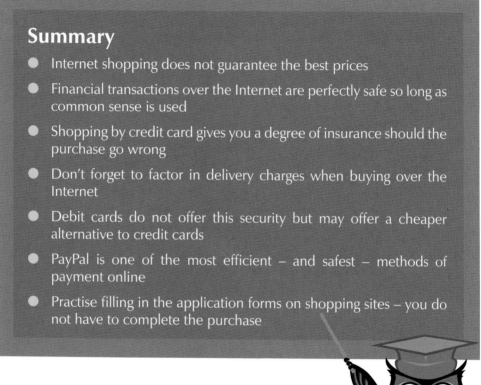

Summary

- Internet shopping does not guarantee the best prices
- Financial transactions over the Internet are perfectly safe so long as common sense is used
- Shopping by credit card gives you a degree of insurance should the purchase go wrong
- Don't forget to factor in delivery charges when buying over the Internet
- Debit cards do not offer this security but may offer a cheaper alternative to credit cards
- PayPal is one of the most efficient – and safest – methods of payment online
- Practise filling in the application forms on shopping sites – you do not have to complete the purchase

Brain Training

There may be more than one correct answer to these questions.

1. What do you need to shop on the Internet?

☐ a) A lot of courage

☐ b) An email address

☐ c) A credit card

☐ d) A firewall setup on your computer

2. Which of these apply to credit card payments over the Internet?

☐ a) You may pay a small premium over a debit card

☐ b) You will get financial protection if the purchase goes wrong

☐ c) You can only use debit cards on the Internet

☐ d) Details of the card are encrypted if the web address starts with **https://**

3. Which of the following applies to shopping online at Tesco?

☐ a) You must register with the company online

☐ b) You may have to pay a delivery fee

☐ c) Fresh food is only delivered mid-week

☐ d) Your minimum order must be over £50

4. What is PayPal?

☐ a) A method of making payments over the Internet

☐ b) A method of payment only used by the eBay auction site

☐ c) A way of transferring money across the globe to email addresses

☐ d) A computer program that has to be downloaded

5. Which of the following shopping sites would you trust?

☐ a) Delboy's Cheap TVs offering a PO box address

☐ b) A checkout page which raises a padlock icon on your browser

☐ c) John Lewis in Oxford Street

☐ d) **www.freewhisky.co.de/malts/cashonly.htm**

6. What can you buy on Amazon?

☐ a) A pedigree Burmese cat

☐ b) DVDs

☐ c) Lawnmowers

☐ d) Books

7. What will iTunes do?

☐ a) Play movies

☐ b) Act as a home music synthesiser

☐ c) Catalogue your music collection

☐ d) Broadcast radio stations

8. What are advantages of shopping online?

☐ a) You can haggle over prices

☐ b) You will probably get better value for money

☐ c) You can return unwanted goods

☐ d) Cheques are an easy method of payment

Answers

Q1 – b and c   **Q5** – b and c

Q2 – a, b and d   **Q6** – b, c and d

Q3 – a and b   **Q7** – a, c and d

Q4 – a and c   **Q8** – b and c

Travel on the Internet

10

Equipment needed: a computer; a printer; Internet Explorer program; an email address; connection to the Internet; a credit or debit card; a firewall; an anti-virus program and a record of usernames and passwords.

Skills needed: knowledge of the keyboard and mouse plus some confidence; knowledge of downloading a program (Chapters 3 and 5); experience of form filling (Chapters 7 and 9).

We all know how much the cost of air travel has come down since the arrival of Internet booking and thousands of previously computer illiterate people are now happily booking their holidays on the Web. This chapter tries to extend that 'literacy' to wider aspects of travel on the Internet.

Flights

Ryanair, EasyJet and Flybe are able to offer these lower costs for the same reasons that online retailers can offer the bargains we discussed in the previous chapter. Central booking reduces the overheads.

The newspaper adverts offer flights to Istanbul for free, charging only the costs of taxes and airport fees. The trouble is that we can never find these free offers when we look them up on the Web. They are there but, as with free lunches, they are few and far between. Let me give you an example.

It is a cold January outside and I rather fancy a mini-break to Malaga's warmer climate, tomorrow, a Saturday. I log in to an airline site and search for a flight, one way, from London Stansted airport. There is only the one flight that leaves at 1.30pm and the cost is £85. A bit steep but I can just about live with that so I continue the booking. If I want to get the sort of seat I want, I need to check in with Speedy Booking (£9.00) and I will need to put one piece of luggage in the hold (£7.50). I decide to forego the one-way travel insurance offer at £9 but I will opt for the Carbon Offsetting charge of nearly two pounds. The total cost of this flight has now risen more than £103 – and that's just one way.

Now let us look at a different scenario. The cost of the same one way flight – from Stansted to Malaga – on a Monday in April is just £27. What this exercise shows is that there are cheap flights out there but you have to bear the following in mind of you are going to take advantage of them:

- Act quickly – ultra cheap flights are booked very quickly.
- Book well in advance.
- Be prepare to travel at unsocial hours and try to avoid weekends.
- Travel light.

Many people are still apprehensive of booking flight tickets over the Internet so let us examine a practical example using the EasyJet website at www.easyjet.com. I will go through this booking procedure in some detail as it involves a lot of form-filling which will be useful practice for use on other websites.

As you can see EasyJet offers a lot more than just flights – hotels, car rental, airport parking and travel insurance are all available from this one site. I have filled in the details of a *return* flight from Stansted to Malaga and I need to click on Show flights to pick a specific time. Use the calendar icons to book a flight further ahead than the present month.

Click on the relevant buttons to show the flight times and then click on Next Step.

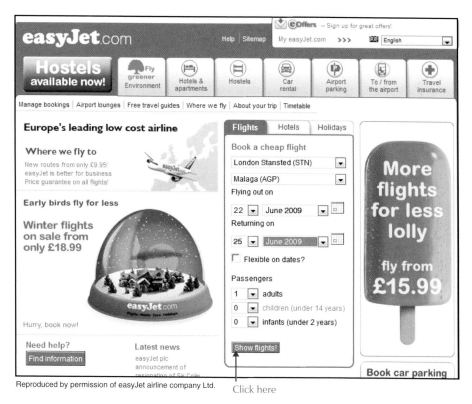

Reproduced by permission of easyJet airline company Ltd.   Click here

Figure 10.1

This is where things start to get complicated. There are several extras and in some cases, essentials, that the airline will be charging you for such as any baggage that has to go in the hold, travel insurance, green taxes and the like. You can remove these at your discretion and activate the appropriate Update buttons. Do you really need Speed Boarding? An annual travel insurance policy is almost invariably cheaper than those policies sold through the airlines.

This screenshot covers only part of the long booking web page and there are extra charges for awkward baggage such as golf bags and skis and options for carbon offsetting so make sure you have selected only those options that you really need. The next page offers the opportunity to book a hotel or hire a car but you will need to choose one of the options at the bottom of the page. I would suggest that, unless you are a regular passenger, you choose the non-login alternative.

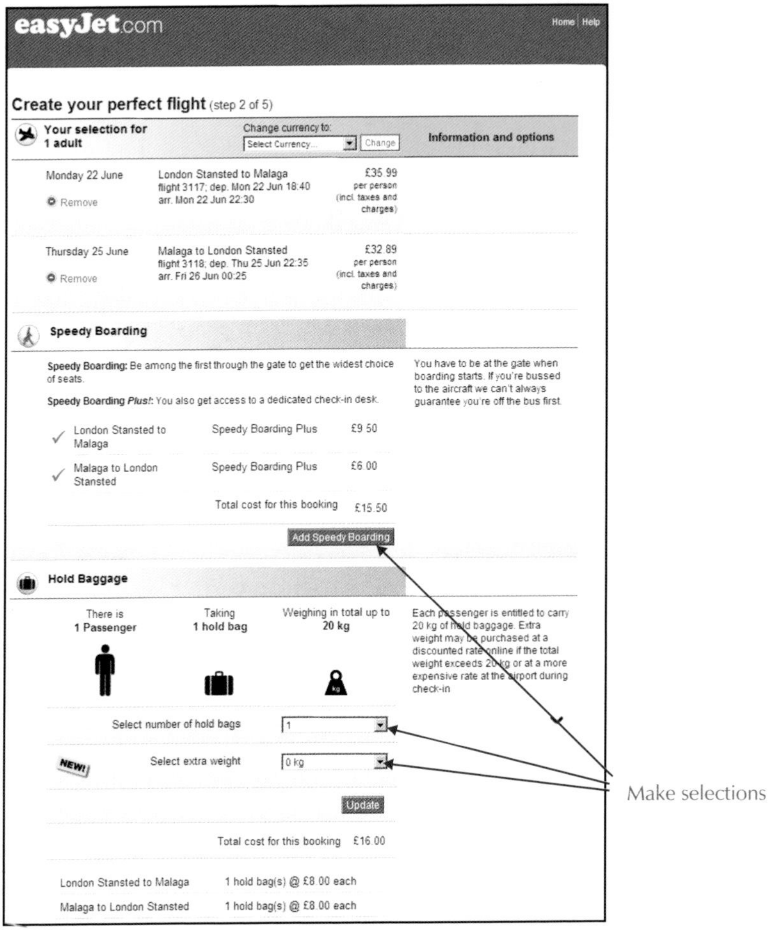

Reproduced by permission of easyJet airline company Ltd.

Figure 10.2

Reproduced by permission of easyJet airline company Ltd.

Figure 10.3

Click on the small orange arrow beside that option rather than the large Login banner. You will have to provide a password later but it might save you from getting a storm of 'special offers' from the airline in your email inbox.

The final page summarises your flight booking followed by your personal details in the boxes provided; here you must enter the particulars of the credit or debit card you propose to use for payment.

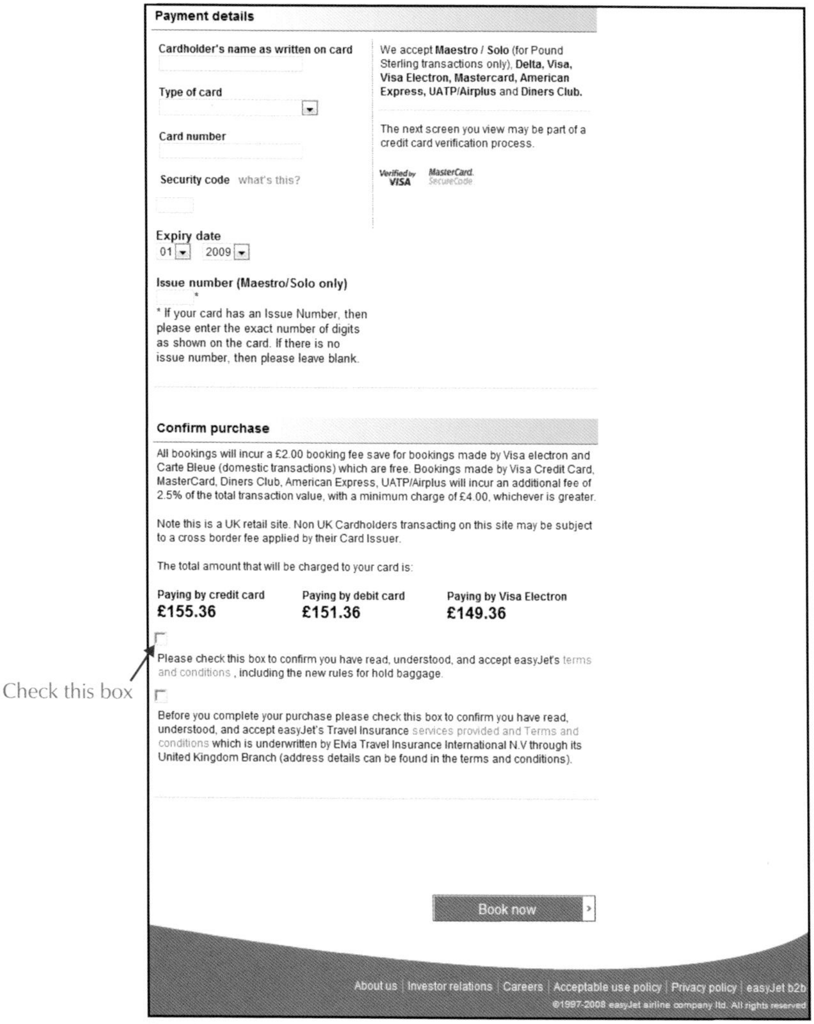
Payment details

Cardholder's name as written on card

Type of card

Card number

Security code what's this?

Expiry date
01 2009

Issue number (Maestro/Solo only)

* If your card has an Issue Number, then please enter the exact number of digits as shown on the card. If there is no issue number, then please leave blank.

We accept **Maestro / Solo** (for Pound Sterling transactions only), **Delta, Visa, Visa Electron, Mastercard, American Express, UATP/Airplus** and **Diners Club.**

The next screen you view may be part of a credit card verification process.

Verified by VISA MasterCard. SecureCode

Confirm purchase

All bookings will incur a £2.00 booking fee save for bookings made by Visa electron and Carte Bleue (domestic transactions) which are free. Bookings made by Visa Credit Card, MasterCard, Diners Club, American Express, UATP/Airplus will incur an additional fee of 2.5% of the total transaction value, with a minimum charge of £4.00, whichever is greater.

Note this is a UK retail site. Non UK Cardholders transacting on this site may be subject to a cross border fee applied by their Card Issuer.

The total amount that will be charged to your card is:

Paying by credit card	Paying by debit card	Paying by Visa Electron
£155.36	**£151.36**	**£149.36**

Please check this box to confirm you have read, understood, and accept easyJet's terms and conditions , including the new rules for hold baggage.

Before you complete your purchase please check this box to confirm you have read, understood, and accept easyJet's Travel Insurance services provided and Terms and conditions which is underwritten by Elvia Travel Insurance International N.V through its United Kingdom Branch (address details can be found in the terms and conditions).

Book now

About us | Investor relations | Careers | Acceptable use policy | Privacy policy | easyJet b2b

©1997-2008 easyJet airline company ltd. All rights reserved

Reproduced by permission of easyJet airline company Ltd.

Figure 10.4

You can move forward from box to box by using the Tab key on the keyboard if you get fed up trying to click in each subsequent box. If you need to go back to a previous box use Shift+Tab.

Don't forget to tick the box whereby you accept the Terms and Conditions of the booking.

The last action, Book Now, is the all important one. Once you have activated this button you are committed to the purchase. You can practise filling in these forms to your heart's content – even to the extent of entering your credit card details – right up to this point so take a deep breath and be sure that everything is as you want it before pressing this final button.

You can cancel your flight but you will have to pay a cancellation fee which will vary according to how close to the flight date you choose to make the cancellation.

This exercise may have seemed a little pedantic but this type of form-filling will become part of your Internet life so it is best to get it right from the beginning.

 The shortest Intercontinental Commercial Flight in the world is from Gibraltar (Europe) to Tangier (Africa). Distance 34 miles, flight time 20 minutes.

Travel by coach

Car, plane and rail are not the only ways to travel. Modern long-distance coaches are a far cry from the charabancs of the 1960s. They afford ample leg room, climate-controlled comfort, washroom facilities and the lack of responsibility of finding your way as you tire towards the end of the journey. The coach companies also offer concessionary fares unlike the airlines.

Scheduled bus journeys run between distant cities, railway stations and airports and avoid the necessity of having to find a parking space at your destination. The biggest operator of coach travel within the UK is National Express at **www.nationalexpress.com** although there are many travel and ticket agencies that will guide you through the maze of connections if your journey is a complicated one.

Booking a coach trip follows very similar operations to those involved in booking a flight so I will not bore with yet more details. You will have got the picture by now.

Lastminute.com

This company is one of the few survivors of the original 'dotcom' boom of the late 1990s when everyone including Uncle Tom Cobley and your mother-in-law was trying to hitch a ride on the bubble of quick and easy money that was to burst at the beginning of this decade. The company offers holidays, tickets and other mini-breaks both here and abroad by collecting all those flights, hotel rooms and theatre tickets that the issuing companies are finding hard to sell. Typing **www.lastminute.com** brings up the following website:

Reproduced by courtesy of lastminute.com

Figure 10.5

The screenshot is only the top part of the home page but it gives you the general idea. As you can see the company does not just deal with last-minute holidays but offers tickets to events and theatres, bookings for restaurants, car hire and gift ideas. Lastminute.com is a great site for getting a bargain but its name does not guarantee that you are getting the very best deal every time – even at the last moment.

Guides and reviews

Many of these reviews will have been written in glowing terms by the hotelier in question but there are a number of independent review sites such as

www.holidaywatchdog.com where the hotel company offered the following recommendation: '...boasts a reputation for its friendliness and welcoming atmosphere. Its cuisine is prepared by award winning chefs...' while the only impartial review describes it as 'What a hole! Don't go.'

> You may be tempted to book a hotel through an airline or a web agency such as Lastminute but can you trust the advertising hype that leads you to expect five-star service when all you find is a two-star Bates motel? The answer is to use a couple of the many hotel guides and reviews posted on the Web.

Bear in mind that this was a single review and the customer may have had a Titanic row with his girlfriend over breakfast.

Trip Advisor – **www.tripadvisor.com** – and Holidays Uncovered – **www.holidays-uncovered.co.uk** – offer a huge number of reviews of holiday destinations across the world.

Here is an example of how to search for a review of a hotel called Hotel Cala Bona that you may have been tempted to book with your flight ticket to Majorca. Call up Trip Advisor on your browser and search for hotels in Majorca and refine your search for 'Cala Bona'.

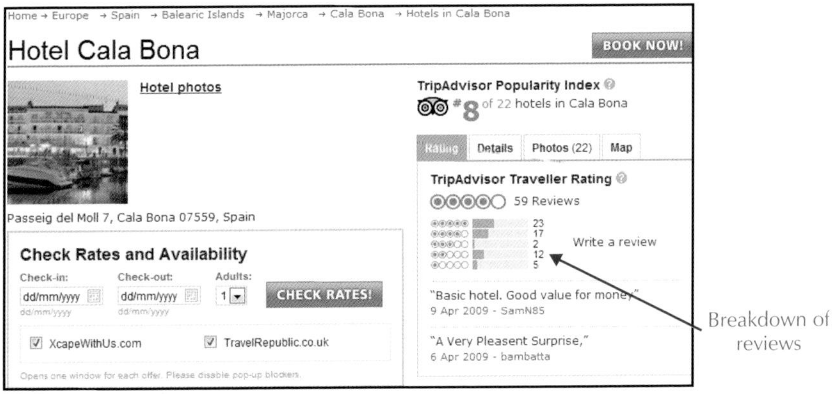

Figure 10.6

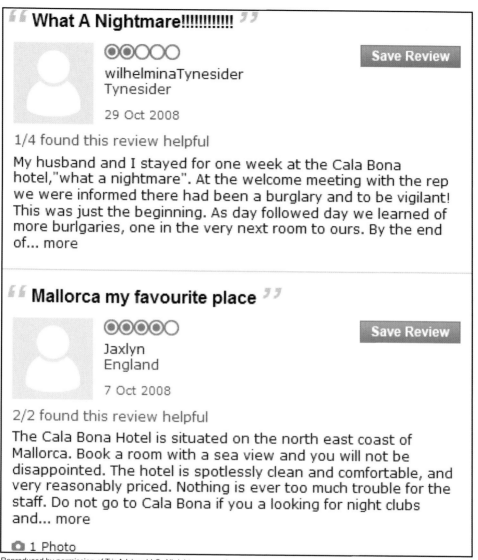

" What A Nightmare!!!!!!!!!!! "

⊙⊙○○○   **Save Review**

wilhelminaTynesider
Tynesider

29 Oct 2008

1/4 found this review helpful

My husband and I stayed for one week at the Cala Bona
hotel,"what a nightmare". At the welcome meeting with the rep
we were informed there had been a burglary and to be vigilant!
This was just the beginning. As day followed day we learned of
more burlgaries, one in the very next room to ours. By the end
of... more

" Mallorca my favourite place "

⊙⊙⊙⊙○   **Save Review**

Jaxlyn
England

7 Oct 2008

2/2 found this review helpful

The Cala Bona Hotel is situated on the north east coast of
Mallorca. Book a room with a sea view and you will not be
disappointed. The hotel is spotlessly clean and comfortable, and
very reasonably priced. Nothing is ever too much trouble for the
staff. Do not go to Cala Bona if you a looking for night clubs
and... more

📷 1 Photo

Figure 10.7

Click on the link and you will find 59 reviews varying from two to five stars with
an average rating of 4 stars. Further down the page you will find the ten latest
reviews together with links to similar hotels in the area, local restaurants, special

offers and other useful links. The two latest reviews suggest that some people have a better time than others. Other reviews praise it to the heavens while one had high praise for all the staff – except the manager! It seems to find more favour with the older generation than the young, single travellers. The one thing you rarely find in these independent reviews is pictures of the hotels in question – although Trip Advisor in an exception in this respect. You could look them up on the hotel's own website – search for the hotel – but these will have been carefully chosen by the advertising agencies. Try searching on Google for images of the resort. Enter 'Cala Bona' as the search terms and select Images rather than Web. The last time I searched for these images I found over 22,000 pictures varying from personal snapshots through commercial advertisements to coloured maps of the village. These images may give you a more representative selection as they come from a huge range of web sources – often private individuals' images of the place.

Ferries

Ferries in all parts of the world, including the cross-channel and Irish lines, can be booked on the Web. The same techniques apply to booking ferries as those used to book flights and coach trips. Check out the Internet links on **www.pcwisdom.co.uk** under the Travel section for links to many of the major steamship companies. If that alternative does not appeal to you then you can find some ferries at:

- **www.ferrysavers.com**
- **www.directferries.co.uk**
- **www.poferries.com**
- **www.hoverspeed.com**
- **www.dfdsseaways.co.uk**

Rail tickets

If you know in advance when you are likely to be travelling you can get good deals from the train operators. If you are thinking of making a long journey cross-country by train then your best option may be thetrainline at **www.thetrainline.com** where they advertise that you can save up to 35 per cent on the cost of a normal fare by using their website. This site is particularly useful if you will be using services operated by a number of different rail companies. You can pick up your tickets at your home station or, if you give a few days notice, they will be posted to you. You also get the opportunity to book a specific seat which, in these days of overcrowding, can be an advantage.

You can also book global train tickets at **www.qjump.co.uk** and use your concessionary cards at **www.raileasy.co.uk**.

Car journeys using the Internet

More and more drivers are making use of satnav machines to help them arrive at their destinations but you will often get useful information from the Web before you set off on your journey. Google maps – **http://maps.google.com/** – are very easy to use and they cover the globe. Simply enter your home town or even your post code and you will get a scalable map of the area. Click on Get Directions and enter your intended end point which, again, can be a place or postcode and Google will list quite detailed driving instructions together with the total distance between the two points and a reasonably accurate estimation of the journey time.

This route map is easily printed out for your navigator but it will not take into consideration any congested areas along the route or details of any temporary diversions and, if you leave the proscribed itinerary, you may find yourself lost in the countryside, outback or desert.

Whatever journey you may be contemplating, using Google maps enter your start and finish destination and, within seconds, you will be told how long the journey should take as well as the distance between the two places

The RAC Route Planner at **http://route.rac.co.uk/** offers further help in setting certain waypoints if you wish to take a particular route. Unfortunately neither of these options cater for hold-ups en route due to accidents or congestion. Frixo at **www.frixo.com** does just this. Just before you leave you can check out any likely holdups on your route by going to Frixo and checking the very latest traffic reports.

Here is an example of the kind of report you can expect when searching traffic conditions on the M4:

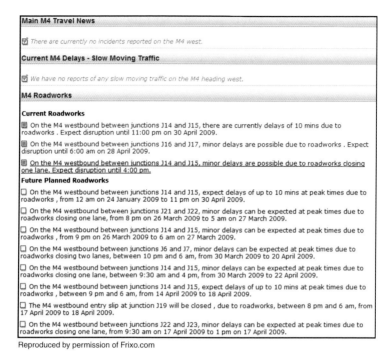

Reproduced by permission of Frixo.com

Figure 10.8

Travel insurance – a cautionary tale

Do not believe or accept everything you find on the Web. My wife and I took the opportunity to visit our family in Singapore at the beginning of this year. We booked our flight online but we also needed travel insurance. The airline did offer insurance but would not cover me as I have undergone heart surgery within the past five years. My brother-in-law had taken out insurance through Age Concern when he visited his sister in the States last year. In spite of suffering worrying health symptoms while he was there, which necessitated wide-ranging and expensive diagnostic tests, the company could not have been more helpful and he was fully reimbursed for all his expenses. I decided to give them a go.

There were two companies that operate within the Age Concern organisation but only one would consider insuring people with previous cardiac history. I filled in the comprehensive questionnaire only to be told that, for our fortnight's trip, the insurance premium would be nearly £1,000. This was far more than the cost of a single air ticket to Singapore but we felt that it would be stupid to travel without insurance and we had to reconsider the whole trip. However, I was pretty certain that I could find a more economical policy so I tried the Saga travel insurance site at **www.saga.co.uk/insurance/travel-insurance**. Once again I completed the seemingly endless questionnaire but this time I was rewarded for my persistence. The policy cost with Saga was just over £150. A savings of over £800!

As it happened both my wife and myself contracted flu out there followed by bronchitis which necessitated two trips to the local doctor whose fees were later reimbursed by the insurance company.

The moral of this story? Don't accept the first offer you get.

Google Earth

This is a fascinating program specifically designed for armchair travellers. Go to the Google home page and select More from the options listed at the top of the page.

Then select Even More from the list and find Google Earth in the Search section. You could also go direct to the website by entering **http://earth.google.com** in the browser address box. Download and install the latest version of Google Earth.

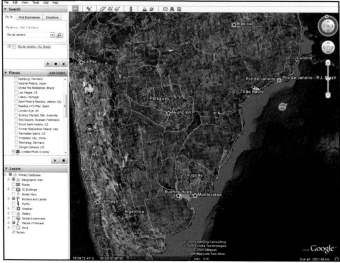

Reproduced from Google™

Figure 10.9

Figure 10.10

A shortcut icon will have been placed on your desktop so double click on it to activate the program and you can begin to explore our world. Type an address, postcode or town into the search box and wait for the map to swing into action and centre itself on your search request. In the example shown I have asked for Rio de Janeiro (see Figure 10.10).

The window displays a map in the main frame with a sidebar offering hundreds of options to add to the display.

The Search section offers the alternatives of 'flying to' a particular place, finding businesses and getting directions.

The Places section offers direct links to renowned places of interest to which you can add your own choices. Just double click on one of the suggestions like The London Eye and you will be whisked off to view the attraction in the map frame

There are other options to view the night sky with its constellations, deep sea oceanography and NASA images from outer space. The latest incarnation of Google Earth is beginning to offer Street View of the larger towns. This option is now available for 25 UK cities with more being added at a later date. The opportunities for exploration are seemingly endless. On Christmas Eve you can even track Santa Claus as he delivers his gifts across the globe – it is an interesting way of teaching young, excited children about geography.

You will have noticed various control options at the top right corner of the map frame. These allow you to pan and tilt the map as well as zoom in for more details. The amount of detail available varies from place to place largely depending upon its population and level of likely interest. The images of Burkina Faso in West Africa show far less detail than Seattle in the state of Washington. In spite of this a number of intrepid travellers have posted photos of Burkina Faso on the Google Earth map of the area.

The Layers options provide an enormous range of potential overlays on the map. You can superimpose roads, current weather conditions, local bars, restaurants, petrol stations, pharmacies, golf courses and grocery stores. Do not try to use all these layers at once because you will be overwhelmed by the amount of information. Check out just the ones you need at the time – but feel free to experiment with the options.

Once you have identified your location you can zoom in and out by using the mouse wheel or drag the mouse pointer to move the map to adjacent areas.

Reproduced from Google™

Figure 10.11

The screenshot above shows Lords cricket ground at a moderate magnification showing the surrounding roads labelled and Carluccio's restaurant identified. Small blue square icons identify the location of an image posted onto the map. Click on these to view the pictures.

Google Earth also offers you opportunities to do a bit of sightseeing without the hassle of packing your bags, parking the car and catching flu on the flight. Type something like 'Central Park, New York' into the search box, click on one of the photo icons and you will be shown the photos together with a sidebar with more options such as User-created content. These are collections of photos of an area which includes your search term.

User-created content

Earth from above ARTHUS-BERTRAND 791 photos&places - Central Park - New-York - Etats Unis

Wakacje z dzieckiem - USA - Central Park

Nerac, Inc. - Central Park

USA Trip Spring 2008 - Central Park

ERICA AND MICHAEL'S GUIDE TO NYC - Central Park

NYC Dog Map - Midtown & ManhattanUpper - Central Park

Reproduced from Google™

Figure 10.12

In this case I have chosen Erica and Michael's Guide to NYC.

Selecting this link opens up your web browser with a map of the area and links to more than 200 images of the New York area including Central Park. Click on any of the locations to see the images.

A friend of mine had been asked to give a talk on his recent trip to Hong Kong. He needed an image of the Tian Tan Buddha, a famous statue on Lantau island, but at the only time he had to visit the site it was pouring with rain and his own photos were a washout.

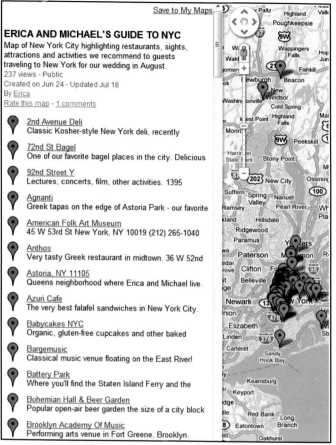

ERICA AND MICHAEL'S GUIDE TO NYC
Map of New York City highlighting restaurants, sights, attractions and activities we recommend to guests traveling to New York for our wedding in August.
237 views - Public
Created on Jun 24 - Updated Jul 18
By Erica
Rate this map - 1 comments

2nd Avenue Deli
Classic Kosher-style New York deli, recently

72nd St Bagel
One of our favorite bagel places in the city. Delicious

92nd Street Y
Lectures, concerts, film, other activities. 1395

Agnanti
Greek tapas on the edge of Astoria Park - our favorite

American Folk Art Museum
45 W 53rd St New York, NY 10019 (212) 265-1040

Anthos
Very tasty Greek restaurant in midtown. 36 W 52nd

Astoria, NY 11105
Queens neighborhood where Erica and Michael live.

Azuri Cafe
The very best falafel sandwiches in New York City.

Babycakes NYC
Organic, gluten-free cupcakes and other baked

Bargemusic
Classical music venue floating on the East River!

Battery Park
Where you'll find the Staten Island Ferry and the

Bohemian Hall & Beer Garden
Popular open-air beer garden the size of a city block

Brooklyn Academy Of Music
Performing arts venue in Fort Greene, Brooklyn.

Reproduced from Google™

Figure 10.13

By using Google Earth he was able to home in on Lantau, click on the blue photo square and found several images that he could download and use in his presentation as well as more facts about the monument.

He could have searched Google images for the Tian Tan statue but he would not have obtained the extra information.

Tian Tan Buddha

Tian Tan Buddha (Traditional Chinese: 天壇大佛;
Simplified Chinese: 天坛大佛; Pinyin:
Tiān Tán Dà Fú) is a large bronze statue of the Buddha,
completed in 1993, and located at Ngong Ping, Lantau
Island, in Hong Kong. Also known as the **Big Buddha**, it
is the world's tallest outdoor seated bronze Buddha.
The statue is located near Po Lin Monastery and
symbolizes the harmonious relationship between man
and nature, people and religion. It is a major center of
Buddhism in Hong Kong, and is also a popular tourist
attraction.
View article on wikipedia.org

By Peter Connolly

Photos

More photos

Videos

User-created content

Sam's India Trip – Tian Tan Buddha
HongKong – Tian Tan Buddha
Hong Kong - November 2007 – Sight Seeing - Tian Tan Buddha
HK – Tian Tan Buddha
Honkers! – Tian Tan Buddha

Sponsored Link

Beautiful Bronze Buddha - www.justimportsuk.com - Affordable Price Bronze Buddha Head
Perfect Idea for Gift & Home Decor

Reproduced from Google™

Figure 10.14

Summary

- Practice filling in forms on the Web – you will doing a lot of this
- Keep an eye on the small print when booking travel on the Web
- Do not rely on the Internet to get the cheapest tickets
- Use independent review sites to assess your proposed accommodation
- Google Earth provides a lot more than just aerial photographs

Brain Training

There may be more than one correct answer to these questions.

1. Why can't I find the free flights advertised?

☐ a) There were less than 100 offered in the first place

☐ b) You were too late in booking

☐ c) They are limited to airline employees

☐ d) You wanted to fly at a popular time

2. What happens if I fill in the form wrong?

☐ a) You will have to start all over again

☐ b) You will be prompted to answer the question correctly

☐ c) You will have to fly at the wrong time

☐ d) You will be banned by the airline

3. What happens if I click twice on the 'Buy It Now' button?

☐ a) You will book a second flight

☐ b) Nothing

☐ c) Your computer will blow up

☐ d) You will have to cancel the second flight

4. Where can I get an independent review of a hotel?

☐ a) From the hotel's website

☐ b) From **www.tripadvisor.com**

☐ c) From a travel agent

☐ d) From **www.holidays-uncovered.co.uk**

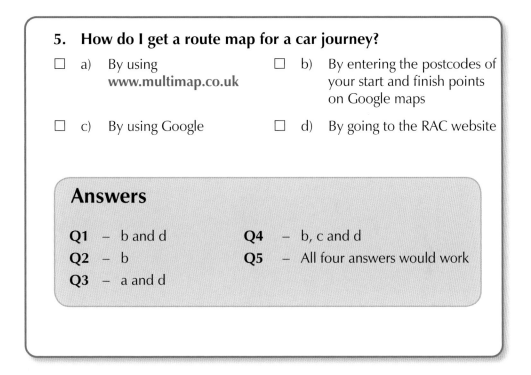

5. How do I get a route map for a car journey?

☐ a) By using
www.multimap.co.uk

☐ b) By entering the postcodes of
your start and finish points
on Google maps

☐ c) By using Google

☐ d) By going to the RAC website

Answers

Q1 – b and d

Q2 – b

Q3 – a and d

Q4 – b, c and d

Q5 – All four answers would work

Save money and get a bargain

11

Equipment needed: a computer; a printer; Internet Explorer program; an email address; connection to the Internet; a credit or debit card; a firewall; an anti-virus program; copies of your latest utility bills and a record of usernames and passwords.

Skills needed: knowledge of the keyboard and mouse; experience of form filling (Chapters 7 and 9).

As we have discussed before, there are many opportunities to save money on the Internet as a result of the lower overheads incurred by online companies. In this chapter we are going to look at specific sites that will lower your household budget.

Cheaper utilities

In the UK we have all been subjected to repeated TV adverts advising us to use hundreds of price comparison sites such as GoCompare.com, Confused. com, MoneySupermarket.com and MoneySavingExpert.com all of which offer to find you the very best deal when paying for utilities. These are reputable companies which, in spite of taking a commission from the utility companies, are able to reduce your annual outgoings – often by very significant amounts. I will use two of these sites to explain what I mean: **www.uswitch.com** and **www.moneysavingexpert.com**.

uSwitch

This is one of the biggest and longest established comparison sites which can save you money on utility bills, telephone charges, credit cards and all forms of insurance. We are going to see if we can reduce our electricity charges so, having opened up the Uswitch site, we select the Gas and Electricity link.

Reproduced by permission of © uSwitch - a Scripps Network Interactive company.

Figure 11.1

Gas & electricity

Your Current Supplier Details

To start your comparison we need to know about your current gas & electricity supplier. The more details we have, the more accurate our results.

Your Gas Supplier

Do you use gas?	◉ Yes ○ No
Current Supplier	▾
How do you pay your bill?	Pay On Receipt Of Bill ▾
Plan name	Standard ▾

Reproduced by permission of © uSwitch - a Scripps Network Interactive company.

Figure 11.2

The first request will be for your postcode so that the search can be limited to your geographical area. The next page will ask you various questions such as whether you receive both gas and electricity from your current supplier and how you normally pay your bill. You will need to have your latest utility bills to hand to answer some of these questions.

On to the next step where you will need to fill in the details of your last bill, how you are prepared to pay your new account as well as a few other questions about how you use your supply.

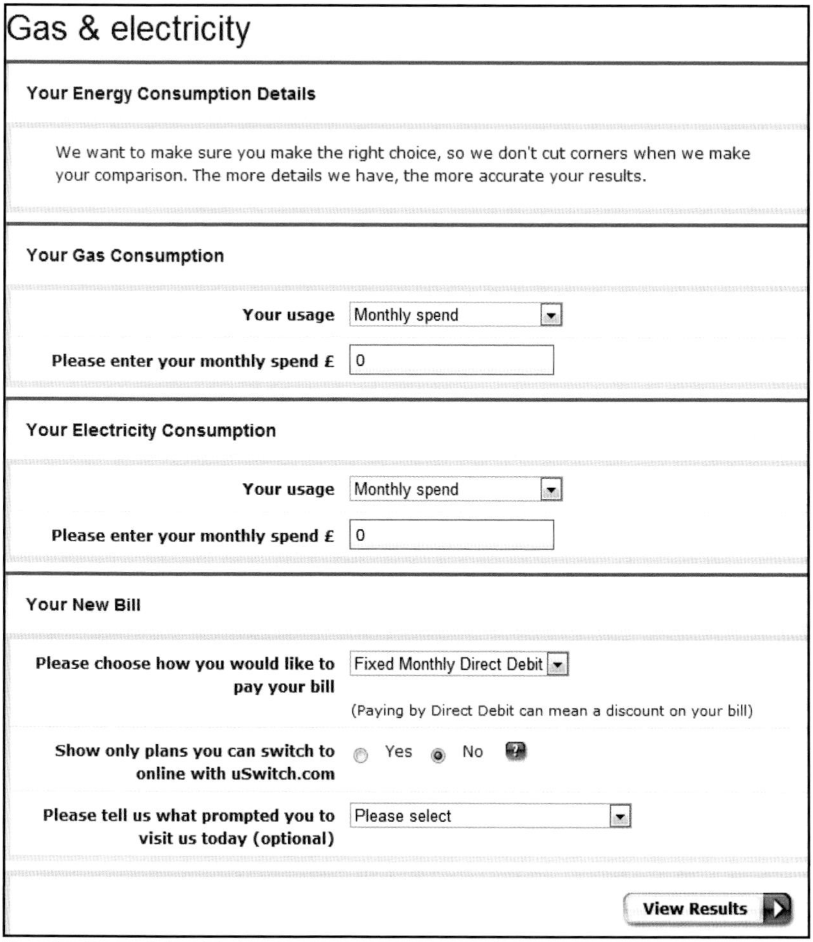

Gas & electricity

Your Energy Consumption Details

We want to make sure you make the right choice, so we don't cut corners when we make your comparison. The more details we have, the more accurate your results.

Your Gas Consumption

Your usage   Monthly spend ▼

Please enter your monthly spend £   0

Your Electricity Consumption

Your usage   Monthly spend ▼

Please enter your monthly spend £   0

Your New Bill

Please choose how you would like to pay your bill   Fixed Monthly Direct Debit ▼

(Paying by Direct Debit can mean a discount on your bill)

Show only plans you can switch to online with uSwitch.com   ○ Yes ◉ No ❓

Please tell us what prompted you to visit us today (optional)   Please select ▼

View Results ▶

Figure 11.3

Finally, click on view results to get an idea of the sort of savings you might expect to achieve by changing suppliers.

Plan features & conditions	Customer rating	Calculated annual price	Start saving
Online Version 6 » • No Termination Fee • Earn Nectar Points	63% ○ 621 reviews	£616.36 Cheapest with uSwitch	Save £183.64 **Save now**
Sign Online V15 - Paperless Billing » • You will receive a discount off your energy bill after you have been with npower and paid by monthly Direct Debit for 12 months. • Paperless Billing ○ more	46% ○ 699 reviews	£651.48	Save £148.52 **Save now**
Sign Online V15 - Standard Billing » • You will receive a discount off your energy bill after you have been with npower and paid by monthly Direct Debit for 12 months. • Extended hours 0845 UK customer contact centres	46% ○ 699 reviews	£651.48	Save £148.52 **Save now**
FixOnline » • Exit fees applicable - £30 dual fuel and £10 single electricity • You may be entitled to an additional £14 annual discount if you do not have a mains gas supply and live in the Norweb, Eastern or East Midlands area. If you are entitled to this discount you will be notified of this within your welcome pack ○ more	59% ○ 962 reviews	£669.58	Save £130.42 Not available on uSwitch.com

Reproduced by permission of © uSwitch - a Scripps Network Interactive company.

Figure 11.4

As you can see from the example above you can look forward to a saving a substantial amount over a period of a year. You can also check out customer reviews of the various companies together with various extras that come attached to the individual plans such as the ability to manage your account online and often some indication of how long these prices will be maintained.

You will notice that some of these companies offer the incentive of No Termination Fee so that you are not locked into an agreement. Check that you are not already locked into such an agreement with your current supplier or you may find that the release fee cancels out much of the anticipated saving.

At any time when utility companies are reducing their prices it might be wise to wait for the flurry of conflicting reductions to die down before committing yourself to a particular supplier. You have probably waited long enough to change your supplier and a short wait will not make a lot of difference to your current bill while you may get far better offers in a few weeks' time.

If you decide that the time is right to make a switch, then select the 'Save now' link next to your chosen supplier. This will take you to a long form which you will need to fill in with details of your home address, bank account or credit card and current readings from your meter. Just follow the forms through, clicking Continue at the end of each one, until you get to the end when you will be asked to commit to the change.

> If you are anxious about the prospect of giving out bank or credit card details you can be reassured by the web address of these pages which will start https:// meaning that the information is secure. A small padlock symbol will also show in your browser window to confirm the security.

And that's it! The rest of the work will be done by uSwitch who will notify the supply companies of your desire to change and complete all the necessary paperwork.

Money Saving Expert

Martin Lewis who runs this site is an award-winning TV and radio presenter, national newspaper columnist and bestselling author. I have been receiving his weekly moneysaving email letter for years and have been able to save a lot of money as a result.

Reproduced by courtesy of ® Martin Lewis and MoneySavingExpert.com

Figure 11.5

> Having gone to **www.moneysavingexpert.com**, the top of this home page gives an inkling of the range and type of moneysaving advice that flows from this site. This is not confined to the usual offers of saving on your heating costs, car insurance, loan offers and bank accounts but covers the whole spectrum of saving money. Some of the links offer just plain common sense while others point out the vast potential of using the Internet to economise and enrich our lives.

The site is full of tips about how to haggle the price of your holiday down; get free offers and often cash for registering with some supermarkets (it costs nothing to register and you can always cancel the registration); get a dozen red roses delivered on Valentine's Day for a reduced price; get a discount off a Family and Friends railcard and hundreds more. They are all perfectly genuine, legal and up for grabs – it is just that people can't be bothered to take a little bit of time to gain the benefits.

You could become seriously addicted to this site but even an hour a week will help save you money and could help pay for your Internet connection. Yes, you can also get advice on the best broadband connection for you as well. Just to clear up any doubts you may have about this apparent promotion of this site, I had better state categorically that I am not paid any commission for this advice or receive benefit in any form at all from the company and I do not know Martin Lewis personally.

Even if you only do one thing when visiting this site at **www.moneysavingexpert.com** sign up for his weekly newsletter.

Price comparison sites

I have already mentioned some of the sites that compare utilities, insurance and mortgages but there are other comparison sites that will help you to get the best price for your more standard purchases. The two I am going to feature – and there are hundreds on the Web (just search for 'comparison sites' using your preferred search engine) – are Kelkoo at **www.kelkoo.co.uk** for UK prices or **www.kelkoo.com** for bargains across Europe and Shopzilla at **www.shopzilla.co.uk** or **www.shopzilla.com** for North America.

Kelkoo

Let us say that you are looking for a replacement coffee maker. You could spend a long time wandering round the various electrical appliance outlets in your neighbourhood or you could just go to Kelkoo. Entering the term 'coffee maker' into the search box brings up the following alternatives:

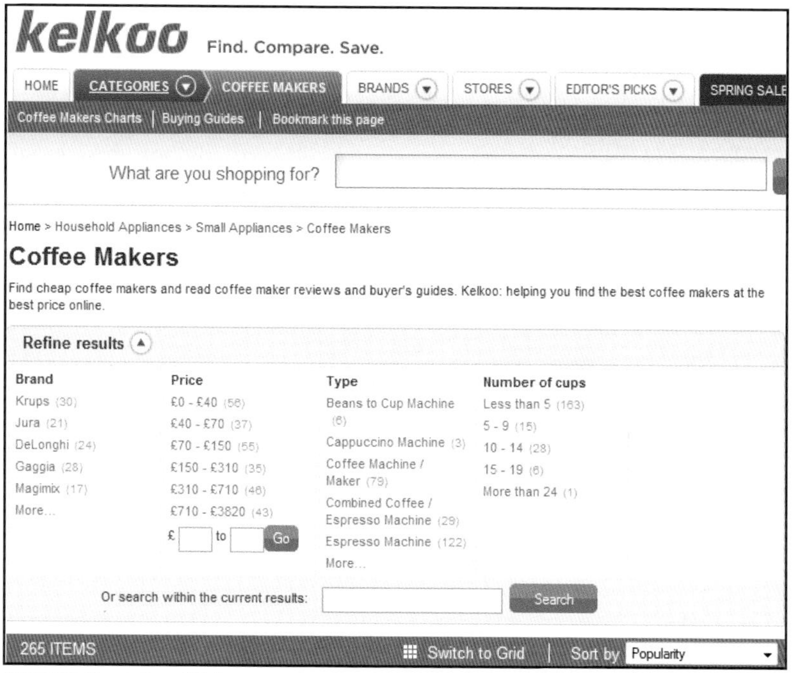

Reproduced by courtesy of Kelkoo

Figure 11.6

This page allows you to choose the type, brand and price of over 200 coffee makers from the comfort of your own home. You even get customers reviews of the individual percolator you are interested in. Check the prices in your local stores but I will bet a pound to a peanut that the Web price is somewhat lower than that on the High Street.

Shopzilla

Searching Shopzilla for coffee makers at **www.shopzilla.co.uk** offers similar results to Kelkoo.

My personal impression is that this site is even more comprehensive than Kelkoo but it is always sensible to check out more than one source if you are going to get a real bargain. I would like to think that you would check out varying prices at normal retail outlets.

Reproduced by permission of Scripps Network Interactive

Figure 11.7

Reproduced by permission of Scripps Network Interactive

Figure 11.8

One glance at the list of departments gives an idea of the range of goods compared by the site – everything from pet food to perfumery and wheel trims to Wii games. If you want to know what Wii games are, ask your grandchildren.

Don't forget that even these sites may prove to be more expensive than sales and special offers on the High Street.

I have only been able to touch the surface of the subject of price comparison sites. There are thousands of them out there and you will find links to them on the PCWisdom website.

Auction sites

If the numbers of TV auction programmes are to be believed the British public has an insatiable appetite for this method of buying and selling. This appetite is confirmed by a Google search for UK Internet auction sites that found over 5 million references.

There are sites offering cars, antiques, art, books, office furniture, houses, computers by the thousand and ballet memorabilia. There are auctions for gays and lesbians, sites offering you free credit and even one calling itself Trotters Independent Tradings! You can buy online from government auction sales, police auctions, car auctions, liquidation sales, property auctioneers, bankrupt stock sales, antique auctions, Customs and Excise sales, computer auctions, goods seized by the bailiffs, courts and the Inland Revenue.

With many of these seized goods auctions condition is everything and I would recommend that, having checked out the goods online, you go to the auction house and view the lots. You will not only get to see the goods themselves but you can find out a lot about the auctioneers themselves. They may be well-established businesses but others could be fly-by-nights and gone the next morning, leaving you holding the baby.

You need to be a professional to use many of these sites profitably but there are two websites that might whet your appetite: **www.ukauctionguides.co.uk** and **www.governmentauctionsuk.co.uk**. The latter sells impounded goods from government, bankruptcy and liquidation auctions, HM Customs and Excise,

Ministry of Defence, lost property offices, police, VAT, tax and court seizures, but you will have to pay a subscription fee to take part in the auctions. Many retired people have found a money-making second career in buying from such auctions and selling the goods on through other auction sites or privately.

You can check them all out on Google but one Internet auction site stands head and shoulders above the rest – eBay.

The American eBay site auctioned a round of golf with Tiger Woods in aid of disadvantaged children. The winning bid was $425,000.

eBay

There are eBay auction sites across the globe from Argentina to Vietnam – some are more active than others and postage costs from foreign parts will cancel out a large part of any saving you may hope to make. You can bid for anything on eBay from a length of old rope to a Gulfstream private jet but we ordinary mortals tend to stick with the more mundane lots.

You can browse eBay to your heart's content but in order to buy and sell on the site within the UK you need to register. Go to **www.ebay.co.uk** and click on Sign In or Register.

You will be presented with a long form similar to those we had to complete when booking a flight or changing our utility supplier so the format should be getting familiar to you. Apart from the usual entries of your name, address and email address you will need to choose your eBay ID together with the obligatory password. Use your imagination to compose a suitable ID – you cannot simply use your name – but it can be a 'play' on your name, address or make of car and even then you may have to add a few numbers to render the ID unique to you. Once you have completed the form click on Register at the bottom and you are ready to go.

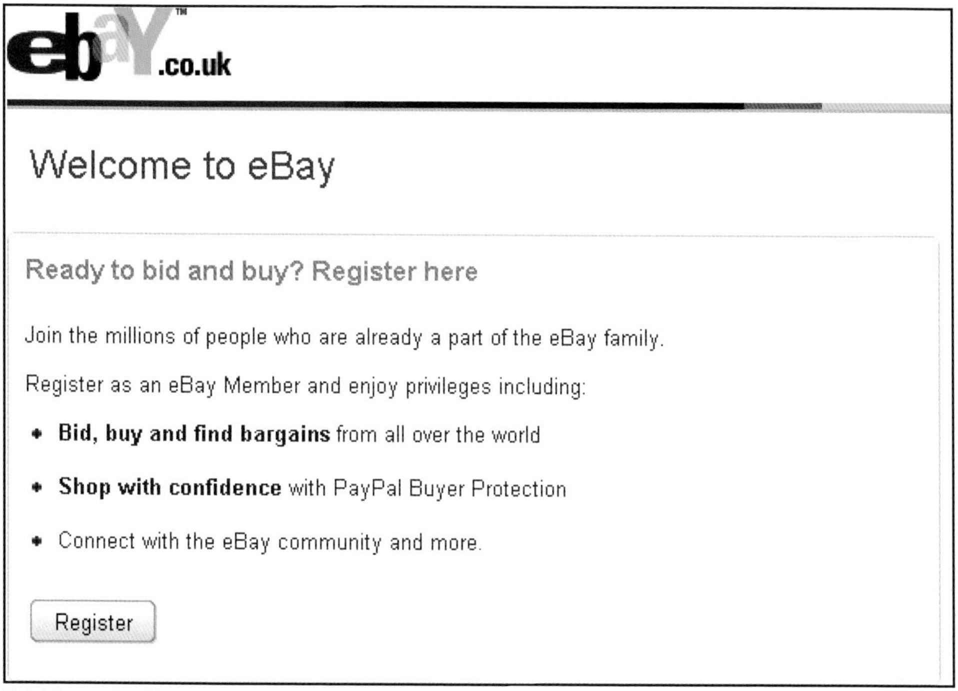
.co.uk
Welcome to eBay
Ready to bid and buy? Register here
Join the millions of people who are already a part of the eBay family.
Register as an eBay Member and enjoy privileges including:
Bid, buy and find bargains from all over the world
Shop with confidence with PayPal Buyer Protection
Connect with the eBay community and more.
Register

Figure 11.9

Buying on eBay

We are going to see if we can add to your mythical collection of woven silk cigarette cards. These cards may have been catalogued under a number of different categories so I have decided to search All Categories.

The initial search brings up 2,953 cards classified under at least eight different categories. The largest selection is found in the Cigarette/Tea/Gum Cards so I selected that category.

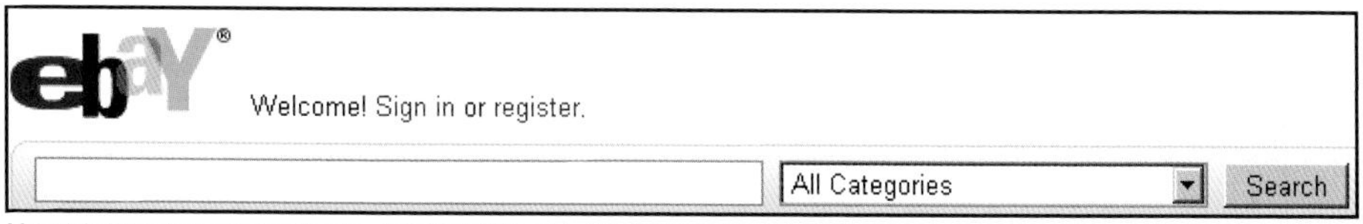
Welcome! Sign in or register.
All Categories
Search

Figure 11.10

Categories ▾	Motors	Stores	Daily Deal NEW	
Antiques	Crafts		Real Estate
Art	DVDs & Movies		Specialty Services
Baby	Dolls & Bears		Sporting Goods
Books	Electronics		Sports Mem, Cards & Fan Shop
Business & Industrial	Entertainment Memorabilia		Stamps
Cameras & Photo	Gift Certificates		Tickets
Cars, Boats, Vehicles & Parts	Health & Beauty		Toys & Hobbies
Cell Phones & PDAs	Home & Garden		Travel
Clothing, Shoes & Accessories	Jewelry & Watches		Video Games
Coins & Paper Money	Music		Everything Else
Collectibles	Musical Instruments		
Computers & Networking	Pottery & Glass		

Figure 11.11

I don't want to spend time wading my way through more than 2,000 lots to find silk cards so I have entered the search word 'silk' in the Find box which has reduced the selection to less than 800 lots.

The lots are listed by the length of time left before the auction of the lot ends. The first entry shows that there are only 20 minutes left before the auction ends but, so far, there have been no bids. The thumbnail picture offers some indication of the appearance of the goods but, by clicking on the blue description of the items, we get far more detail.

eBay conducts more transactions every day than either the New York Stock Exchange or the NASDAQ.

Study this screenshot carefully and you will realise how much information it contains. There will be a more detailed description of the item below this screenshot. In this case the auction is due to end in just over three days. As the end time approaches you could add it to your watch list which you will find under your Account details. Note also that this seller has completed over 634 transactions on eBay and that he has a customer satisfaction rating of 100% so I would be inclined to trust him.

Enter your bid here   Details of the seller

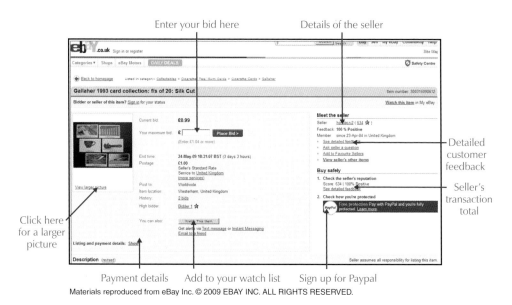

Detailed customer feedback

Seller's transaction total

Click here for a larger picture

Payment details   Add to your watch list   Sign up for Paypal

Materials reproduced from eBay Inc. © 2009 EBAY INC. ALL RIGHTS RESERVED.

Figure 11.12

To enter a bid, simply click within the Place Bid box and type in the maximum amount you are prepared to pay. This does not mean that this is the price you will have to pay – only the amount you are prepared to spend. Once you have submitted a bid, eBay will enter the lowest amount that exceeds the previous highest bid. There have been two bids for this item so far and the current highest bid stands at £0.99 so, if you have offered £10, you will automatically become the highest bidder at £1.04. Your bid will continue to be raised automatically by eBay until someone exceeds your original £10 offer. You will be notified by email of changes in your bid status and offered the option of increasing your bid, should you wish.

You will find all you need to know about ebay – including tutorials – at **http://pages.ebay.com/education/index.html**.

Bids tend to come rather slowly at first but build up as the end of the auction approaches and you can always increase your bid if someone offers more than your maximum amount. If you really want to acquire an item it is a good idea to stay on the computer while the auction draws to a close.

You can often find a real bargain by looking for misspelled items. It is amazing the number of times lots are misspelt which means that they are omitted from a standard search. There is even a website that will check out these errors for you at **www.bargainchecker.com**.

If you are successful with your bid you will be notified by email and then comes the matter of payment. If you look at the last screenshot you will notice that the seller is prepared to accept cheques but prefers payment by PayPal (eBay now insists on all subscribers having a PayPal account). So what is PayPal?

PayPal

With the increasing demise of the cheque a number of alternate methods are becoming available on the Internet. One of the first and most reliable is the service offered by the PayPal company. The principle behind the system is payment to email addresses but, first of all, you must set up your PayPal account.

Go to PayPal at **www.paypal.com** and click on Signup. Choose your home country from the dropdown menu and choose the Personal account option. Fill in the necessary boxes with your email address, name, address and telephone number, choosing a suitable password as one that you are going to remember and other people are unlikely to guess.

Click on Agree and Create Account. On the following page choose whether you wish to pay through your bank account or your credit card. I would suggest using your bank account since these details are less likely to change than those of your credit card. Fill in the details of your account. You may have noticed that the web address of the PayPal page now starts with **https://** and a small padlock 🔒 icon will appear on the screen showing that the details are to be securely encrypted and therefore safe from criminal interference.

Once you have registered your credit card or bank account details PayPal will set about verifying your information. When the company is satisfied with its initial checks it will debit your account with two small payments. You will be notified by email that you should verify these payments. Find the two figures on your card or bank statement and enter them on the secure verification site. Once you have verified that you are indeed the holder of the account you will be able to use the PayPal system.

Selling on eBay

Once you have registered an account on eBay and you have had a little practise in using the site to buy a few small items, you can start to sell your unwanted paraphernalia on the site.

The most expensive item ever bought on eBay was a Gulfstream II Jet for US$4.9 million.

There are two methods of selling – Quick Sell and Advanced Sell. The former chooses the most popular listing options while the latter affords more control over your listing. I would suggest using the Quick Sell option for your first few lots.

Choose your descriptive words carefully – and honestly – to make every word count towards attracting potential buyers. Having entered the description eBay will suggest a number of likely categories under which you will list your item. A suitable category will normally present itself but, if not, you can always browse for other categories.

A clear digital image of the item is a must if you are going to achieve the best price for your item. Click on Add a Photo to upload the images – you can have more than one but each one, after the first, will incur further small charges – more details about these charges on the website.

Now comes the detailed description of your lot. Give as much information as possible but avoid any 'embellishment' of the description as the eventual buyer may refuse to complete the transaction if your description is in any way misleading.

The next stage is to choose a starting price. The lower you set the original asking price, the lower the fee you will be charged by eBay which is based on the starting price. A lower starting price will also attract more interest in your offering but beware of setting the price so low that you are giving the item away if you only get one bid. You could also set a 'Buy It Now' price to attract those people browsing the site who are interested but unwilling to wait for the end of the auction. Setting such a Buy It Now price will incur a higher fee from eBay.

One you have set the initial price you will have to set the length of time the auction is to last. This can be 3 days, a week or 10 days. You should also bear in mind the timing of the end of the auction. Set it to end at a time when potential bidders are likely to be active on their computers rather than breakfast time when the family are busy trying to get the children ready for school.

Now you have to enter the postage and packaging costs. Be fair in your estimation to avoid discouraging potential bidders. eBay even provides a postage cost calculator to help you with this estimation.

Finally you must choose the methods of payment you are prepared to accept. If you have set up a PayPal account this would be the method of choice but you can always choose payment by cheque or credit card if you have the facility to accept such payments. You should wait to ensure that any cheque paid clears through your bank before posting the item to the buyer and this can add several days to the transaction time.

Once you have completed the selling details click on Save and Preview to see what your entry will look like and make any further alterations to improve the listing before you commit to the listing of your lot. You will be notified of all the charges incurred by your listing before you commit yourself to selling your goods.

All you have to do now is sit back and wait for the bids to come in. Do not be discouraged by the absence of bids during the first few days. The bidding tends to become much more active in the final hours of the auction.

If all of this sounds a bit complicated you could use a company like Auctiva (**www.auctiva.com**) which is free and leads you through the process of listing your cast off goods and places the listing to start and finish at times of your choice.

As a registered user of eBay you will get email notification of occasional offers from the company such as free listing days which can cut your selling costs considerably.

Have fun!

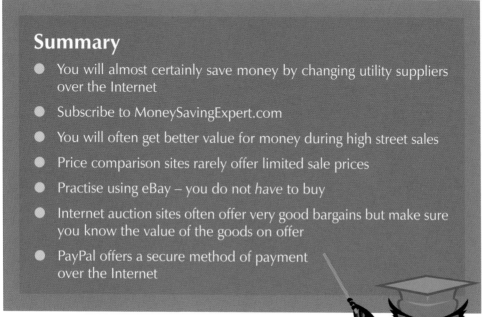

Summary

- You will almost certainly save money by changing utility suppliers over the Internet

- Subscribe to MoneySavingExpert.com

- You will often get better value for money during high street sales

- Price comparison sites rarely offer limited sale prices

- Practise using eBay – you do not *have* to buy

- Internet auction sites often offer very good bargains but make sure you know the value of the goods on offer

- PayPal offers a secure method of payment over the Internet

Brain Training

There may be more than one correct answer to these questions.

1. Which is the best comparison site?

☐ a) **www.kelkoo.co.uk** ☐ b) There isn't one

☐ c) Google ☐ d) A web directory

2. What is available on eBay?

☐ a) A length of old rope ☐ b) Cars

☐ c) Firearms ☐ d) Dodgy antiques

3. What do you need to buy an item on eBay?

☐ a) An eBay account ☐ b) A PayPal account

☐ c) A security code ☐ d) A credit reference from your bank

4. Which household budget items can I change on the Internet?

☐ a) Your Council Tax ☐ b) Your mortgage

☐ c) Your telephone supplier ☐ d) Your life insurance

5. Where will I find a bargain?

☐ a) High street shop sales ☐ b) Travel agents special offers

☐ c) Internet auction sites ☐ d) On a website offering something that is too good to be true

Answers

Q1 – b

Q2 – a, b and d

Q3 – a and b

Q4 – b, c, and d

Q5 – a, b and c

PART III
Projects

Digital photography online

12

Equipment needed: a computer; Internet Explorer program; an email address; connection to the Internet; a credit or debit card; and a record of usernames and passwords.

Skills needed: knowledge of the keyboard and mouse plus some confidence; knowledge of downloading a program (Chapters 3 and 5); use of a digital camera.

The digital camera has largely replaced the old film cameras in the photographic market. There are thousands of amateur paparazzi out there with only a very basic knowledge of how to use both their camera and their home computer. Very often the nearest they get to actually viewing a photo is by peering at the tiny screen on the back of the camera, or by staring at it on the computer screen. This chapter aims to change all that by showing you how to use the Internet to order prints of your best shots, and share your digital photos with the world online.

2003 was the first year when digital cameras outsold conventional film cameras.

Getting prints from the Web

You may have reached the stage with your digital photography where you have taken your camera's memory card down to the local photo shop or supermarket and printed out copies of your favourite photos. Unfortunately this means a car journey, parking and higher costs when you could do it all from the comfort of your own home. There are hundreds of photo print websites on the Web which will print your pictures at a lower cost – and initially even free – even taking into account the postage costs.

Internet sources for such services can be found at **www.tescophoto.com**, **www.kodakgallery.co.uk**, **www.truprint.co.uk** and **www.snapfish.co.uk**. You simply select your chosen images, upload them to the website, enter your credit card details, type in your address and wait for the post. They usually arrive within a day or two.

These sites also offer many more photographic services than simply printed photos. You can get coffee mugs, coasters, place mats, T-shirts, cards, calendars and canvas prints from these companies. You can even get giant posters and customised newspapers from your images. The Web is your photographic oyster.

Snapfish

I have chosen to use Snapfish as an example of how to use such a website. Open up the website at **www.snapfish.co.uk**, fill in your name and choose a password

© Hewlett-Packard Development Company, L.P.

Figure 12.1

and move on to the next page where you enter a name for the album with any extra details you care to mention.

Go to 'upload to this album' then, on the next page, you will choose your photos.

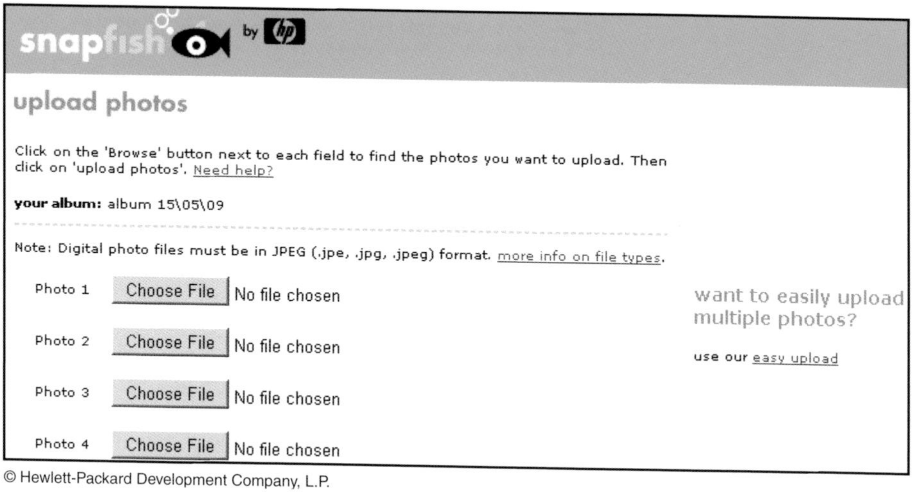

© Hewlett-Packard Development Company, L.P.

Figure 12.2

Click on Choose File for the first picture and navigate your way to the folders that contain the images you want to have printed. Having made your selection click on upload photos. This may take some time depending on the size of the image files you have chosen. The larger the file, the better the end result but uploading is always much slower than downloading so be patient. You can always minimise the upload page and get on with other things while this is happening. Eventually the images will finish uploading and you will be invited to view your album or add more photos. On the album page you can then choose to print the images.

Select those images you want printed and choose whether you want a matt or gloss finish and the size of the prints and any other alterations you may need.

You are perfectly safe at this stage. You have not committed yourself to any payment contract – they do not even know your credit card details yet. You have simply uploaded a few pictures to an online album. You can even copy the web page address and post it to your friends and they can see your pictures online.

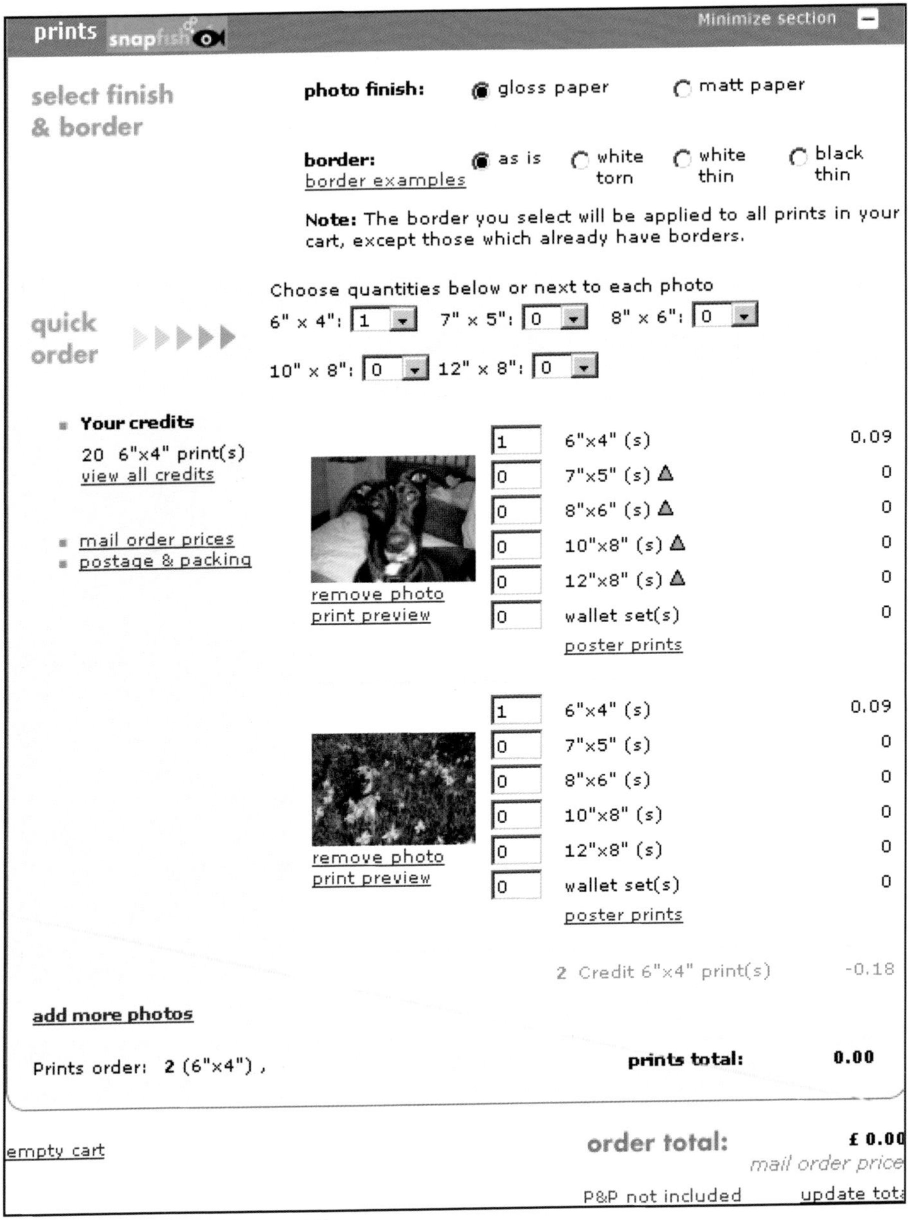

prints snapfish ⚬

select finish & border

photo finish: ◉ gloss paper ○ matt paper

border: ◉ as is ○ white torn ○ white thin ○ black thin
border examples

Note: The border you select will be applied to all prints in your cart, except those which already have borders.

Choose quantities below or next to each photo

quick order ▶▶▶▶

6" x 4": [1 ▾]   7" x 5": [0 ▾]   8" x 6": [0 ▾]

10" x 8": [0 ▾]   12" x 8": [0 ▾]

■ **Your credits**
20 6"x4" print(s)
view all credits

■ mail order prices
■ postage & packing

[1]	6"x4" (s)	0.09
[0]	7"x5" (s) ⚠	0
[0]	8"x6" (s) ⚠	0
[0]	10"x8" (s) ⚠	0
[0]	12"x8" (s) ⚠	0
[0]	wallet set(s)	0
	poster prints	

remove photo
print preview

[1]	6"x4" (s)	0.09
[0]	7"x5" (s)	0
[0]	8"x6" (s)	0
[0]	10"x8" (s)	0
[0]	12"x8" (s)	0
[0]	wallet set(s)	0
	poster prints	

remove photo
print preview

2 Credit 6"x4" print(s)   -0.18

add more photos

Prints order: **2 (6"x4")** ,

prints total: **0.00**

order total: **£ 0.00**
mail order price

P&P not included   update tota

Figure 12.3

When you have finished stipulating how you want to have your photos delivered click on Check Out at the bottom of the page and fill in your details together with your credit card details. Having provided all the necessary information click on Continue. If you have made any mistakes or omitted certain information you will be returned to the checkout page with a notice of where you have gone wrong.

Eventually you will see your completed order.

If you are still happy with your order click 'buy now' to submit your order. You are not committed until you take this final step. If you are uncertain or unhappy in any way just close the web page down and you have not spent any money. You will have gained a lot of confidence in going through the process.

Another commercial company that regularly features in the list of best photo labs is Photobox at **www.photobox.co.uk** which offers a wide range of photographic options as well as good value for money.

Picasa (see below) does not restrict its links to photo labs in the US and Europe. Simply select the country and Picasa will offer the commercial options for that country. This means that even if you live thousands of miles away from your intended recipient, you only have to pay local postage.

Storage on the Web

If you really want to keep your most precious photos even safer you can store them on the Web. There are many companies that offer a certain amount of free storage space for photographers to use but this can get used up quite quickly bearing in mind that modern cameras are producing larger and larger files. If you reach your allotted limit you can pay a storage charge for increased space. Check out these sites by doing a Google search for 'photo storage' and check out the results. Storage fees are usually based on annual subscriptions which vary from $50 for the home snapper to $250 for a professional photographer.

You will need a reasonably fast broadband connection if you are going to upload a significant number of files. Remember that upload speeds are often far less than a third of the speed of the usual download speed.

Web albums

While we are talking about uploading images to the Web it might be a good idea to mention web albums. As you will have gathered you can store your images on the sites of the commercial photo print companies but the addresses of these tend to be very long and convoluted. For example:

www3.snapfish.co.uk/thumbnailshare/AlbumID=279857812/a=160602377_160602377/t_=160602377

which would be impossible to remember. However there are websites devoted solely to the storage and display of Joe Public's pictures. The two I will be dealing with are Picasa and Flickr albums.

Flickr

This website is part of the Yahoo group. The address is **www.flickr.com**. You will have to complete a registration form to establish your own page on the site. The process is similar to many of those we have discussed in previous chapters.

Figure 12.4

This is my home page on Flickr. As you will see there are a number of options whereby you can search for Contacts and Groups, Explore the Flickr site, Search for images and Organize your pictures into different albums. Click on the various options and explore the possibilities to your heart's content.

You can also search for images by name. To give you some idea of the size of the Flickr site, I found over 1,200,000 images of Venice when I typed the single word Venice into the search box while refining the search to the word 'rialto' brought up 54,000 pictures.

By joining Groups and making other Contacts you will be able to share your photos with people across the globe.

You can also upload your pictures via the website but Flickr offers a more efficient method of doing this by using the Flickr Uploadr which is a small program that you will need to download and install. You will find this at **www.flickr.com/tools/uploadr** (watch for the spelling of Uploadr).

Having installed the Flickr Uploadr you will be automatically logged in to your Flickr account and you can choose Add to start uploading your pictures.

By adding descriptive text and keywords (or Tags) you will make the image more available for searching under a variety of words. You can also set the privacy of the images by hiding then from the public or restricting them to certain people. Instead of having all your pictures in one folder you can create supplementary albums called Sets.

Once you have collected all the images just select Upload Photos and wait for the process to finish. You can then tell your friends that they can view the latest pictures of your holiday in Sausalito by going to your Flickr album.

Figure 12.5

Picasa web albums

The Picasa system works in a very similar way to Flickr but is operated via the Picasa program. You select the files that you want to add to your album and then choose the Upload function. You can also upload your photos directly from the website.

The Picasa album offers description facilities comparable to those of the Flickr albums as well as similar search options.

Picasa is supplied by the respected Google company and comes completely free. Download it from **picasa.google.com**. (You may need to put **http://** in front of this address if you have an old web browser.) Select Download Picasa 3 and let the computer do its stuff. (You may already done this if you have followed the instructions in Chapter 3.)

Once Picasa is installed and you open the program it will ferret its way through all the picture files on your computer and catalogue them by folders. Every time you open Picasa it checks to see if you have added any more images and adds then to the program. You will see little popup images emerging from the right side of the screen as it loads these new images.

Picasa is more than just a way to upload photos to the web. It's a complete photo catalogue and editing program with many options available. Most of these options are beyond the topic of the Internet, so I'll be just hitting the highlights in order to concentrate on the parts pertinent to web albums.

Picasa menu bars

You will have come across menu bars before and you are probably getting the hang of them by now so just click on a few of the options and see what is available.

To get the hang of all of the features I would suggest that you select a few pictures or video files, click on a button and see what happens. You will learn far more from personal experience than reading from a book. To identify the action of each button hover the mouse pointer over the required button.

Reproduced from Google™

Figure 12.6

I cover the use of Picasa in far more detail in the digital photography chapter of *Computing for the Older and Wiser* (ISBN 9780470770993), available at your favorite book seller. In the alternative, you might want to explore Google's Picasa Getting Started Guide online at **http://picasa. google.com/support/bin/answer.py?answer=93183**.

Picasa's Internet features

Picasa provides four main Internet features that you can use to share your photos online, attach them to an email to send to family and friends, or order a nice set of prints.

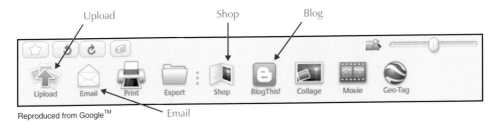

Figure 12.7

Upload to web album

Picasa offers its own web album on the Google site so that you can direct your friends to the site where they can enjoy your latest pictures without having to download them onto their computer.

> You will get a better idea of how to use the Picasa albums by selecting a few images within the program and then choosing to upload to the web album when you will be taken through the registration process and establishment of your personal album.

> One big advantage of using web albums is that instead of attaching lots of photos of your grandchildren or latest holiday to email messages that you send to your friends you simply provide the web link to your images. It can be rather tedious having to open each one of twenty or more photos – one at a time – attached to an email message.

Email

Just select the images you want to send and hit this button. Your email program will be activated with the photos, not only attached, but ready for compression to reduce their file size. Just add your message and click on Send.

Shop

We have already discussed the advantages of having your photos printed via the Internet. This button allows you to upload photos for printing by a wide range of commercial companies.

Another tip to save you some money. If you want to send some of your pictures to friends and relatives living abroad choose a printing company in the country to which you want them sent. You will save on airmail postage rates and they will arrive much quicker. These companies, like the ones mentioned previously, can also produce very attractive photo albums, coffee mugs and T-shirts directly from the Picasa program.

Blog

A blog is an online diary kept by many people on the Web. You can use this button to upload your images to your blog. I will discuss blogs later in Chapter 15.

Google Images

If you want to find a picture of a particular subject, place or person, use the Google Images option from the main Google search page. There are millions of images available on Google but to see the better ones I would advise you to search for the Large images from the dropdown menu.

Reproduced from Google™

Figure 12.8

Commercial software

This is not the place to explore the potential offered for digital manipulation of images by commercial software. You can develop this hobby by using such books as Photoshop Elements for Dummies and PaintShop Pro for Dummies – both published by John Wiley & Sons, Ltd. These programs offer a wider spectrum of editing tools than Picasa for those who take the subject even more seriously. These programs such as Photoshop Elements or PaintShop Pro are not free and you will be charged for these programs.

> In my opinion, one of the best websites for all things photographic can be found at **www.dpreview.com** which carries authoritative reviews, photo galleries, discussion forums, buying guides and some tutorials.

Video editing

If you want to try your hand at editing some of your family videos you can do a lot worse than using the free Windows Movie Maker program that comes ready installed with both Windows Vista and Windows XP.

To make the best use of this program you will need a fast connection between your computer and the video camera called Firewire. This requires a special cable and socket but the latter will be found on most computers manufactured within the past three or four years.

The program has a comprehensive Help facility that will guide you through the process. There are also over 2,500 video tutorials on the use of Movie Maker on the YouTube website at **www.youtube.com**.

We will be discussing the use of this website in the next chapter on learning new skills.

Summary

- There are no developing and printing costs for poor digital photos
- Getting prints from the Web are normally cheaper than from a high street outlet
- Download Picasa and play around with your images
- Uploading your images to the Web will save disk space on your computer

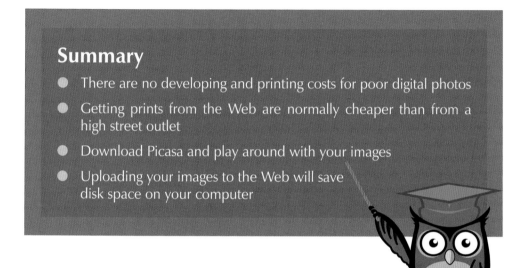

Brain Training

There may be more than one correct answer to these questions.

1. What is the cheapest way to get my photos printed?

☐ a) Print them on your own machine
☐ b) Take them to the local supermarket
☐ c) Use online commercial photo printers
☐ d) Use a specialist camera shop

2. How can I store copies of the photos away from my computer?

☐ a) You cannot store photos
☐ b) Transfer to an external hard disk
☐ c) Copy them to a DVD
☐ d) Use a scanner

3. What would be an optimum file size to send a photo by email?

☐ a) You cannot send amateur photos by email
☐ b) 250 megabytes
☐ c) Five kilobytes
☐ d) 200 kilobytes

Answers

Q1 – c   Q3 – d
Q2 – b and c

Learning a new skill

Equipment needed: a computer; a printer; Internet Explorer program; an email address; connection to the Internet; a firewall; an anti-virus program and a record of usernames and passwords.

Skills needed: knowledge of the keyboard and mouse; knowledge of downloading a program (Chapters 3 and 5); experience of form filling (Chapters 7 and 9).

The song tells us that you're never too old to fall in love and I hope that this chapter will convince you that you are never too old to learn a new skill. It may take a bit longer, but most of our generation enjoy the benefits of more spare time.

Knowledge

> Just because you have a computer does not mean that you should cut down on your social life but the Internet can enlarge and enhance the knowledge you acquire from such meetings. You may have joined a birdwatching group and you happen to see a spotted woodpecker enjoying the peanuts you set out in the bird feeder. But is it a Greater or Lesser Spotted Woodpecker? No problem. Just search for 'spotted woodpecker' on Google images and you will have the answer in minutes.

Let me give you a few more examples of what I mean.

Languages

You may be contemplating a trip to the Black Forest in Germany but any elementary German you may have learnt at school is probably rusty to the point of non-existence by now. You could join a U3A course offering German for Beginners and you can supplement this training in a number of different ways. You could tune in to a German news radio programme at **www.listenlive.eu/germany.html** or, even better, take a free tutorial in either audio or video format at **www.multilingualbooks.com/freelessons-german.html**. I found these sites by searching Google for 'german news radio tutorial' but you can perform your own searches for the language that interests you.

There are two very good language learning sites at **www.bbc.co.uk/languages** – with audio and video courses in 36 languages and **www.ilovelanguages.com** – which is a site based in the US but there are lessons in 76 tongues.

YouTube

I have mentioned this site before as a great source of information. In essence YouTube is a vast library of video clips on every subject you can imagine and many that you would never have thought of. The address (URL) is **www.youtube.com**. Put it in the Favorites folder of your web browsing program. Searching YouTube for German language tutorials brought up over 200 videos on the subject varying from pronunciation to basic German for the occasional traveller.

> You will find instructional videos to help you with any hobby from creating a ribbon rose in embroidery to replacing a cistern ball valve in plumbing. While on the subject of YouTube, try lifting your spirits by going to the web address **http://www.youtube.com/watch?v=4OT_kw48rl4**. I challenge you not giggle – even if suppressed – when you view this video.

Information

Searching the Web for information using a search engine is what this book is all about but if the search engine results tend to overwhelm you then you can restrict certain searches to an encyclopaedia. The first computing encyclopaedia was

Windows Encarta at **www.encarta.msn.com**. This was originally developed as a loadable program by Microsoft and has since found its way onto the Web but, in the headlong rush to get more and more information onto the Web, many more online encyclopaedias have appeared notably the Encyclopaedia Britannica at **www.britannica.com** and Wikipedia - **http://en.wikipedia.org**.

Reproduced by courtesy of Wikipedia®

Figure 13.1

The latter is a curious beast in that it is a community based project in which members of the public make their own contributions to the site. All submissions to Wikipedia are examined for accuracy and content but – and this is occasionally a big 'but' – incorrect entries do slip through and some are downright wrong in the information they provide. The scrutiny of submitted material has been tightened up a great deal in recent years but I would suggest that you check any vital information from a secondary source. I would suggest you do this with *any* information you may glean from the Web. Having said that, you can while away a few profitable hours following up the links found on every page of the Wikipedia site.

The Encyclopaedia Britannica (**www.britannica.co.uk**), or Britannica Online as it is known, provides thousands of authoritative articles and videos for general consumption but if you need to use it to obtain educational or specialist information you may have to take out a subscription and subscription charges are detailed online.

Finally, there is the encyclopaedia of encyclopaedias, **www.encyclopedia.com** (check the spelling!). This online resource combines the results of 49 published encyclopaedias and 73 dictionaries and thesauruses. It is an Aladdin's cave of human knowledge.

Games and pastimes

You will probably have realised by now that you can learn almost anything on the Web. You can learn to play bridge, find out your nearest bridge club and even play the game online to get practice. You can brush up your knowledge of older card games such as whist and cribbage and check out a chess tutorial.

Crosswords, both normal and cryptic, and Sudoku puzzles can be found across the world. You can print the puzzles out and complete them in the comfort of the fireside armchair. There are Scrabble games, dictionaries and competitions as well as sites devoted to other board games like Monopoly.

If you find yourself in dispute about the rules of some esoteric game you can always get the definitive answer at **www.pagat.com**.

Hobbies

At our age we may not want to take up downhill skiing or even bungee jumping but there is a multitude of hobbies available to keep our hands and minds active. I have been surprised at the number of my female pupils who are absorbed by the hobby of card-making. They have also been surprised to find how much cheaper their craft supplies cost on the Web compared to local shops and mail order.

Patterns for embroidery, knitting and crochet work are all available on the Internet. A friend of mine who is painstakingly building a model steam engine from scratch was able to find some essential parts from online sources.

A couple of my pupils were ardent supporters of the TV programme, *Strictly Come Dancing*, and learnt the basic steps of the Paso Doble without the help of Len Goodman. They simply checked out one of the many dance tutorials on YouTube.

Fancy an interesting country walk? There are suggestions and maps that you can print out anywhere in the country and throughout the world. Try **www.ramblers.org.uk** – the definitive site for hikers of all abilities or **www.ramblersholidays.co.uk** for hiking holidays across the globe.

Health advice

You may not have been totally reassured by your latest visit to the health centre. Why not check out the advice by going to sites such as **www.nhsdirect.nhs.uk** or join a group of similar sufferers and carers? My earlier advice about getting more than a couple of opinions is particularly apt in these situations. These remarks are not intended to devalue the medical advice you get from your general practitioner in any way but it may help you ask more pertinent questions. Another health information site which gives good advice is **www.netdoctor.co.uk**.

History

It is a funny thing but it is a fact that the older we get, the more interested we become in both local and national history. The Internet offers access to millions of history sites from the Sumerian dynasty to memories of your home town or village. You can also contribute your own memories to many of these sites so that they do not get lost in the mists of time. I will look at the question of creating your own family history in the next chapter as this is a subject that deserves explanation in greater detail.

If you are interested in personal memories of the Second World War you will find fascinating accounts as **www.wwiimemories.com** and the BBC archive at **www.bbc.co.uk/ww2peopleswar**. To research the history of your home town or village or those of your ancestors' homes you will find an invaluable site at **www.visionofbritain.org.uk**.

Homework

No, I am not suggesting that you need help with your English or Maths homework but your grandchildren may appreciate a little help with their own. You may be able to give guidance to the very young without the help of a computer but the teaching of quite young children has changed so much since our day that you will soon begin to feel out of your depth with the latest teaching methods. Whatever the current vogue in teaching history or French you should be able to help even Year 4 students with their homework, with the help of your computer, while enjoying their company and imparting some of the knowledge you have acquired in a lifetime of experience. Beyond Year 4 you will find that the children are more adept in searching the Web for information than you will be – even after you have finished this book!

Answering questions

You do not have to undertake a new venture to make use of the knowledge available on the Web. It can be used to answer those questions that have lurked in the back of your mind but to which you have never found an answer.

Questions such as, 'Why is the sky blue?' or 'Why do autumn leaves change colour?' are the sort of thing I have in mind. To get answers to these and the many other questions that may jump into your head you can get them by typing the question in as a phrase, that is, by enclosing the whole phrase in inverted commas. There is one website specifically designed to answer this sort of question and that is Ask.Com which can be found at **www.ask.com**. It is a very useful search engine and often comes up with more specific answers than either Google or Yahoo.

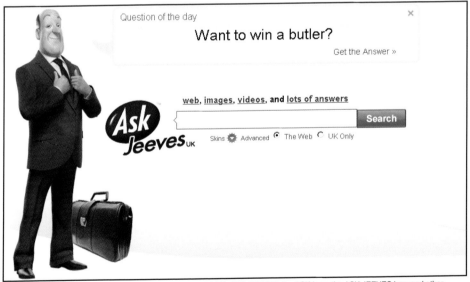

Figure 13.2

Your mind is like the local Post Office – use it or lose it.

Summary

- Whatever your interests you will find tutorials and information on the Web

- Find video tutorials on the YouTube website

- Use the Web to research a medical condition but always confirm your findings with your GP

Brain Training

There may be more than one correct answer to these questions.

1. Which of the following sites may demand a subscription fee?

☐ a) Encyclopaedia Britannica

☐ b) YouTube

☐ c) Which? reports

☐ d) The National Health Service

2. What does YouTube provide?

☐ a) Video clips

☐ b) Comedy

☐ c) Advice on making model trains

☐ d) Political speeches

3. What action would you take if a website advised eating spinach to cure your cough?

☐ a) Seek medical advice

☐ b) Get three more opinions from different websites

☐ c) Get a recipe for spinach soup

☐ d) Go down to the allotment

4. Which of the following can you play on the Internet?

☐ a) Hopscotch

☐ b) Bridge

☐ c) Poker

☐ d) Chess

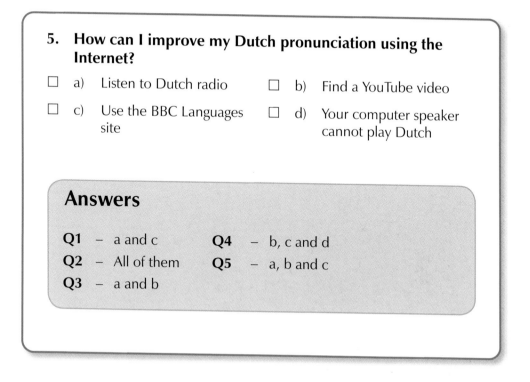

5. **How can I improve my Dutch pronunciation using the Internet?**

☐ a) Listen to Dutch radio   ☐ b) Find a YouTube video

☐ c) Use the BBC Languages   ☐ d) Your computer speaker
           site   cannot play Dutch

Answers

Q1 – a and c   **Q4** – b, c and d
Q2 – All of them   **Q5** – a, b and c
Q3 – a and b

Managing your finances

Equipment needed: a computer; a printer; Internet Explorer program; an email address; connection to the Internet; details of your bank account; personal finance software; a firewall; an anti-virus program and a record of usernames and passwords.

Skills needed: knowledge of the keyboard and mouse plus some confidence; knowledge of downloading a program (Chapters 3 and 5); experience of form filling (Chapters 7 and 9).

Online banking

Online banking has become so much part of modern life over the past decade that I thought it important to spend a little time on the subject. Those of us who grew up with the old-fashioned bank manager, cheque books and handwritten statements are naturally rather sceptical about these modern developments in the banking industry.

For all their faults, the one thing that the banks – with the aid of government funds – can do is to keep your accounts safe from Internet theft. The security measures that have been put in place by the banks to protect your banking identity are second to none. By using these security measures and allying them with common sense your online account is just as safe as it was before.

So what are the advantages of banking online? They are very similar to those that we have already discussed when using the Web for shopping. Internet banking keeps overhead costs down and therefore enable the banks to offer better rates of interest both to savers and borrowers. The cost of transferring funds electronically are minuscule compared to those involved in completing a written cheque payment. The counter staff and expensive high street premises are less needed now that we do not have to present our passbooks, count our cash or verify the cheques when we make financial transactions.

We have been using the cashless form of money transactions for years in the form of credit and debit cards and these are far more prone to loss or theft than the login details of an online bank account. Statements are available for printing at the touch of the keyboard; direct debits can be made at times of our own convenience and incoming receipts can be checked at any time – day or night – even on bank holidays.

The greatest concern of those who use Internet banking is theft. There is a risk of online identity theft, theft of passwords and pin codes. There are concerns about viruses attacking the bank's computers and bringing the system to a halt, or hackers getting in and stealing all the money. These may be genuine concerns but, as I have mentioned in Chapter 9, the risks of having your house burgled or your being mugged in the street far outweigh the risks of losing your identity online. The banks have lots of protection against such eventualities.

To maintain this security you have your own part to play. First, you must never give out your passwords or pin codes to anyone. They are for your use only and allow you to access your bank accounts safely, to pay your bills or transfer money between accounts. If you keep these to yourself you are protecting your bank accounts and the money they are holding.

Although there are some risks connected with Internet banking overall it is proving to be a safe, efficient and convenient method of banking that is satisfying consumers all over the world.

Next, never pay your bills by accessing your banking needs through anything that is not directly associated with your bank. Do not use pop-up windows, hyperlinks rooted in emails or search engines. Anything that looks suspicious probably is and so should be deleted permanently. Your bank has its own website and its specific steps for paying your bills, use them and nothing else. There is never a reason for any company to request your banking information that includes a password or pin code. If this happens do not complete the transaction. Leave the site immediately and do not return to it.

Setting up an online account

Despite everything I have said in the previous paragraphs you may have to visit your bank branch to arrange for the setup of your online facilities. It will probably take less than half an hour to set up the account during which time you will get an identity number, username and password, all of which you will need to keep in a safe place. Following this visit to the bank it may be a couple of days before you can actually start using your account.

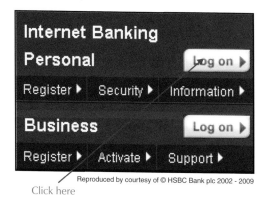

Reproduced by courtesy of © HSBC Bank plc 2002 - 2009

Click here

Figure 14.1

Using the URL or web address given to you by the bank you will first need to open up the website. Each website will have its own layout but all will offer the option of logging in to your own account. The login process will differ slightly between the banks but the following procedure will help you through most of the pitfalls. You will probably be asked for your identification number followed by your username and specific characters of your password. Most of the institutions do not ask for your full password but for certain characters within that password. This is to avoid anyone peering over your shoulder gaining access to it by watching your keystrokes. It is all part of the security system.

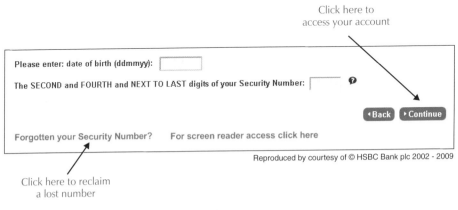

Figure 14.2

Once you have completed the security checks you will have access to your bank account. From here you will be able to pay off any outstanding bills, alter your direct debit instructions or transfer cash to other accounts at any time, day or night, whenever the mood takes you.

Home finance software

We all dread the time of year when the television ads start to remind us of our need to submit our tax returns. Even if we are in the fortunate situation where we have an accountant or book-keeper to help us complete the endless forms we still need to have access to our financial records. Before I got a computer these records were filed away in several different places – even pinned to a nail on the desk – but now I have them entered on my computer and it is a comparatively simple process to print out the necessary details for submission to the Inland Revenue.

Several people I know keep their household and investment accounts on a spreadsheet but the commercial programs now available will make these tasks much easier and provide integrated reports. The sum invested in such a program will more than pay for itself in the first year.

Even if you think you have a good command of your cash flow, the scope of these programs could surprise you. From simple tracking of bank and credit card accounts, such programs can go much further. Perhaps you may be thinking that you are spending too much in the supermarket? An analysis of your spending will quickly tell you what percentage of your money is going to whom. Car playing up? A few clicks of the mouse and you will discover how much of your budget it is eating into. Should you buy a new one? Software programs can help you plan a repayment schedule on a loan for it.

Your accountant won't like this, but you could even save yourself his or her fee and do your tax return yourself with the help of personal finance software. Some will even help you with VAT. If you have children growing up, these programs can ease your planning for school fees, university fees or even a wedding, however far in the future that might be. And, if you need lots of reminders, software can remind you to pay bills on time or even to move your credit card balance if you are coming to the end of a low-rate introductory offer.

If your horizons are broader, many programs allow you to run accounts in other currencies – useful if you have a property or bank account abroad, and especially so if you rent a property out.

Most of these financial programs remain resident on the computer's hard disk but there are a number of Internet sites that can keep you abreast of your financial commitments. For many years I have used a program called Quicken for all my personal and small business accounting. The company was later taken over by Microsoft who incorporated the benefits of Quicken into their own financial program, Microsoft Money. In my opinion Money is not as intuitive as the original Quicken so I have stuck with the older program. You do not have to have the very latest software to do the job.

You could pick up a copy of the Quicken software on eBay but the new contender seems to be Personal Accountz Home Edition available from Amazon.

What can you expect from a computer-based home accounts program such as Personal Accountz? The following list will give you a taste of what you can achieve:

● Control bank accounts, credit cards and loans.

● Track savings, investments and more.

● Automatic direct debit and standing order processing.

● Schedule recurring transactions.

● Import and convert MS Money files.

● Download and import bank statements.

● Manage assets and funds.

● Allocate and track budgets to individual or multiple accounts.

● Create unlimited accounts and entries.

● Forecast up to a year ahead.

The screenshot below shows a typical account register which looks very similar to a bank statement.

 95% of the money printed in the US each year is used to replace old money that has worn out. 45% of all printing is for $1 bills.

There is a comprehensive list of over 45 different reports, all of which can be customised to suit your personal requirements. You can submit your own tax returns with the aid of the De Luxe packages of MS Money and Personal Accountz – even the very basic packages allow you to present financial records to your accountant or tax advisor making their job a lot easier and therefore incurring much lower fees.

Account Register

HSBC No1 Account

Change register view

View: All Transactions covering All Dates, Sorted by Date (Increasing)

	Num	Date ▲	Payee	C	Payment	Deposit	Balance
	Maestr	26/05/2006	PC World		196.96		6,637.12
	601164	30/05/2006	Southern Electric		360.91		6,276.21
	601165	01/06/2006	Command Pest Control		176.25		6,099.96
	601166	01/06/2006	KD Radcliffe		47.00		6,052.96
	ATM	01/06/2006	Cash		51.75		6,001.21
	DEP	01/06/2006	The "A" Trust			1,000.00	7,001.21
	DirDeb	01/06/2006	Colchester Borough Council		160.00		6,841.21
		05/06/2006	Orange		5.09		6,836.12
		05/06/2006	Morgan Stanley		2,407.51		4,428.61
		05/06/2006	Total Butler		55.00		4,373.61
	601170	05/06/2006	Post Office		175.00		4,198.61
	DEP	05/06/2006	Prudential Annuity			92.94	4,291.55
	DEP	05/06/2006	National Pension			202.00	4,493.55
	DEP	05/06/2006	National Pension			309.52	4,803.07
	DirDeb	05/06/2006	Toucan		38.73		4,764.34
	601168	07/06/2006	Post Office		175.00		4,589.34
	ATM	07/06/2006	Cash		51.75		4,537.59
	601169	12/06/2006	Scrutton Bland		427.65		4,109.94
	601171	14/06/2006	Panther Security		487.33		3,622.61
	DirDeb	16/06/2006	Bank Account Fee		177.98		3,444.63
	DirDeb	21/06/2006	Deposit			4,443.25	7,887.88
	601172	23/06/2006	JE Arnold		1,000.00		6,887.88
		26/06/2006	HSBC Mastercard		95.22		6,792.66
		26/06/2006	Sky Digital		36.00		6,756.66
	ATM	26/06/2006	Cash		51.75		6,704.91
	601173	29/06/2006	Anglian Water		56.21		6,648.70
	601174	29/06/2006	Inland Revenue		40.93		6,607.77
	DEP	29/06/2006	Deposit			873.00	7,480.77

☐ Show transaction forms

Dropdown list of other accounts

Running balance

Figure 14.3

Both programs allow you to keep track of your investments, direct debits, credit card accounts, transactions by payee, monthly budgets and even your frequent flyer miles.

The screenshot Figure 14.4 gives an idea of the enormous range of financial reports that are available at the touch of a button.

Most of the leading financial software programs provide links to any online bank accounts you may have set up to provide a seamless interface between the two.

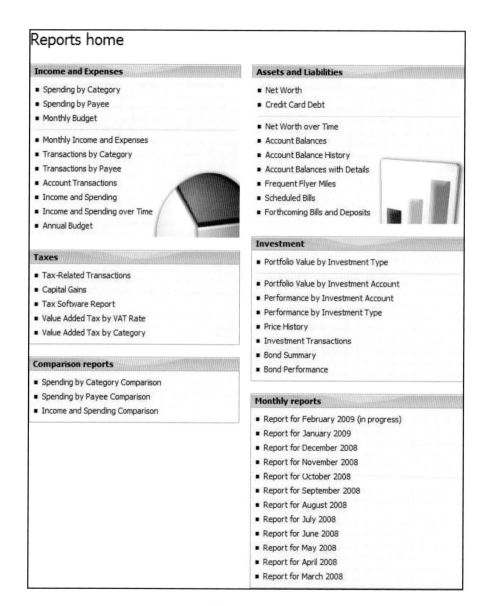

Reports home

Income and Expenses

- Spending by Category
- Spending by Payee
- Monthly Budget

- Monthly Income and Expenses
- Transactions by Category
- Transactions by Payee
- Account Transactions
- Income and Spending
- Income and Spending over Time
- Annual Budget

Taxes

- Tax-Related Transactions
- Capital Gains
- Tax Software Report
- Value Added Tax by VAT Rate
- Value Added Tax by Category

Comparison reports

- Spending by Category Comparison
- Spending by Payee Comparison
- Income and Spending Comparison

Assets and Liabilities

- Net Worth
- Credit Card Debt

- Net Worth over Time
- Account Balances
- Account Balance History
- Account Balances with Details
- Frequent Flyer Miles
- Scheduled Bills
- Forthcoming Bills and Deposits

Investment

- Portfolio Value by Investment Type

- Portfolio Value by Investment Account
- Performance by Investment Account
- Performance by Investment Type
- Price History
- Investment Transactions
- Bond Summary
- Bond Performance

Monthly reports

- Report for February 2009 (in progress)
- Report for January 2009
- Report for December 2008
- Report for November 2008
- Report for October 2008
- Report for September 2008
- Report for August 2008
- Report for July 2008
- Report for June 2008
- Report for May 2008
- Report for April 2008
- Report for March 2008

Figure 14.4

Investments online

Programs like MS Money will also keep track of any investment portfolio you may have in which case I can strongly recommend the Money Extra website at www.moneyextra.com. This site and others such as www.iii.co.uk will allow you to keep details of your portfolio up to date with regular updates of your investment performance. The stock market valuations are delayed by 20 minutes unless you want to pay a subscription fee for minute by minute valuations of your stocks and shares. You don't have to have a huge portfolio to take advantage of these facilities and you can check out the price and past history of all stocks traded on the world's exchanges. You will also gain access to the latest company reports as well as investment advice simply by registering on the sites. There is no cost involved unless you opt for the very latest prices and other professional services.

Keep your family in the picture

While we are on the subject of personal finances I have recently found a very useful suggestion on the Age Concern website. They offer a Life Book either free through the post or you can use it online. So what is a Life Book?

During a long active life we accumulate a large number of details about ourselves that our family – and executors – will need to know about should we become incapacitated or die. Details such as bank account numbers, National Insurance numbers, usernames and passwords as well as information about our solicitors, doctors and insurance policies will be invaluable to those who have to deal with our affairs when we are unable to do so ourselves. The Age Concern Life Book has been very carefully thought out to prompt you to record such details for the benefit of your family in the event of your death.

You do not have to spend days collating all the information but, if you gradually complete the sections over a period of time, you will make the job of handling your affairs so much easier. It need not be a morbid exercise. You can enter facets of your life history that will be of interest and amusement to your next of kin.

Details of the Life Book can be found at **www.ageconcern.org.uk/lifebook**. In the meantime continue to live your life to the full.

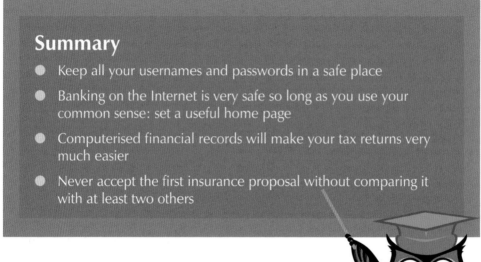

Summary

- Keep all your usernames and passwords in a safe place
- Banking on the Internet is very safe so long as you use your common sense: set a useful home page
- Computerised financial records will make your tax returns very much easier
- Never accept the first insurance proposal without comparing it with at least two others

Brain Training

There may be more than one correct answer to these questions.

1. When can you feel safe in giving out your credit card number?

☐ a) Never

☐ b) On the telephone

☐ c) On a website that starts with https://

☐ d) Only when you have a firewall on your computer

2. What can home finance software do?

☐ a) Increase your overdraft limit

☐ b) Prepare your annual tax return

☐ c) Remind you of payments due

☐ d) Guarantee you 15% on your savings

3. Where can you get advice on improving your mortgage terms?

☐ a) Price comparison sites

☐ b) **www.moneysavingexpert.com**

☐ c) Your local mortgage broker

☐ d) A spam email offer

4. What financial products can you buy online?

☐ a) Pet insurance

☐ b) A cheaper mortgage

☐ c) A bet on a horse

☐ d) A car loan

5. Which of these online services will cost you money?

☐ a) Instant share quotes

☐ b) Maintenance of an investment portfolio

☐ c) Investment advice

☐ d) Personal investment advice

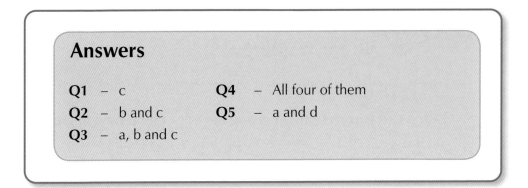

Answers

Q1 – c	**Q4** – All four of them
Q2 – b and c	**Q5** – a and d
Q3 – a, b and c	

Staying in touch

Equipment needed: a computer; a printer; Internet Explorer program; an email address; connection to the Internet; a credit or debit card; a firewall; an anti-virus program and a record of usernames and passwords.

Skills needed: knowledge of the keyboard and mouse; knowledge of downloading a program (Chapters 3 and 5); experience of form filling (Chapters 7 and 9); and a desire to communicate.

We have already discussing several forms of communication using the Internet such as email and online photo galleries but the opportunities for social interaction do not stop there. It is simple to combine the speed of the computer with the personal touch of a message delivered by post to those friends and relatives who have no access to a computer by using one of the many eCard sites. You can make telephone calls across the world free of charge – yes, really – by using the telephone from your computer and a simple program called Skype. A couple of friends work on the North Sea oil rigs and avoid expensive mobile phone bills using this program. If you are still of an age when you can use and understand text messaging then this is also available from your laptop computer.

Online diaries, known as 'blogs', are one of the current rages on the Internet. You do not have to be a journalist or 15 minute celebrity to publish your thoughts on the Web although you can read Jeremy Paxman's diatribes or Robert Peston's latest views on the current financial situation if you so wish.

Alexander Graham Bell, inventor of the telephone, was originally an instructor for deaf children and invented the telephone to help his deaf wife and mother to hear.

eCards

You may have left it too late to go out and buy a birthday card for Maisy's fifth birthday tomorrow but you can still have a card delivered the next day using an eCard company. One such site is **www.moonpig.com**. You simply choose the occasion, select your card, add your personal message, pay by credit or debit card and the company posts it off by first-class mail to get there on time. You don't have to stop at cards. You can send personalised cakes, calendars, jelly moulds and even doormats.

Don't forget to save on airmail postage costs by selecting a card site in the recipient's country if they happen to live abroad.

If you have really left it too late for a greeting card to be delivered by post you can always send an electronic card using the Internet. The recipient will get an email telling them that they have a card waiting for them and providing a link to the card which will then appear on their screen. Not only are many of these cards completely free but they can be personalised to a very large extent and the range of options is enormous. There are birthday cards, anniversary cards, cards for commiseration, congratulation and compassion while the range of occasion cards is almost limitless including births, deaths, marriages and even a successful driving test or school exam.

Skype telephony

Families are spreading across the globe as travel becomes more accessible but international telephone calls can quickly add a financial burden to the emotional costs of distance. One way of keeping in touch with distant relatives without incurring any costs whatsoever – apart from your monthly ISP subscription charges which you are paying anyway – is to use your computer to make the telephone calls. With a good broadband connection you can add video to your telephone conversation by using a web camera. We are talking Skype.

First of all you need to set up the Skype program on your computer and persuade your friends and relatives to do the same by going to **www.skype.com** and downloading the program.

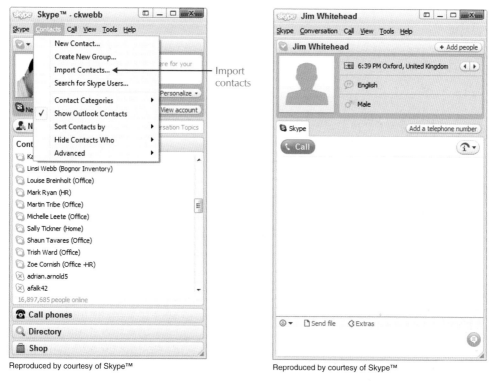

Reproduced by courtesy of Skype™

Reproduced by courtesy of Skype™

Figure 15.1   **Figure 15.2**

Once installed, I suggest that you begin by importing your contacts from your address book in your mail program. You can always phone a landline number from your Skype program but this will cost you money.

To make a free telephone call you need to know your connection's Skype address and you can check out whether any of your contacts are subscribers to Skype by searching for Skype Users in the Contacts dropdown menu on the Menu bar. All you have to do is to enter the email address of any potential subscriber and the system will check its database and inform you of their status. If they are a subscriber you will be offered the option to add them to your Contacts list.

To make a call simply double click on the contact's name and click on either the Call or Video call buttons. If you choose to make a video call the program will automatically start up any webcam you may have installed on your system. The success of any call depends upon the receiver having their computer turned on and being in front of the screen so it is a good idea to agree a set time and day when you are likely to make the call.

You can always dial their landline and get them to fire up their machine and call you back at a suitable time. Calls between Skype subscribers are completely free no matter how long you spend talking or wherever they happen to be in the world. They just need to have the program installed and activated. There is no monthly fee or other costs involved in Skype-to-Skype calls.

If you feel uncomfortable with communicating by phone via the computer, there are many standard Skype telephone handsets on the market. Check their availability out on eBay.

Sound, and especially, video transmission require a reasonably fast broadband connection. I live in the country where broadband speed is measured in snail's paces so video calls are very patchy and we tend to use the standard voice connection which even at 480 kilobytes per second is perfectly adequate (480 kps is like driving at 5 mph on a derestricted highway!)

Blogging

I have mentioned this modern phenomenon before but, to recap, blogging is simply the keeping of an online diary. This can take many forms. You can use a blog to record your daily thoughts or write an account of your latest holiday or activities for the family to view at their leisure. I have only recently joined the blogging community and I am still finding my way around the possibilities that blogging offers. You can check out my blog at **http://adrianarnold.blogspot.com**.

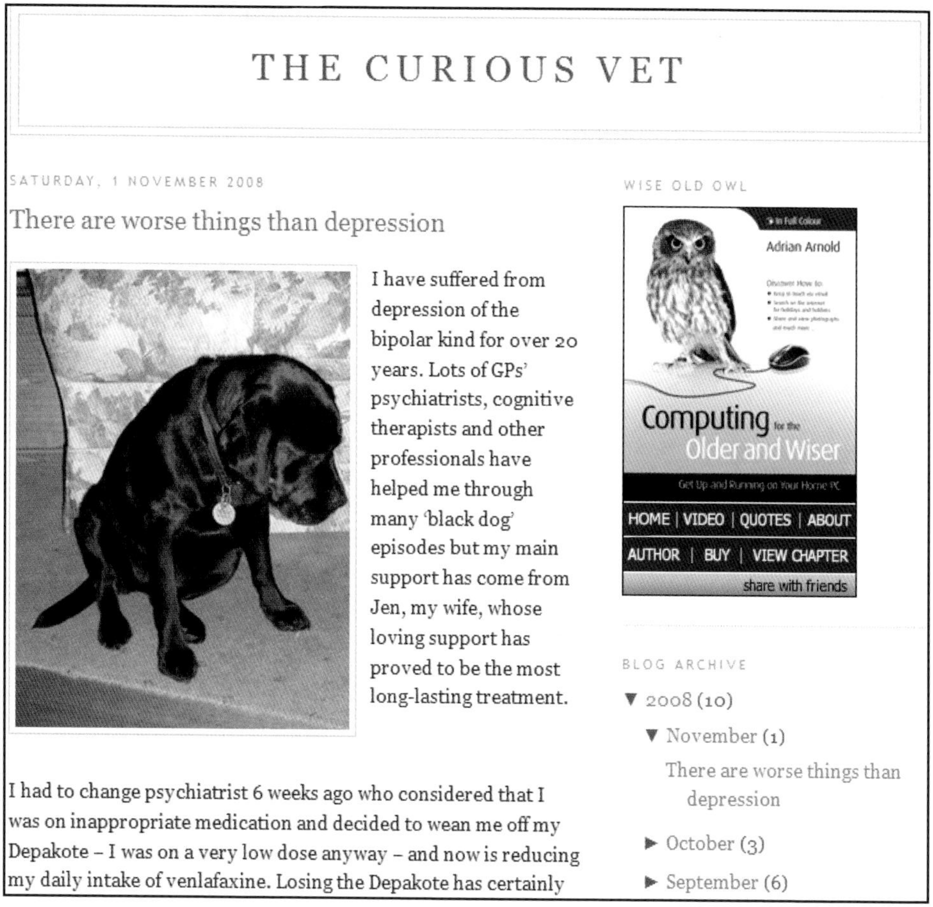

THE CURIOUS VET

SATURDAY, 1 NOVEMBER 2008

There are worse things than depression

I have suffered from depression of the bipolar kind for over 20 years. Lots of GPs' psychiatrists, cognitive therapists and other professionals have helped me through many 'black dog' episodes but my main support has come from Jen, my wife, whose loving support has proved to be the most long-lasting treatment.

I had to change psychiatrist 6 weeks ago who considered that I was on inappropriate medication and decided to wean me off my Depakote – I was on a very low dose anyway – and now is reducing my daily intake of venlafaxine. Losing the Depakote has certainly

WISE OLD OWL

BLOG ARCHIVE

▼ 2008 (10)

   ▼ November (1)

     There are worse things than depression

   ► October (3)

   ► September (6)

Figure 15.3

There is a mass of blogging sites on the Web but I would suggest that you test the waters by using one of the oldest and best sites aptly named, Blogger, at **www.blogger.com** which is part of the Google stable of thoroughbred facilities.

Set up a blog

To start using Blogger, simply sign in with your Google Account. (If you use Gmail or Google Groups, you already have an account.) If you don't have a Google

Account yet, you can create one by going to **www.google.com/accounts** and complete the form. This will have the added advantage of providing you with an alternative email account as well as access to a blogging account and the Picasa photo albums discussed in Chapter 12. Once you have established an account – which is free – you can begin the process of setting up a blog by clicking on the appropriate link.

Reproduced from Google™

Figure 15.4

This will open the Blogger home page where you will enter your username and password, and click Sign In. Enter a display name and accept Blogger's Terms of Service. Then click the Create a Blog link and you are ready to post your first blog.

Reproduced from Google™

Click to start a new blog

Figure 15.5

Pick a name and address (URL) for your blog. Then, choose a template (this is how your blog will look when you publish it). Now get creative; add information to your personal profile, and customize how your blog looks, if you feel up to it. Start blogging now!

Click the NEW POST button and enter anything you want to share with the world. Next, you'll see the Create New Post page. Start by giving your post a title (optional), and then type the blog entry. As you become more proficient you will find that you can add web links and photos to your blogs.

Remember that you can always delete any blog you are not happy with so give it a try. Only practice will tell you if the blogging experience is something that you will enjoy.

Using Blogger you can search for like-minded souls and add their profiles to your contacts list. You may even find a few 'pen pals' in different continents with whom you can share your experiences.

If you have any problems using your Blogger account there is a very useful Help site at **http://help.blogger.com/**.

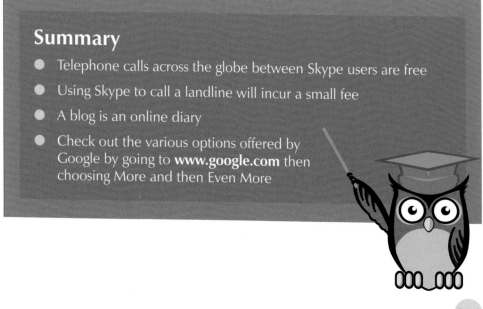

Summary

- Telephone calls across the globe between Skype users are free
- Using Skype to call a landline will incur a small fee
- A blog is an online diary
- Check out the various options offered by Google by going to **www.google.com** then choosing More and then Even More

Brain Training

There may be more than one correct answer to these questions.

1. Which country is the most expensive to phone using Skype?

☐ a) USA

☐ b) Antarctica

☐ c) New Zealand

☐ d) Russia

2. What is a blog?

☐ a) A dangerous object floating on a river

☐ b) A binary log

☐ c) A Beginner's or Learner's Own Goal

☐ d) An online diary

3. What will you find at www.blogger.com?

☐ a) A British Columbian lumberjack's website

☐ b) A blogging website

☐ c) Lots of technical jargon that you need to know nothing about

☐ d) A method of creating your very own diary online

4. How can you contact friends using Skype?

☐ a) Enter their landline number

☐ b) Use their Skype name

☐ c) Use their email address

☐ d) You will need a specially adapted handset

5. Which of the following methods of using Skype is free?

☐ a) You will have to pay a
subscription fee for any
type of call

☐ b) Using their landline number

☐ c) Using their Skype name

☐ d) All Skype calls are free

Answers

Q1 – They are all free
using Skype names

Q2 – d

Q3 – b and d

Q4 – a, b and c

Q5 – c

Social networking

Equipment needed: a computer; a printer; Internet Explorer program; an email address; connection to the Internet; a credit or debit card; a firewall; an anti-virus program and a record of usernames and passwords.

Skills needed: knowledge of the keyboard and mouse; knowledge of downloading a program (Chapters 3 and 5); experience of form filling (Chapters 7 and 9).

I mentioned the idea of 'pen pals' in the previous chapter but there are many ways of keeping in touch with distant friends and relatives, and even make new friends on the Web. There are forums that you can join free of charge; newsgroups that offer advice on a multitude of subjects; websites that put you back in touch with long lost friends and social networking sites which, although frequented mainly by the younger generations, are now being enjoyed by computer users of a more mature age. In fact, there are social networks that cater exclusively to those of us who are 'older and wiser'.

I have discussed forums and newsgroups in Chapter 6 so I will concentrate on the use of social networking sites in this chapter.

What are social networks?

Simply put, social networks are online communities made up of people with shared or similar interests. Most social networks have some basic features in common, such as the ability to create a profile page, share photos, exchange messages with other members, join groups and post content.

In the rest of this chapter, I will introduce to you several of the more popular social networks. While they may share some characteristics, each is unique and offers different levels of community and communication. You should not feel as though you need to join and maintain an account at every one of the networks I describe in this chapter. Instead, sample the ones that seem the most interesting to you, and frequent the ones that seem to make you feel the most comfortable.

Facebook

Founded in 2004, Facebook membership was initially limited to Harvard students, but later expanded to include other colleges in the Boston area, the Ivy League, and Stanford University. It then expanded still further to include any university student, then high school students, and, finally, to anyone aged 13 and over. The website currently has more than 200 million active users worldwide, and has grown nearly 200 per cent in the last year among those aged 55 and older.

Facebook has a number of features with which users may interact, including the Wall, a space on every user's profile page that allows friends to post messages for the user to see; Pokes, which allows users to send a virtual 'poke' to each other (a message that tells a user that they have been 'poked'); Photos, where users can upload albums and photos, and Status, which allows users to inform their friends of their whereabouts and actions. A user's Wall is visible to anyone who is able to see that user's profile, which depends on their privacy settings.

To sign up to Facebook go to **www.facebook.com** and fill in the application form. Registration is free. Once you have registered you can start adding details about yourself but beware of giving away too much information that might be used nefariously.

Having entered your details and included a photo if you wish, you can start searching for friends and relatives on Facebook by going to the Friends tab and searching for names, email addresses or even places of work or schools. Once you have found someone you know you will be invited to send them a message suggesting that they become a 'friend' and in this way you can begin to build up your own social network.

Facebook © 2009

Figure 16.1

Over time, Facebook has added several new features to its website. In 2006, a News Feed was announced, which appears on every user's homepage and highlights information including profile changes, upcoming events, and birthdays related to the user's friends. In 2007, Facebook began allowing users to post attachments to the Wall, whereas the Wall was previously limited to textual content only.

Initially, the News Feed caused dissatisfaction among Facebook users; some complained it was too cluttered and full of undesired information, while others were concerned it made it too easy for other people to track down individual activities (such as changes in relationship status, events, and conversations with other users). In response to this dissatisfaction, The company issued an apology for the site's failure to include appropriate customisable privacy features. Since then, users have been able to control what types of information are shared automatically with friends. Users are now able to prevent friends from seeing updates about different types of activities, including profile changes, Wall posts, and newly added friends.

One of the most popular applications on Facebook is the Photos application, where users can upload albums and photos.

Facebook allows users to upload an unlimited number of photos, compared with other image hosting services such as Photobucket and Flickr, which apply limits to the number of photos that a user is allowed to upload. In the past, all users were limited to 60 photos per album. However, some users report that they are able to create albums with a new limit of 200 photos. It remains unclear why some members have a 200-photo limit while others do not. Privacy settings can be set for individual albums, limiting the groups of users that can see an album. For example, the privacy of an album can be set so that only the user's friends can see the album, while the privacy of another album can be set so that all Facebook users can see it. Another feature of the Photos applications is the ability to 'tag', or label users in a photo. For instance, if a photo features a user's friend, then the user can tag the friend in the photo. This sends a notification to the friend that they have been tagged, and provides them a link to see the photo.

MySpace

This is a very similar setup to Facebook and you may find more friends on one or the other so try both of them out. You can always cancel your membership of either site if the idea does not hold any appeal for you.

Reproduced by courtesy of MySpace

Figure 16.2

Signing up involves a similar process to that of Facebook. Click on the Sign Up tab and complete the form before creating your own profile. There are the same opportunities to search for friends on the site.

Try both sites out and you will find out which one appeals to you more. Social networking sites are like recipes. Some people prefer meat to fish – there is no best option – both provide necessary nutrition – or you could decide that you are an Internet vegetarian and decide against joining such sites. The choice, as with the rest of the Internet, is yours.

Twitter

This is the latest member of the social networking community. It is comparatively lightweight, and a bit less overwhelming compared to Facebook and MySpace and may be the site you are looking for if you desire interaction with others, but don't feel the need to be involved with posting photos and the like. The service is currently free, and only takes a few seconds to get started after signing up at **http://twitter.com**.

Twitter actually began as a status notification service by where users kept others updated on their whereabouts and activities by posting 140 character messages that answered the question, 'What are you doing?' However, since its start in 2006, Twitter has emerged as more of a conversation and 'micro-blogging' tool where users engage in conversations with others, provide helpful information, answer questions and post links to interesting sites on the Web.

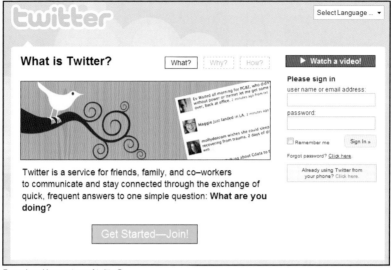

Reproduced by courtesy of twitter©

Figure 16.3

Users are limited to 140 characters per message which might contain the words, 'I am feeling really rather lousy so I have run a bath and intend to indulge myself in some nostalgic music from Neil Diamond' (125 characters). Or you might ask the question, 'Where is the best carvery in Chichester?' Chances are, someone on Twitter knows!

Twitter is also a great place to get news and other information. For example, the *Guardian*, the BBC, and *The New York Times* all send updates via Twitter. And if you have ever wanted to interact with a favourite celebrity, increasingly you will find them on Twitter. British comedian Stephen Fry is one of the most followed celebrities on Twitter, and there are many others.

Friends Reunited

The main Friends Reunited site aims to reunite people who have in common a school, university, address, workplace, sports club or armed service; the sister site Genes Reunited enables members to pool their family trees and identify common ancestors; the Dating and Jobs sister sites link members with similar attributes, interests and/or locations.

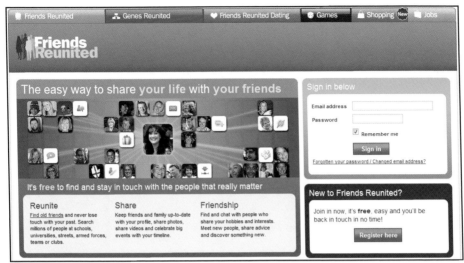

Reproduced by permission of Friends Reunited

Figure 16.4

Go to **www.friendsreunited.co.uk** to register and enter your places of education and work when you will be shown contemporary members with whom you may have lost touch many years ago. You never know you may find that boy or girl who temporarily stole your heart when you were just entering your teen years. Aaaah! Who knows? That spotty-faced youth may now be a pillar of their local community.

You may be bereaved and lonely and yet there could be a friend of yesteryear living just a few miles away. You will never know unless you try.

Saga Zone

Saga Zone is a hugely popular online social community for the over 50s. And, 'over 50s' is not just a marketing line. Saga Zone does in fact require all new members to be over the age of 50. Join Saga Zone and you can make a whole new network of friends from the comfort of your home. What's more, Saga Zone is completely free and great fun to use.

Create your own personal profile page and share your interests with others in the lively online forums. Or why not write your own web diary, blog or even create a photo album, where you can share pictures with your new friends.

You will find Saga Zone at **www.sagazone.co.uk**.

Reproduced by permission of SagaZone©

Figure 16.5

Silver Surfers

There is a mind-boggling number of links to sites of interest to the older generation on this site – **www.silversurfers.net** -- but one of its greatest strengths is the Find People search which, as the screenshot below demonstrates, offers you plenty of ways to get in touch with lost friends.

Although the site is based in the UK it has links across the world to search sites linked to addresses, religion, telephone numbers, electoral rolls, postcodes and adoption agencies. I can almost guarantee that that in less than an hour spent on this site you will find someone from your past. Whether you want to renew their acquaintance is entirely up to you.

Tracing, finding lost friends, people, birth parents, adoption, reunited, directories, electoral roll, bad debtors & missing persons.

Find People & Friends

Other pages you may be interested in:	Address Book, Online	Find where people are on the Map	Who Are Your Ancestors?	Try these sites
Ancestry	Address Book	Google Latitude	First Name	192.com
Ancestry Tips	Adopted & Adoptions		Last Name	Address Book
Ancestry: Scottish	Missing You	Find People & Lost Friends	Search	Genes Reunited
Chatrooms	Norcap	Around	Powered by Ancestry.co.uk	Tracesmart
Family History Tracing Organisations & Societies	People Finder UK	Classmates		Tracing People: Chargeable Services
	UK Birth	Find a Parent or Child	Phone Directories	192.com
Famous People	Ancestors, Trace	Friendster (USA)	192.com	Finder Monkey (UK People Finder)
Find a New Partner	Ancestry	Friends Reunited	The Phone Book from BT	People Finder UK
Find a Travelling Companion		Genes Reunited	Switchboard (US businesses)	People Search
	E-mail / Address Directories: USA based	Jewish Reunion		People Tracer
Genealogy & Research	Addresses	Lost Amigos	Worldwide Telephone Directories	Trace People (Private Investigator)
Irish Genealogy	E-mail Address Directory	My Old Mate	Yell	Tracesmart
		Reunite		UK People Finder
Meet New Friends & Partners	Internet Address Finder	Language Learning Community	Postcodes & Addresses, Find UK	Track friends around the World
Search Engines & Directories	US Search	Babbel	Royal Mail	Where are you now?
Scottish Genealogy	WhoWhere?	Military Services	Telephone Dialing Codes, Worldwide	UK Missing Persons Helpline
	Electoral Registers: UK	Service Pals	Country Calling Codes	National Missing Persons
	192.com	Missing Persons		
	Tracesmart	Look4Them	Trace Heirs	
		Lookup UK	Heirtrace	

Figure 16.6

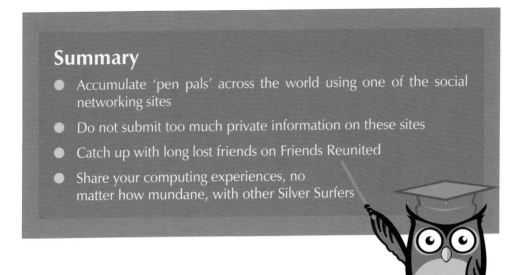

Summary

- Accumulate 'pen pals' across the world using one of the social networking sites
- Do not submit too much private information on these sites
- Catch up with long lost friends on Friends Reunited
- Share your computing experiences, no matter how mundane, with other Silver Surfers

Brain Training

There may be more than one correct answer to these questions.

1. What is Twitter?

☐ a) The call of a wren

☐ b) An idiotic comment

☐ c) A form of social networking

☐ d) A short message limited to 140 characters

2. Which of the following can you place on Facebook?

☐ a) Photographs

☐ b) Friends' birthdays

☐ c) An urgent message

☐ d) A video file

3. What organisations can be included in Friends Reunited?

☐ a) Workplaces

☐ b) Armed Forces

☐ c) Schools

☐ d) Dating agencies

4. How much does membership of Saga Zone cost?

☐ a) Nothing

☐ b) £3.50 per month

☐ c) £24 per year

☐ d) Nothing if you subscribe to the magazine

5. What do you need to access MySpace?

☐ a) An Internet connection

☐ b) A credit or debit card

☐ c) A digital camera

☐ d) An email account

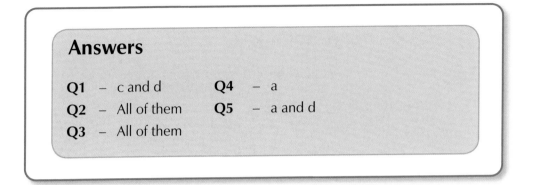

Answers

Q1	– c and d	**Q4**	– a
Q2	– All of them	**Q5**	– a and d
Q3	– All of them		

Publishing online

17

Equipment needed: a computer; Internet Explorer program; an email address; connection to the Internet; a credit or debit card; a firewall; an anti-virus program and a record of usernames and passwords.

Skills needed: knowledge of the keyboard and mouse; knowledge of downloading a program (Chapters 3 and 5); experience of form filling (Chapters 7 and 9).

We have discussed the submission of photos to online albums and thoughts to blogging sites but if you want to establish a full presence on the Internet you may consider creating your own website. This is not as difficult or technologically challenging as it might seem to begin with.

You may not have realised it but when you signed up to an ISP for your email and Internet connection they almost certainly offered you free web space to which you can publish a website. You may need to access your account on the ISP's website and activate your web space when you will be given the opportunity to create a web address or URL for your proposed site. The address would look something like **http://myspace.tiscali.co.uk/fredjones**. It does not quite trip off the tongue but it is a perfectly valid web address. These ISP websites are free up to the point when they become very large indeed by which time you should be paying for a commercial site in the first place.

Yes, I could introduce you to the construction of a website using Hypertext Markup Language (HTML) with its tags, metatags, titles, keywords and the like but it would probably bore you rigid or scare the living daylights out of you so I will give that approach a miss. If you are determined to make website construction your new hobby then there are many books in the marketplace far better suited to that type of approach than this one.

Weebly

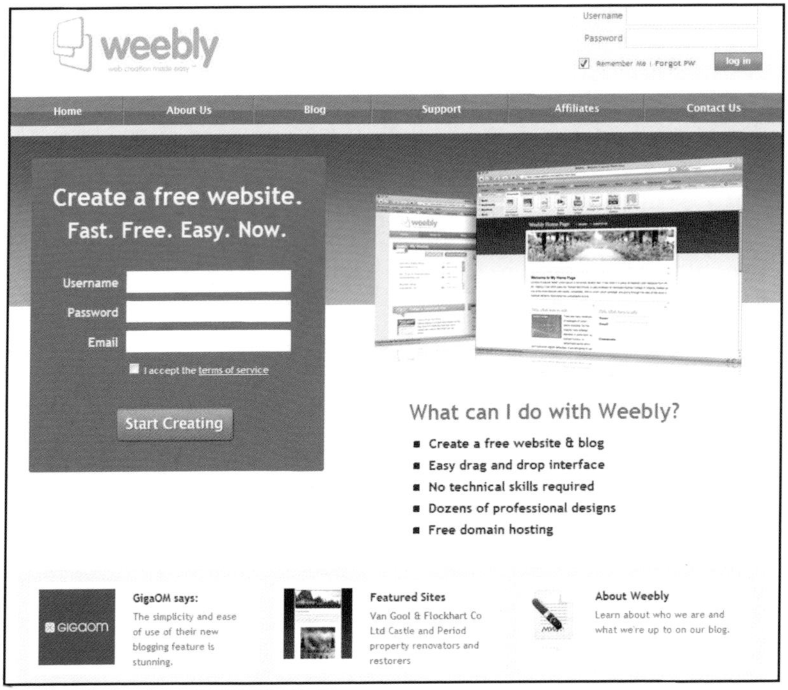

Reproduced by permission of ©2009 Weebly, Inc.

Figure 17.1

Several ISP websites include basic site building tools but these vary from company to company so I am going to suggest that you try out the free web hosting server offered by Weebly. Go to **www.weebly.com** where you will need to create an account by choosing both a username and password. Once you have registered you can choose to have your site hosted free of charge by Weebly such as www.another.weebly.com or opt to have your very own web address in the form of www.another.co.uk for which there will be a small fee.

Once you have registered and logged in you will be presented with a screen similar to Figure 17.2:

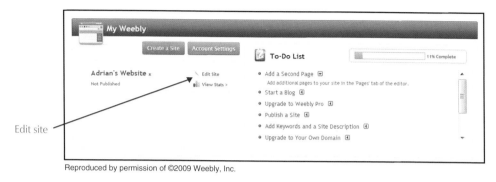

Reproduced by permission of ©2009 Weebly, Inc.

Figure 17.2

Click on Create a site or, if you need to edit a site in progress, go to Edit Site to access the Weebly Editor. As you can see from the Actions list below there are many features that you can add to your site so that it really does become your own creation.

Reproduced by permission of ©2009 Weebly, Inc.

Figure 17.3

The site offers many options for the insertion of pictures, paragraphs, titles and columns with even more option available under the Designs and Pages tabs. To insert an element you simply drag the item such as Paragraph with Picture into the underlying page and insert your own images and text. The Designs tabs offers over 60 different layouts which you can customise to your heart's content as seen in Figure 17.4. Simply drag your chosen option onto the main page and upload any photos or text you wish to add to the site.

Once you have created your Home page you can begin to add further pages that can incorporate maps, music, images, slide shows, clocks, sports results – in fact there are over 20,000 of these 'widgets' that you can incorporate into your site. To get an overview of the capabilities of this program watch the video tutorial at **www.youtube.com/watch?v=18JiQn_FWBU** – if this address seems too long you can also access it at **http://tinyurl.com/p9em37**.

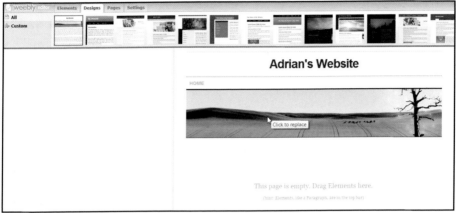

Figure 17.4

The beauty of the Weebly site is that virtually everything is free. You do not have to pay a penny for any of its core services such as website creation and hosting. You can even sell goods and services from your site using PayPal. The site is so comprehensive that it would take a whole book to explore its potential but you can find a list of comprehensive tutorials at **www.weeblytutorial.com/weebly-help.html** and the Help facility offers very useful advice.

Getting your own web address

Weebly and your ISP websites will have generated a web address for you but they may sometimes appear clumsy and unprofessional. This is fine if the website is aimed at friends and family but, if you want to reach a wider audience, you may be better served by a registered URL or web address. Many hosting companies will offer you a service whereby you can experiment with a number of web address options. As an experiment I went to Network Solutions at **www.networksolutions.com** to see what addresses were available for a website devoted to card making called 'Cardcraft'. www.cardcraft.co.uk had already been taken as well as cardcraft.org, cardcraft.com, cardcraft.net and cardcraft.biz but www.cardcraft.info and www.cardcraft.gb.com were both available. These names are so much more appropriate than **www.adrianarnold.weebly.com** or **http://myspace.tiscali.co.uk/fredjones** and the asking prices for such URLs are not excessive. The more expensive plans include such options as unlimited web space, secure internet shopping facilities and a mass of statistics relating to your site.

> This subscription will include the registration of your domain or web address with the appropriate registry which will have to be renewed every year or two but this would involve a minimal sum.

Serif WebPlus

The penultimate stage of your web building career would be to use another free program such as Serif WebPlus SE which can be found at **www.freeserifsoftware. com**. This is a much bigger program which will enable you to create semi-professional websites that reflect more accurately your own design ideas.

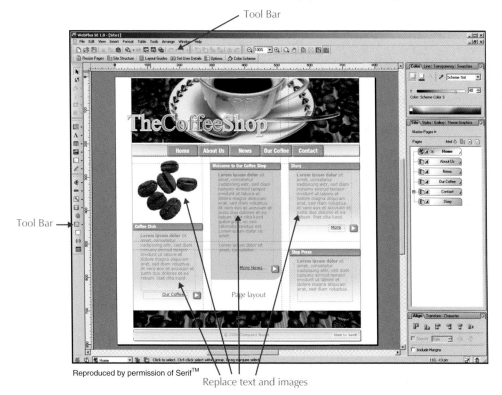

Reproduced by permission of Serif™

Figure 17.5

You ought to be familiar with the downloading and installing processes by now so I will assume that you have the program loaded onto the computer.

As you will see this is a much more comprehensive program with tool bars and other options spread around the screen. This may be all too much for you at this stage so I would suggest that before you begin you start to work your way through the Help menu which is very comprehensive. Once you have begun to get the hang of the program go to File then New and you will be offered the choice of starting from scratch or using a pre-designed template. The latter option is a little bit easier for beginners.

Reproduced by permission of Serif™

Figure 17.6

You can also use this menu to take a few of the tutorials which will quickly bring you up to speed.

Publishing your website

Throughout this book we have discussed the use of the Internet for surfing the Web and sending email messages but there is a third function of the system that we need to use if we are to publish our artistic creation to the Web. This is called File Transfer Protocol or FTP for short. Using FTP we can upload files from our personal computer to the huge 'server' computers that store these files for public access. While there are a number of FTP programs available for download many of the web development programs have their own integrated FTP facility.

Before uploading your masterpiece you should preview it using the Serif WebPlus program to make sure that it looks the way you want it – that the spelling is correct, the pictures sit nicely on the page and all the links work. You can preview and publish the site by using the File menu. You will need to have your FTP username and password to hand before you start uploading the files. These details will have been provided by email by your service provider.

This has been a very cursory look at the subject of publishing your own website but I hope that it may have whetted your appetite to achieve something extraordinary. If you achieve your goal by successfully publishing a new website please let me know the web address by mailing me at **bu33kin@tiscali.co.uk**. You can even put your queries to me via the website at **www.pcwisdom.co.uk**.

Best of luck!

Brain Training

There may be more than one correct answer to these questions.

1. What does FTP stand for?

☐ a) Fairly Typical Page ☐ b) File Transfer Protocol

☐ c) File Termination Procedure ☐ d) Fail To Produce

2. What is the average ISP fee for hosting your own website?

☐ a) £10 per year ☐ b) £10 per month

☐ c) Free with your ISP contract ☐ d) Nothing

3. What is a web template?

☐ a) A web page that you can customise ☐ b) A free website

☐ c) An alternative layout of your desktop ☐ d) A temporary website

4. Where can you get your own URL or website address?

☐ a) Your ISP ☐ b) A hosting company

☐ c) A registrar ☐ d) From a computer shop

5. What is a domain?

☐ a) A geographical area

☐ b) A web address

☐ c) The home page of a private website

☐ d) The last part of a URL

Answers

Q1 – b

Q2 – c

Q3 – a

Q4 – a, b and c

Q5 – d

Research your family tree

Equipment needed: a computer; a printer; Internet Explorer program; an email address; connection to the Internet; a credit or debit card; a firewall; an anti-virus program and a record of usernames and passwords.

Skills needed: knowledge of the keyboard and mouse; knowledge of downloading a program (Chapters 3 and 5); experience of form filling (Chapters 7 and 9); and some details of your family history.

There is inevitable sadness when an older member of one's family dies. We miss their presence, their character and their company but we have also lost a vital source of information about our ancestors. We can no longer get answers to questions like, 'What sort of a man was Great-Grandfather Huxtable?' Great Aunt Mabel knew him well but she died three years ago and we will never know. You can prevent this sort of knowledge passing away with us by creating a family tree and leaving it as a living memory for the younger generation. They might not be particularly interested while they are busy raising a family of their own but the chances are that the interest will grow as they themselves grow older.

In the same way that someone with the surname of Cholmondeley is called Chumley, the unlikely surname of Woolfhardisworthy is pronounced Woolsey.

Genealogy on the Web

There are many hundreds of websites devoted entirely to genealogy and family history, so much so that it can be a problem deciding on which sites to concentrate on. In this chapter I hope to lead you through this jungle of information and I will be concentrating on three websites that I have found to be a cut above the rest – Genes Reunited, Ancestry and Roots UK.

All of these web facilities offer you access to every census from 1841 (the latest one to go online is the 1911 census, birth, marriage and death records kept by the National Archives at Kew), military records and passenger lists of ships bringing more people to these islands and carrying them to foreign parts. UK censuses are carried out every 10 years. These records as well as local parish records provide a mine of information although you may have to pay a physical visit to these records to get the full information.

Genes Reunited

Found at **www.genesreunited.co.uk**, Genes Reunited have more than 9½ million members with nearly 6 million names added each month. The current annual fee – incurred when your free trial runs out after seven days – is £9.50. If you want to gain access to the actual records themselves you will have to pay an additional fee of £5 for 50 credits (most record details cost 5 credits), but these credits only last for seven days so prepare yourself in advance before you make a series of searches to take full value of this offer. You will be led through the payment process when you need to make your first search. Payment is made by credit card or PayPal which was explained in Chapter 11.

As you can see from the screenshot of my own home page I have managed to find 266 family members with the oldest record dating back to the 17th century and that I now have 67 contacts who have contributed to my tree as well as to their own. Under the Hot Matches section I am told that the tree owner, Graham, has 35 entries that match my own.

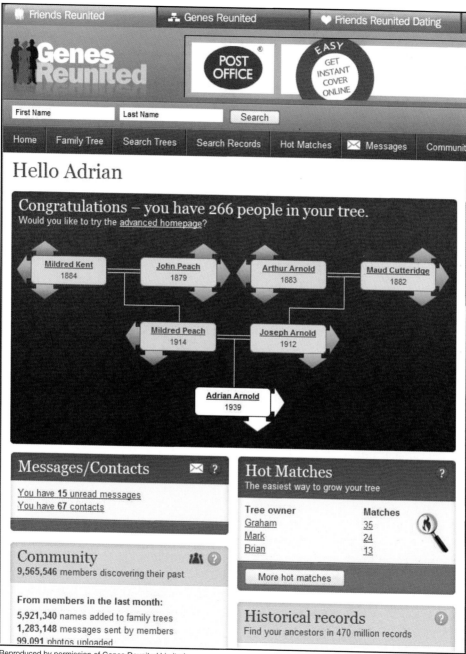

Reproduced by permission of Genes Reunited Limited

Figure 18.1

Getting started

Your first task should be to accumulate as much information as possible from living relatives. This will give you a head start before searching the records. Many years ago I learnt that my grandmother was named Maud Cutteridge and that she was born in the town of March in Cambridgeshire. I knew that she died in 1960 at the age of 78 but I had no knowledge of other members of the family and so I decided to do a search for her in the 1901 census.

Census search

Search Records

What are Census Records?

Amend Search   ?

1841 1851 1861 1871 1891 1901

Forename	Maud
Surname *	Cutteridge
Year of birth	1882
Give or take	5 years
Place keywords	

* = mandatory fields

Search

1 matches for Maud Cutteridge in the 1901 Census   ?

Show this result on a map

These matches have been found in the 1901 Census. If you think they could be your ancestor then click the view button to find out more.

Page 1 of 1

Surname	Forename	▼ Year of birth	Place of birth	Location in 1901		
Cutteridge	Maud	1882	Cambs March	Cambridge, March	View	Census

Page 1 of 1

Reproduced by permission of Genes Reunited Limited

Census

View

Figure 18.2

I was pretty certain that I had got my facts right but decided to accept a five year leeway in the date of her birth and got her details within a few seconds. Now I need to get some more information by using the View or Census options. The Census option which costs 5 credits (50p) will display a printable image of the relevant census page.

These pages are a mine of information giving details, not only of the immediate family – the actual address, their occupation, age and place of birth – but also

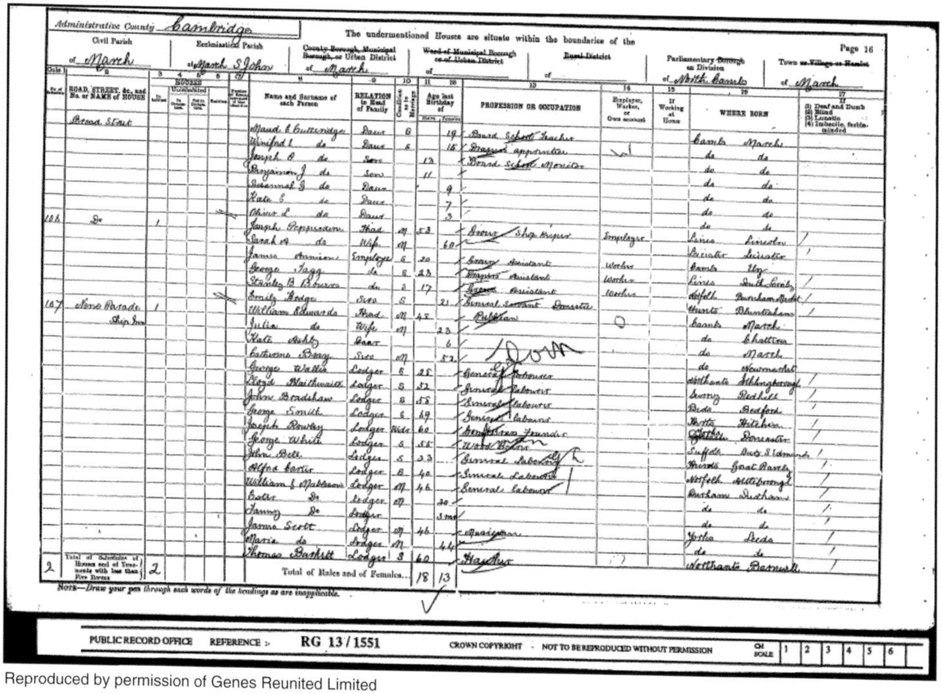

Administrative County Cambridge

The undermentioned Houses are situate within the boundaries of the

Civil Parish of March | Ecclesiastical Parish of March St John | County Borough, Municipal Borough, or Urban District of March | Ward of Municipal Borough or of Urban District of | Rural District of | Parliamentary Borough or Division of North Cambs | Town or Village or Hamlet of March | Page 16

No. of Schedule	Road, Street, &c., and No. or Name of House	Houses Inhabited	Name and Surname of each Person	Relation to Head of Family	Condition as to Marriage	Age last Birthday of Males	Age last Birthday of Females	Profession or Occupation	Employer, Worker, or Own account	If Working at Home	Where Born	(1) Deaf and Dumb (2) Blind (3) Lunatic (4) Imbecile, feeble-minded
	Broad Street		Maud E Butteridge	Daur	S		19	Board School Teacher				
			Winifred L do	Daur	S		15	Drapers apprentice			Cambs March	
			Joseph A do	Son		13		Board School Monitor			do do	
			Benjamin J do	Son		11					do do	
			Susannah J do	Daur			9				do do	
			Kate E do	Daur			7				do do	
			Olive L do	Daur			3				do do	
186	Do	1	Joseph Pepperdine	Head	M	53		Grocer Shopkeeper	Employer		do do	
			Sarah A do	Wife	M		60				Lincs Lincoln	/
			James Ammon	Employee	S	20		Grocer Assistant			Leicester Leicester	/
			George Tagg	do	S	23		Drapers Assistant	Worker		Cambs Ely	
			Stanley B Bowers	do	S	17		Grocer Assistant	Worker		Lincs South Scriby	/
			Emily Hodge	Serv	S		21	General Servant Domestic	Worker		Norfolk Burnham Market	/
187	Nene Parade Ship Inn	1	William Edwards	Head	M	47		Publican	O		Hunts Bluntisham	/
			Julia do	Wife	M		23				Cambs March	
			Kate Ashly	Daur			6				do Chatteris	
			Catherine Bray	Serv	M		52				do March	
			George Wallis	Lodger	S	25		General Labourer			do Newmarket	
			Lloyd Blaithwaite	Lodger	S	52		General Labourer			Northants Kettering	/
			John Bradshaw	Lodger	S	58		General Labourer			Surrey Redhill	/
			George Smith	Lodger	S	69		General Labourer			Beds Bedford	/
			Joseph Rowley	Lodger	Wid	60		Iron Founder			Herts Hitchin	/
			George White	Lodger	S	56		Wood Bottom			Yorks Doncaster	/
			John Bell	Lodger	S	33		General Labourer			Suffolk Bury St Edmunds	/
			Alfred Carter	Lodger	S	40		General Labourer			Hunts Great Raveley	/
			William J Mableson	Lodger	M	46		General Labourer			Norfolk Attleborough	/
			Esther Do	Lodger	M		30				Durham Durham	/
			Fanny Do	Lodger			3 mo				do do	/
			James Scott	Lodger	M	46		Musician			do do	/
			Maria do	Lodger	M		44				Yorks Leeds	/
			Thomas Baskett	Lodger	S	60		Hawker			do do	/
2	Total of Schedules of Houses and of Tenements with less than Five Rooms	2	Total of Males and of Females			18	13				Northants Barnwell	/

Note—Draw your pen through such words of the headings as are inapplicable.

PUBLIC RECORD OFFICE REFERENCE :- RG 13/1551 CROWN COPYRIGHT - NOT TO BE REPRODUCED WITHOUT PERMISSION

Reproduced by permission of Genes Reunited Limited

Figure 18.3

those of their neighbours which gives some idea of their social standing. You may notice that two doors down the road there is the Ship Inn which housed 18 people. Even more importantly, it shows the age and birth place of Maud's parents so that I can search for them in an earlier census.

> Unfortunately family records can spread over two pages as in this case, where the details of the head of the household and his wife appear on the previous page, and only the 'searched for' individual's page is shown.

This is where the View option comes in useful. Basically this is a transcription of the census entry giving full details of the family which consisted of nine members of which Maud was the oldest.

The screenshot below shows just part of the View page

Householder 1	
Name	Benjamin J Cutteridge
Relation to Head of Family	Son
Condition as to Marriage	
Age Last Birthday	11
Sex	Male
Profession or Occupation	Juvenile
Employment Status	
Where Born	Cambs March
Language	
Infirmity	
Householder 2	
Name	Joseph O Cutteridge
Relation to Head of Family	Son
Condition as to Marriage	
Age Last Birthday	13
Sex	Male
Profession or Occupation	Board School Monitor
Employment Status	
Where Born	Cambs March
Language	
Infirmity	

Figure 18.4

A further advantage of the View record is that some of the census images can be difficult to read even when printed in high resolution. Genes Reunited have done the hard work of interpreting the handwritten entries. Accessing the View record will cost another 5 credits. As you will see you can run through credits quite quickly when searching for these details.

Creating your family tree

Once you have accumulated a number of antecedents you can begin to compile your family tree starting with yourself.

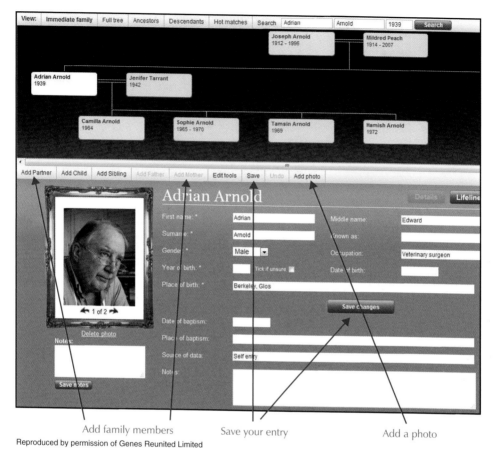

Add family members   Save your entry   Add a photo

Reproduced by permission of Genes Reunited Limited

Figure 18.5

To add parents, children and siblings select the relevant family member and type in their details and even submit a scanned photo of the individual if you have a copy.

In this case I need to add Winifred's husband whose details I have found by searching marriage records.

> As your family tree grows and the details are added to the database on Genes Reunited, the program will begin to search for likely matches in other family trees and you will start to get emails notifying you of possible matches in other private family trees and other records such as military service.

Save changes

Reproduced by permission of Genes Reunited Limited

Figure 18.6

Reproduced by permission of Genes Reunited Limited

Figure 18.7

By clicking on any of the 'Find out more' links you will be shown a contact form whereby you can send a message to the owner of the other family tree asking for further details of their ancestor. In the example shown here it looks as though it is a good match.

Below the message box you will find a small box which renders your current tree available to the other genealogist. In this way you will begin to build up contacts whose trees interlink with your own and you can add more family members.

Be aware that your correspondent's accuracy of information may not be as certain as your own research criteria. If you have any doubts about dates tick the box beside the entry to acknowledge this fact.

The great advantage of keeping your family history online is that it is permanently secure and viewable by other members of your family so long as you let them have your login details.

The most common surname on the planet is Li, the second is Wang.

Ancestry.co.uk

This genealogical program at **www.ancestry.co.uk** works in a similar way to Genes Reunited but the main difference is that your subscription covers the costs of searches. You can pay for annual or monthly subscriptions and you can choose from three different plans depending upon the range of search facilities you may need to compose your family tree. Currently the basic Essentials membership fees is £10.95 a month or £83.40 for a year and covers the Birth, Marriages and Deaths index, the various censuses, military records of World War I, school and university alumni as well as phone book records. The most expensive plan, Worldwide membership, adds pre-1837 Parish Records, Irish records and worldwide genealogical databases currently costs £18.95 a month or £155.40 for the annual membership. Ancestry.co.uk has an American parent site – **www.ancestry.com** – which houses the millions of North American records and this will detail their subscription fees on their website.

This inclusive payment has the advantage that you have permanent access to your chosen records without having to top up your search credits but, if your enthusiasm wanes, you may find yourself paying for a transitory whim. There is no charge to create and store your family tree on the Ancestry site.

📄 1891 England Census	NAME: **Edward Arnold**
Census & Voter Lists	SPOUSE: Eliza
★★★★	BIRTH: abt 1848 - Great Shelford, Cambridgeshire, England
View Image	RESIDENCE: 1891 - March, Cambridgeshire, England
📄 1881 England Census	NAME: **Edward Arnold**
Census & Voter Lists	BIRTH: abt 1848 - Grt Shelford, Cambridgeshire, England
★★★★	RESIDENCE: 1881 - March, Cambridgeshire, England
View Image	
📄 1901 England Census	NAME: **Edward Arnold**
Census & Voter Lists	SPOUSE: Eliza
★★★★	BIRTH: abt 1848 - Great Shelford, Cambridgeshire, England
View Image	RESIDENCE: 1901 - March, March, Cambridgeshire, England
📄 1861 England Census	NAME: **Edward Arnold**
Census & Voter Lists	BIRTH: abt 1848 - Great Shelford, Cambridgeshire, England
★★★★	RESIDENCE: 1861 - Great Shelford, Cambridgeshire, England
View Image	

Figure 18.8

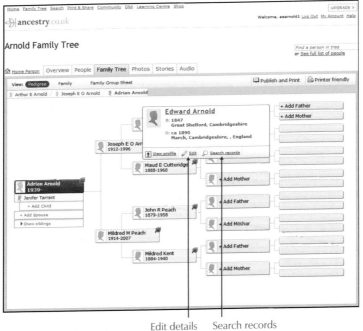

Edit details   Search records

Figure 18.9

Having entered a number of family ancestors you can begin to search the record databases by clicking on Search records.

Searching the records will trawl through the Ancestry records and present the most likely results at the head of a very long list. These records will include all the census details, Birth, Marriage and Death registers, military records, photos, newspaper articles and details of recorded wills among many others. To get to a copy of the individual records click on the underlined record link. This will produce a transcribed version of the entry and the option to view and print the actual record.

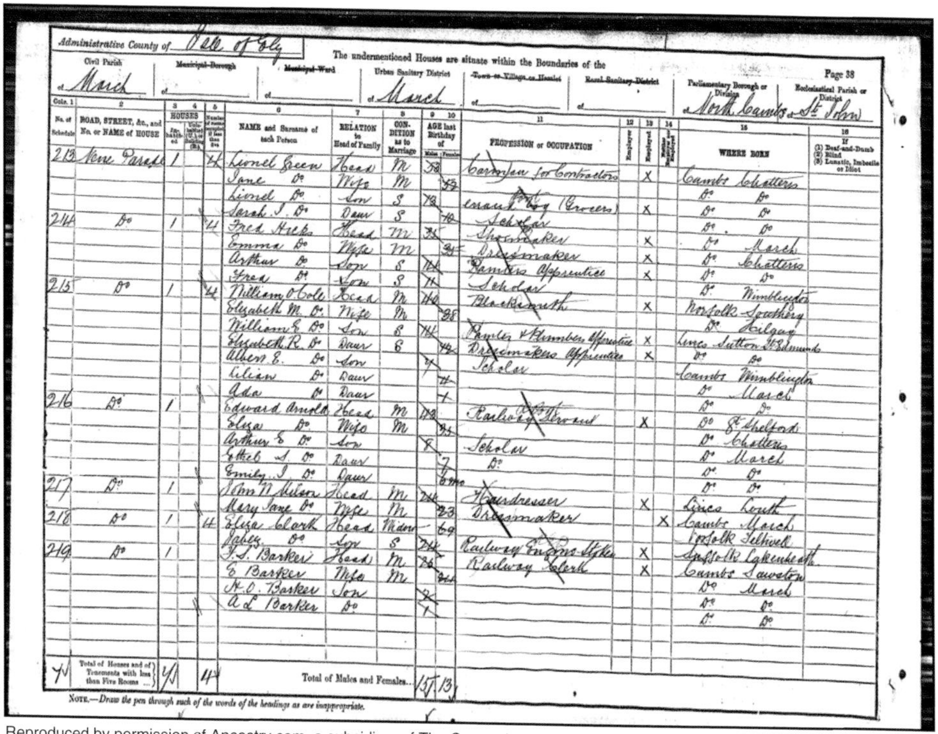

Administrative County of Isle of Ely. The undermentioned Houses are situate within the Boundaries of the Civil Parish of March; Municipal Borough of —; Municipal Ward of —; Urban Sanitary District of March; Town or Village or Hamlet of —; Rural Sanitary District of —; Parliamentary Borough or Division of North Cambs; Ecclesiastical Parish or District of St John. Page 38

1 No. of Schedule	2 Road, Street, &c., and No. or Name of House	3 Houses Inhabited	4 Uninhabited	5 Number of rooms occupied if less than five	6 Name and Surname of each Person	7 Relation to Head of Family	8 Condition as to Marriage	9 Age last Birthday of Males	10 Age of Females	11 Profession or Occupation	12 Employer	13 Employed	14 Neither Employer nor Employed	15 Where Born	16 If (1) Deaf-and-Dumb (2) Blind (3) Lunatic, Imbecile or Idiot
213	Nene Parade	1		4	Lionel Green	Head	M	53		Carpenter for Contractors		X		Cambs Chatteris	
					Jane Do	Wife	M		53					Do Do	
					Lionel Do	Son	S	13		Errand Boy (Grocers)		X		Do Do	
					Sarah J. Do	Daur	S		10	Scholar				Do Do	
214	Do	1		4	Fred Hicks	Head	M	35		Shoemaker		X		Do March	
					Emma Do	Wife	M		34	Dressmaker		X		Do Chatteris	
					Arthur Do	Son	S	14		Painters Apprentice		X		Do Do	
					Fred Do	Son	S	11		Scholar				Do Wimblington	
215	Do	1		4	William O Cole	Head	M	40		Blacksmith		X		Norfolk Southery	
					Elizabeth M. Do	Wife	M		38					Do Hilgay	
					William E Do	Son	S	14		Painter & Plumber Apprentice		X		Lincs Sutton St Edmunds	
					Elizabeth R. Do	Daur	S		12	Dressmakers Apprentice		X		Do Do	
					Albert E. Do	Son		9		Scholar				Cambs Wimblington	
					Lilian Do	Daur			11					Do March	
					Ada Do	Daur			1					Do Do	
216	Do	1			Edward Arnold	Head	M	33		Railway Servant		X		Do St Shelford	
					Eliza Do	Wife	M		35					Do Chatteris	
					Arthur E Do	Son		8		Scholar				Do March	
					Ethel S. Do	Daur			7	Do				Do Do	
					Emily J. Do	Daur			6 mo					Do Do	
217	Do	1			John N Wilson	Head	M	24		Hairdresser		X		Lincs Louth	
					Mary Jane Do	Wife	M		23	Dressmaker			X	Cambs March	
218	Do	1		4	Eliza Clark	Head	Widow		69					Norfolk Feltwell	
					Jabez Do	Son	S	24		Railway Engine Stoker		X		Suffolk Lakenheath	
219	Do	1			J.S. Barker	Head	M	26		Railway Clerk		X		Cambs Sawston	
					E Barker	Wife	M		24					Do March	
					H.O. Barker	Son		2						Do Do	
					A L Barker	Do		1						Do Do	
7	Total of Houses and of Tenements with less than Five Rooms	7		4			Total of Males and Females	15	13						

Note.—Draw the pen through such of the words of the headings as are inappropriate.

Reproduced by permission of Ancestry.com, a subsidiary of The Generations Network, Inc.

Figure 18.10

From this page from the 1891 census we can see the makeup of my great grandfather's household in March, Cambridgeshire. His profession is given as Railway Worker, his wife, Eliza, was born in Chatteris and in their road, Nene Parade, the neighbours worked variously as dressmakers, hairdressers, blacksmiths, errand boys and a railway engine stoker. (March was a thriving railway town at the time.) With more time spent searching earlier records for the marriage details of Edward Arnold to Eliza I could find out her maiden name and then the details of her family in Chatteris. It is just like detective work – you will have to put in the hours.

If anything the range of recording detail such as the facility to add audio files and family stories on Ancestry is greater than that of Genes Reunited. On the other hand Genes Reunited has more of a sense of community.

Roots UK

This is another web-based genealogy site and program which operates in much the same way as the other two but has one important extra facility. That of offering a computer based program, Roots Magic, which you can buy from the site at **www.rootsmagic.co.uk**. The price varies from the Basic edition currently priced at £16.95 to the full Platinum program which costs £49.95 at this time. The website is normally search fee based but with the full Roots Magic program you get over £1,000 worth of credits to the British Data Archive CD set.

It can be a bit of a pain displaying one's family history to family members on the Web when it is easier to open a program with all the details – and search facilities – from your computer's hard disk.

Using such a program you can publish your very own genealogical website, create a large wall chart and print out your family history in book form.

Local History

Once you have started to create your family tree you may be interested to find out more about the places where your ancestors lived out their lives. A great resource for this can be found at **www.visionofbritain.org.uk** where I searched for my own village and came up with the following linked web page:

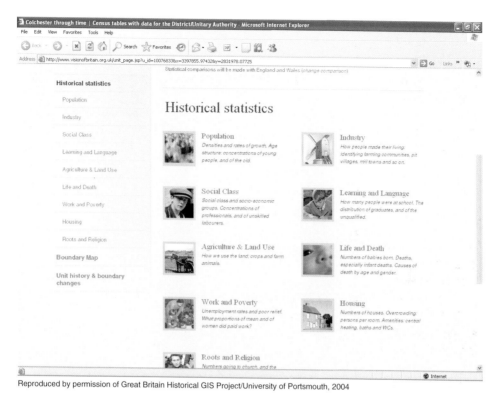

Reproduced by permission of Great Britain Historical GIS Project/University of Portsmouth, 2004

Figure 18.11

These sites are a wonderful way of adding flesh to the dry bones of a family tree.

Family Tree Maker

Now owned by Ancestry.com this is possibly the grand-daddy of all computer-based family tree programs. The Platinum edition is currently priced at £59.99 and includes a six month basic membership to Ancestry so you get the best of both worlds. It is very similar to the Roots Magic program and each has their devotees. You can find out more details at **www.familytreemaker.com**.

Each program has a different layout but you will soon get used to that of your chosen program after making the first few entries and experimenting with the options. Like Roots Magic, Family Tree Maker offers many different ways of displaying your family tree.

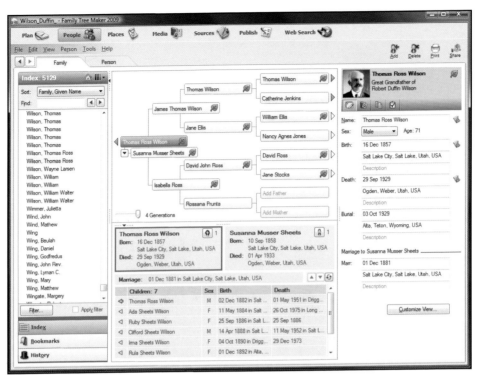

Reproduced by permission of Ancestry.com, a subsidiary of The Generations Network, Inc.

Figure 18.12

Summary

- Get as much information as you can from living relatives before searching your family tree online

- Check out the subscription fees before joining any genealogical website

- You can maintain your family tree on both your own computer and the web

- Certificates of birth, marriage and death are not available on the web. You must apply in writing or in person to the National Archives

Brain Training

There may be more than one correct answer to these questions.

1. How frequently are UK censuses taken?

☐ a) Every five years   ☐ b) Every 10 years

☐ c) There is no regular interval   ☐ d) Every 15 years

2. What was the last census to be put online?

☐ a) 1871   ☐ b) 1891

☐ c) 1919   ☐ d) 1911

3. What are the advantages of viewing an actual census page?

☐ a) You can tell where a person was born   ☐ b) You can establish the professions of the neighbours

☐ c) You can see all the members of the household   ☐ d) You can tell whether they were deaf

4. Where can you store details of your family tree?

☐ a) On a computer file   ☐ b) On the Web

☐ c) In the family Bible   ☐ d) On a DVD

5. Where is the best place to get started with your family tree?

☐ a) On the Internet

☐ b) By using a commercial family tree program

☐ c) By talking with your oldest relative

☐ d) By visiting the National Archives at Kew

Answers

Q1 – b

Q2 – d

Q3 – a, b and d

Q4 – All of them

Q5 – c

PART IV
Appendices

Don't panic! I've just accessed the helpline...

Appendix: Internet links

This is a list of websites featured in this book. A much fuller directory of useful web addresses can be found on the PCWisdom website at **www.pcwisdom.co.uk**

All these sites have been personally checked by me prior to going to press. Unfortunately websites have an annoying habit of disappearing without trace, changing their address and revamping the content, so please accept my apologies for any of the following sites that become unavailable.

Auctions

www.ebay.co.uk	Everything from bits of old rope to military jet aircraft for sale
www.governmentauctionsuk.co.uk	Government auctions
www.ukauctionguides.co.uk	Listings of auctions throughout the UK

Books and audio books

www.abebooks.co.uk	Millions of new and second-hand books; easily searched
www.amazon.co.uk	Not just books but toys, computers, clothes and DIY; useful reviews and book lists

www.whsmith.co.uk	Sometimes cheaper than Amazon
www.waterstones.co.uk	Another great British bookseller

Cars

www.autotrader.co.uk	Comprehensive catalogue of new and used cars
www.classiccarsforsale.co.uk	Worldwide catalogue of classic cars from Abarth to Willys Jeep
www.whatcar.com	Very good site for information and valuations
www.parkers.co.uk/cars/used-prices	Another good car prices site
http://route.rac.co.uk	Accurate route information
www.streetmap.co.uk	A very good road atlas and route planner

Computing advice

www.speedtest.net	Test your broadband speed
www.pcwisdom.co.uk	The website of this book. Full of advice and tutorials
www.delicious.com	Internet book marking and recommendation site
www.google.com/chrome	Download the latest web browser
www.mailwasher.net	A good spam filtering program
www.cloudmark.com	A very good commercial spam filtering program
www.scantips.com	Contains invaluable scanning hints and tips

Consumer advice

www.which.co.uk

Reviews of everything under the sun for £7.75 per month

www.uswitch.com

Very efficient comparison site for utilities, insurance, mortgages and current accounts

www.moneysavingexpert.com

A brilliant money-saving site

DIY

www.youtube.com

Video demonstrations of simple DIY projects

Finance

www.checkout.google.co.uk

Online payment facility

www.paypal.com

Online payment facility

www.moneysavingexpert.com

Each week there are tips on how to save money. Subscribe to the newsletter

www.moneysupermarket.com

Lots of good financial, insurance and travel deals

www.moneyextra.com

Keep track of your personal investment portfolio

www.iii.co.uk

Another very good site for investors

Food and drink

www.sainsburys.com

Online supermarket

www.tesco.com	Save yourself the hassle of carrying heavy shopping
www.epicurious.com	Hundreds of thousands of recipes
www.bbc.co.uk/food/recipes	All the BBC food program recipes

Genealogy

www.genesreunited.co.uk	A really good site to start your family research
www.ancestry.co.uk	Another good research site
www.rootsuk.com	Comprehensive genealogy site with its own family tree program

Health

| www.nhsdirect.nhs.uk | Self-help from the NHS |
| www.netdoctor.co.uk | Highly respected website for all your health problems |

History

| www.wwiimemories.com | Personal histories of the last world war |
| www.visionofbritain.org.uk | A supreme site for local history buffs |

Hobbies

www.yahoo.co.uk/recreation/hobbies	Links to every hobby you could think of
www.ebooks.com	Over 130,000 books to download
www.gutenberg.org	Over 27,000 books to download free

www.audiobooksonline.co.uk	Rent or buy thousands of audio books
www.abebooks.com	Find that elusive second-hand book for a song

Holidays

www.tripadvisor.com	Check out that holiday before you book
www.lastminute.com	Flights, holidays, theatre tickets and much, much more at bargain basement prices
www.holidaywatchdog.com	More customers reviews
www.holidays-uncovered.co.uk	Unsolicited testimonials

Information

www.about.com	Information on any subject; brilliant
www.ask.com	Answers all your questions
www.wikipedia.com	Everything you ever wanted to know

Leisure

www.ebooks.com	Over 130,000 books to download
www.gutenberg.org	Over 27,000 books to download free
www.audiobooksonline.co.uk	Rent or buy thousands of audio books
www.spotify.com	A wonderful way to listen to the music of your choice while online
www.abebooks.com	Find that elusive second-hand book for a song

Miscellaneous

www.moonpig.com	Another greeting card site that posts your greetings for you
http://earth.google.com	Load the program and view your own home

Motoring

www.autotrader.co.uk	Comprehensive catalogue of new and used cars
www.theaa.com	Lots of advice and route maps
www.rac.co.uk	Route maps and traffic reports
www.streetmap.co.uk	A very good road atlas and route planner
www.frixo.com	Check out the road conditions before you leave

News

http://news.bbc.co.uk	Comprehensive news site that makes a good home page for your browser
www.telegraph.co.uk	Daily Telegraph
www.timesonline.co.uk	The Times
www.dailymail.co.uk	The Daily Mail
www.thisislondon.co.uk/standard/	Evening Standard
www.guardian.co.uk	The Guardian
www.express.co.uk	Daily Express

www.thesun.co.uk	The Sun
http://observer.guardian.co.uk/	The Observer
www.newsoftheworld.co.uk	News of the World

Over 50s

www.silversurfers.net	A great directory of websites of interest to the older generation and one of the few that is not US based
www.friendsreunited.co.uk	Find that friend from years ago
www.sagazone.co.uk	Specifically designed for the Over 50s
www.pcwisdom.co.uk	The website of this book; full of useful advice

Photography

www.dpreview.com	The most comprehensive digital photography site on the Internet
http://picasa.google.com	The best free photo cataloguing program with some powerful editing facilities
www.scantips.com	Contains invaluable scanning hints and tips
www.flickr.com	Great for sharing photos

Price comparison sites

www.uswitch.com	Great for reducing your utility bills
www.mysupermarket.co.uk	Checks your shopping list against all the major supermarkets and then takes you to the best value site

www.moneysupermarket.com	Lots of good financial, insurance and travel deals
www.gocompare.com	More ways of reducing your household budget
www.confused.com	Track down the best insurance deals

Reference

www.wikipedia.org	Collaborative encyclopaedia with all the latest facts and a few errors!
www.which.co.uk	Online version of the consumer magazine; membership fee applies (check website for details)

Shopping

www.amazon.co.uk	Not just books, but music, videos, toys, phones, computers and even jewellery!
www.tesco.com	Save yourself the hassle of carrying heavy shopping
www.sainsburys.com	Supermarket shopping delivered to your door
www.kelkoo.co.uk	Best prices on the Net
www.google.co.uk/products	This used to be Froogle; search for the best bargains
www.shopzilla.co.uk	Compare prices from coffee makers to bicycles
www.abebooks.com	Find that forgotten book for a couple of pounds

www.yell.com	The online Yellow Pages makes searching a pleasure

Software

http://mail.google.com	Get a second email address
www.download.com	Extensive library of downloadable programs
www.tucows.com	Authoritative reviews and download site
http://downloads.zdnet.co.uk	A great source of downloadable programs
www.mailwasher.net	A good spam filtering program
www.cloudmark.com	A very good commercial spam filtering program

Television and radio

www.bbc.co.uk	Auntie's doorway to the media
www.itv.com	The commercial alternative to the Beeb
http://tv.sky.com	Sky TV offerings
www.bbc.co.uk/radio	All the Beeb's audio offerings
www.liveworldradio.com	All the world is a radio studio
www.bbc.co.uk/iplayer	Watch the TV programs you missed
www.itv.com/ITVPlayer/default.html	ITV's response to iPlayer
http://demand.five.tv	Watch Channel Five programs

Travel

www.tripadvisor.com	One of the best holiday and hotel review sites on the whole of the Web
www.holidaywatchdog.com	More customers reviews
www.holidays-uncovered.co.uk	Unsolicited testimonials
www.easyjet.com	Cheap flights to European destinations
www.ryanair.com	Flights, hotels, car hire at knock down prices if you book early
www.directferries.co.uk	The gateway to Europe by sea or Tunnel
www.nationalexpress.com	The great way to book your coach trips
www.thetrainline.com	Great place for booking cheaper rail tickets
http://route.rac.co.uk	Accurate route information
www.streetmap.co.uk	A very good road atlas and route planner
www.frixo.com	Check out the road conditions before you leave

Utilities

www.uswitch.com	Wonderful comparison site to reduce your household expenses; they do it all for you
www.gocompare.com	Enormous site for insurance, mortgages, travel and utilities
www.comparethemarket.com	An alternative comparison site

Appendix: Glossary

ADSL. Asymmetric Digital Subscriber Line. Broadband internet connection (3–200 times faster). You need to be close to a digital telephone exchange, on cable or have a satellite dish. You can remain connected permanently. See also RADSL.

ANTIVIRUS program. Something that can spot a virus attached to an email or already on your computer and deal with it.

APPLICATION. A program such as Word or Internet Explorer. Applications almost always end in EXE.

ASP. Application Service Provider. Computer companies are hoping to provide you with programs and data storage over the net for a rental, rather than buying them outright.

BACKUP. Keeping copies or programs or work in a separate place in case of corruption of the first version. There are various methods. See Help, Backup in Windows. See Floppy disk, CDR, ZIP drive.

BANDWIDTH. A measure of the maximum amount of data that can be transferred over the Internet or phone system at any one time.

BETA. A program which is being tested, which is given out to users to find any problems.

BITMAP. A graphic image which is made up of many tiny dots.

BLOG, BLOGGER. A weblog or person who writes a website about the boring things they do each day.

BLUE SCREEN 'of death'. The screen that comes up in Windows 95 and 98 when your computer can't cope with something. It suggests you press a key to continue. Called the 'Blue Screen of Death' because pressing a key doesn't help at all and the technical details shown are no help. The only thing you can do is to *reboot!*

BLUETOOTH technology. Using radio transmission from your PC for controlling everything from printers to lights to the washing machine anywhere within a building. See also Wi-Fi.

BOOT. Start a PC from cold. To reboot is to restart.

BROADBAND. High bandwidth Internet connections such as cable or ADSL for faster connections.

BROWSER. Program for browsing the Internet, e.g. Internet Explorer, Netscape Navigator, Firefox, Safari, Opera etc.

BYTE. A number of digits which make up a character, number or space on a hard, floppy disk or CD.

CAB file. A compressed file. In Windows they contains all the files necessary to create the Windows operating system.

CABLE MODEM. Cable companies such as NTL and Telewest can pipe fast Internet connections to you providing you have a special modem fitted to your PC.

CHAT. Text messaging to others on line using messaging software such as MSN, Yahoo, AOL and others.

CHAT ROOM. An area on the Internet where people chat (usually written) to each other in 'real time'.

COOKIE. A small text file which is downloaded to your computer without you knowing anything about it. Mainly they are used to trace your activities for marketing purposes. Can be deleted by using Windows Explorer or prevented by Internet Explorer security. The latter may prevent you from accessing certain sites.

CD/CDROM/CD-R/CDRW. Compact Disk Read Only Memory but they are not really memory like RAM. They are the familiar disks on which programs arrive. They are Read Only because the tracks are 'burnt' into them and cannot be changed. The RW type can be rewritten to many times but cannot be read on another machine, so they are less useful for safe backup.

CHIP. Silicon chip – the silicon base used to mount the millions of components that go to make up a computer processor.

CLIPART. Ready-made picture on disk.

CONTROL PANEL. An important set of icons which allow you to configure the basic functions of your computer.

CONTROL KEY. Marked Ctrl on the keyboard. Like Alt and Function keys its use can vary from program to program.

CUT or COPY & PASTE. Most Windows programs allow you to cut or copy a **selected** item (text or picture) and paste it into another place or even another program. So you can copy a picture from one program and paste it into another. Use Ctrl with X, C and V for shortcuts.

CYBERCAFE or INTERNET CAFE. Cafes where you can get access to the Internet. They are all over the world and are a major method of communication for travellers.

DATABASE. A list of items of data kept on a computer disk so that it can be amended, searched or printed.

DESKTOP. The main, first page in Windows.

DIGITAL. The method of storing or transmitting things as a series of numbers. Surprisingly these numbers never get past one so they are made up of noughts (zeros) and ones. The speed and accuracy with which these can be stored has enabled most information to be stored in this way, from television, photography, all computing and – of course – the Internet.

DIRECTORY. An organised search facility on the **WEB.**

DIRECTX. A free downloadable Windows program that ensures that graphics programs work with all the different types of graphics hardware.

DIVX is a new video format that will compress to one-hundredth the size of the current ones, thus enabling you to put films onto CDs.

DOS. Disk Operating System. The original Operating System used on PCs without which the machine would be a just a collection of useless electronic parts, which has now been more or less superseded by Windows.

DOWNLOAD. The process of transferring files from the Web to your machine's hard drive. You can download pictures, text and programs.

DPI. Dots per inch. Used in connection with printers, scanners and monitors.

DRAG AND DROP. The facility in most programs to select text or a file and drag it to another position.

DTP. Desktop Publishing. Creating print ready documents on a computer.

DVD-ROM. Digital Versatile Disk Read Only Memory. A disk capable of containing much more than a CD. Used for music, films and *big* programs.

DVD-RW. A rewriteable DVD.

DVD Player. Special disc player for DVD discs. Capable of playing CDs as well.

EBOOK. Electronic book.

ECOMMERCE. Business conducted over the Internet.

EMAIL. Messages sent to people over the Internet. Email addresses always contain the symbol @ somewhere.

EMAIL CLIENT. Program you use to send and receive emails, such as Outlook Express, Eudora, Netscape Communicator.

EXABYTE (EB). A thousand million **GIGABYTES.** That's a lot of bytes!

FAT, FAT32. File Allocation Table. This is the file system used on a disk and stands for File Allocation Table. It is a form of index which is constantly updated to keep track of everything on the disk. **FAT** is limited to 4 Mb per partition. **FAT32** is almost unlimited but cannot cope with files that are more than 4 GB. See also NTFS.

FAVORITES. Or bookmarks. All web browsers enable you to add favourite sites to a list for easy retrieval.

FIREWALL. A program that ensures that your PC has no open 'ports' which allow hackers to access it.

FIREWIRE. A socket on some PCs that enables much faster transfer of data than via Serial, Parallel and even faster than a USB2 port. Needed if you are transferring large amounts of data, e.g. from a digital video camera for editing purposes. An add-on card is currently quite expensive but will eventually come down in price.

FIXED PITCH. Sometimes it is better to use a typewriter style of character which has the same width whatever the letter. Courier is an example of such a font.

FLOPPY DISK. Hardly floppy these days. 3.5″ disks you can use to save data so you can copy it to and from your hard disk. See also **HARD DISK**.

FONT. A collection of characters of a predefined style such as Times or Arial.

FREEWARE. Computer programs that are distributed free of charge, often missing some elements of the full product or having a set time limit.

FRIACO. Flat Rate Internet Access Call Organisation.

FUNCTION KEYS. Programmable keys F1 to F12, which may vary in their use.

GEEK. Someone obsessed with computers. I didn't hear that!

GIGABYTE (GB). A thousand million bytes.

GIGAHERTZ. A thousand megahertz.

GPS. Global Positioning System. Use of satellites to tell you where you are. Used by boats; now used by cars, soon to be used with mobile phones. Just in case you forgot where you were going. Can it also remind me what I was going for?

GRAPHICS. The general term used for pictures and drawings.

GRAPHICS CARD. The part of the PC that sends signals to the monitor or display.

GSM. Global System for Mobile Communication. A standard whereby you can use your telephone abroad.

HACKER. A person who delights in breaking into other people's computers.

HARD DISK. A set of spinning disks coated with recording material. Can retain details of programs and data indefinitely.

HARDWARE. Any piece of equipment such as the computer or a printer.

FIREWALL. A program that can detect intrusion onto your computer and check whether you mind.

GRAPHIC. Any picture.

HOME PAGE. The first page of a website, usually Index.htm.

HOTMAIL. It is possible to get an email address before you get a computer and pick up mail at a cybercafe. It might take the form of Yourname@hotmail. com.

HOTSPOT. An area (cafe, airport, hotel etc.) enabled for connection to the Internet by WiFi enabled laptops, Smartphones or PDAs.

HTML or HTM. Hypertext Markup Language. The agreed language that websites are built from. Your browser interprets the language to show you intelligible pages. DHTML stands for Dynamic HTML, which is an advanced form which can make web pages more animated. See also **XML**.

HYPERLINK. A link on a web page that takes you to another web page. Usually blue and underlined. See **SURFING**.

HYPERTEXT links. These are the addresses of other sites or pages, which might be on the same site or on the other side of the world. They always are coloured blue and are underlined. When the cursor arrow hovers over one it will change its shape to show it is a link. Mostly you will see hypertext when connected to the Net but you may also find them in things like encyclopaedia CDs. When clicked your computer may go online then access the site.

ICON. A graphic representation of something such as a shortcut to a program (or a religious picture or other form of representation).

IDE. The standard interface (connection) used to attach hard disks and CD players.

IM. Instant Messaging. Text based messages to people online, using Microsoft or AOL Instant Messenger.

INKJET or BUBBLEJET printer. The commonest form of printer which squirts ink onto the paper. Normally colour + black.

INTERNET. A conglomeration of linked computers which can be accessed by people who are connected to the Web.

INTERNET EXPLORER. The web browser issued by Microsoft.

INTRANET. This is a network of private computers used in homes and businesses. It is separate from the Internet.

ISDN. Integrated Services Digital Network. A faster (than standard) Internet connection, requiring a special cable.

ISP. Internet Service Provider. A company which provides you with access to the Internet.

JAVA and JAVASCRIPT. A programming language used on some web pages.

JPG or JPEG. The most commonly used compressed graphic format. JPEG stands for **J**oint **P**hotographic **E**xpert **G**roup, a body which sets common standards.

KILOBYTE (KB). 1,000 bytes.

LAN. Local Area Network. Computers connected 'locally', e.g. within a company or home, so they can communicate and share programs and data.

LASER PRINTER. A printer which uses a laser to create an image on a light sensitive drum, which then loads toner powder onto paper. Often just black printing. Faster and more economical than inkjets.

LED. Light Emitting Diode. Some 'laser printers' use this type instead of a laser.

LINUX. An operating system, like Windows but *free* and *stable*. It requires software written especially for it.

MACRO. A small program within another program which, at the touch of a couple of keys, performs a series of actions.

MEGABYTE (MB). A million bytes. See also **BYTE KILOBYTE GIGABYTE EXABYTE**.

MEGAHERTZ. A measure of how fast your PC processor works. Basically a million vibrations a second. One instruction takes place each vibration.

MIDBAND. BT's new 'broadband' which runs at 128 k (twice the speed of a normal dialup service). Although it is not permanently connected like broadband it is possible to use the telephone on the same line at the same time.

MONITOR. The computer screen. Also called a VDU – **V**isual **D**isplay **U**nit.

MOTHERBOARD. The main circuit board of a computer, to which other components are attached.

MP3. A highly compressed form of music, which can be downloaded from the Net and played on a computer or a portable MP3 player. It stands for **M**usic **P**rogram **E**xpert **G**roup Audio Layer **3** (or MPEG3).

MSN. Microsoft Network.

NET. A term used loosely to mean the Web.

NETSCAPE COMMUNICATOR. Netscape's email client program (an alternative to Outlook Express).

NETSCAPE NAVIGATOR. Netscape's Browser. An alternative to Internet Explorer.

NETWORK. General term for connected computers. See also WAN and LAN.

OCR. Optical Character Recognition. Some software can convert scanned text into word processable documents.

OEM software means that the software is sold *only* with a certain piece of hardware and/or the software manufacturer provides no technical support. Some OEM software is a cutdown version of its retail counterpart. Always make sure the software has all of the features you need.

OFFLINE. Not connected to the Internet. Some things, like writing emails, can be done before going online.

ONLINE. Connected to the Internet.

OUTLOOK EXPRESS. The free Microsoft program for handling emails. Netscape's is called Messenger.

PARALLEL PORT. Almost always a 25 pin 'female' socket on the back of a computer which is used for printing but also to attach things like scanners and other external equipment. See also USB port.

PATH. The location of a file or program on a disk, e.g. Word is at C:\Program Files\Microsoft Office\Office\winword.exe.

PCI slot. Peripheral Component Interface. A type of connector – usually white – which enables you to add components to your PC.

PCMCIA. Originally stood for Peripheral Component MicroChannel Interconnect Architecture. This awkward acronym was jokingly expanded as 'People Can't Memorize Computer Industry Acronyms' or 'Personal Computer Manufacturers Can't Invent Acronyms'. It was then renamed after the standards organization, the **P**ersonal **C**omputer **M**emory **C**ard **I**nternational **A**ssociation. Difficulty with the acronym led to the simpler term 'PC Card' for the version 2 specification. It was originally for memory expansion, but the existence of a usable general standard for notebook peripherals led to all manner of devices being made available in this form. Typical devices include network cards, modems and hard disks.

PHISHING. This is the name give to a scam where you get an email supposedly from your bank, requesting that you confirm your password. If you give out a password like this you can expect your account to be robbed shortly afterwards!

PIM. Personal Information Manager. Software which acts as a diary – even an alarm clock.

PIXEL. Picture element. A small element on a screen or in photograph. Cameras are sometimes referred to in megapixels. A megapixel is a million pixels. The more pixels the better the quality of the picture and the more memory is used up.

PLUG AND PLAY. Modern machines and hardware (printers, sound cards, CD players etc.) are able to recognise when they are connected, so enabling easy installation or use.

POINT SIZE. The height of a printed character. Correspondence is usually around 12 point.

PORT. Either a socket on your computer, such as USB, parallel (printer) or serial (communications) or part of the system which allows communication with your computer (the latter are numbered, e.g. Port 110). See also Hacker.

PS/2. The smaller type of socket used for modern keyboard and mouse connections.

PROPORTIONAL FONT. Some fonts use much less space (width), e.g. for a small L (l) than for a capital W.

QUICKTIME. A program from Apple which enables you to view moving pictures.

RAM. Random Access Memory. Chips in your PC which work on programs temporarily.

REGISTER. A most important file used in Windows 95 onwards. Contains details of everything within Windows.

RSS FEED. Standing for Really Simple Syndication, it is a format that allows the regular updating of rapidly changing web pages such as news pages.

SAFE MODE. This is when you start Windows in its most basic form with no background programs in operation. As a result the screen changes to its very basic (large) layout. Safe Mode is used to cure various problems including Virus and Defrag. difficulties. To get into Safe Mode (on most PCs) press F8 as Windows begins to load.

SCANNER. A piece of equipment capable of digitally recording a picture or some text for saving on the computer.

S-VIDEO. A higher quality video connection. It carries brightness and colour information separately.

SCSI. Small Computer System Interface. A fast interface (connection) for attaching peripherals to your computer. See also IDE.

SEARCH ENGINE. A program, usually accessed through the Net, which enables you to search for what you want by entering a few words.

SERIAL PORT. A 9 or 25 pin (male) socket on the back of a computer, which can be used to attach a mouse, a modem or a printer. Referred to as a COM (Communication) port. Most PCs have two built in.

SERVER. A large computer that stores information which can be accessed by other computers.

SHAREWARE. Computer programs or software that are free to use but you are invited to make a contribution towards its costs – usually about $15.

SITE or **WEBSITE** is an area on the Internet that has its own unique web address (URL). It has a Home page followed by other pages linked to the Home page.

SKYPE. A program that allows you to make free telephone calls from your computer.

SOFTWARE. Programs of all kinds which make the computer act in a particular way.

SPAM. Unsolicited advertising that usually arrives as emails.

SPYWARE. Software which is installed on your computer without your knowledge to monitor and report back what you are doing. Scary.

SPREADSHEET. A mathematical program which contains formulae to automatically work on the figures that are entered.

STREAMING. Receiving sound or pictures continuously over the Internet (rather than downloading first).

STYLE sheet. A previously arranged document with specific type styles, weights and sizes. See also Template.

SURFING the Web means using hypertext links to jump from one site or page to another.

SVGA. Super VGA. The later type of screen (and video card) capable of displaying more colours and higher definition.

TAB key. The key on the left of the keyboard which allows you to jump certain fixed distances across the page when using a word processor (or even a steam age typewriter).

TEMPORARY FILES. The Internet, some installation programs and even your own programs may use a part of your hard disk to enable them to work. They often end in TMP. They can be deleted later to create more disk space.

TEMPLATE. A standard letter or spreadsheet which can be amended to suit your needs.

TFT. Thin film transistor. The technology used to create those popular flat screens.

TOOLBAR. A list of icons often found at the top of a program such as a word processor.

TROJAN. A virus program that is disguised as something else. It invades your PC and can be accessed by a hacker.

TWAIN is a standard for acquiring images from image scanners. The word TWAIN is not officially an acronym; however, it is widely known as a backronym for 'Technology Without An Interesting Name'.

UPDATE. This is a later version of a program which may contains more features or improve security. Windows updates are free but you may have to pay for other program updates.

URL. Universal Resource Locator or Web address. It always starts with http:// and is usually followed by www. And then other parts of the address.

USB PORT. Universal Serial Bus. A more recent versatile communication port, which can transfer data faster and also enables equipment to be 'hot swapped', whilst the machine is on. The sockets are about half an inch long. It also contains a power supply so equipment such as webcams do not need a transformer. An add-on card is available for older machines but early Windows 95 did not support this connection.

USB2. At 480 MBs is even faster than USB. Looks the same as USB and the slower devices can also be attached to it.

VDU. Visual Display Unit. The screen.

VGA. Video Graphics Array. The older type of colour screen.

VIDEO-CONFERENCING. Using the PC as a video phone.

VIDEO-PHONE. Using a microphone, speakers and a webcam to see and hear others over the Internet.

VIRUS. A malicious program which can harm your computer. It is spread through programs – either from disks or from the Internet. It is the graffiti of the Internet. They may also be called Trojans or Worms.

VOiP. The technology that allows telephone calls to be made from a computer – usually for free (see Skype).

WAP. Wireless Application Protocol. A system of sending (restricted) Internet pages to the screen of a mobile phone.

WEB BROWSER. A program to help you navigate the Internet, e.g. Internet Explorer, Firefox or Google Chrome.

WEBCAM. A small camera which is attached to a computer and captures images of you working hard at the keyboard.

WIFI. A wireless interface, using radio to link computers and other devices. A snappier name than the 802.11b standard. See also Bluetooth.

WINDOWS 95. The 1995 version of the Windows system, which replaced version 3.11. It did not support the USB sockets.

WINDOWS 98. The 1998 version of the Windows system, which replaced Windows 95. Only the Second Edition (SE) had USB support.

WINDOWS ME. Windows Millennium Edition. A halfway house between Windows 98 and Windows XP.

WINDOWS VISTA. Microsoft Windows latest computer operating system soon to be replaced by Windows 7.

WINDOWS XP. Microsoft's last operating system before Vista arrived, intended to replace all previous Windows formats. There are Home and Professional versions.

WIZARD. A program which helps you through a process such as installing new software or hardware.

WORD PROCESSING. Creating documents on a computer that can easily be amended (processed).

WORM. A virus program that spreads by sending itself to people in your email address book.

WWW. World Wide Web. The Internet.

ZIP file. Compressed file that ends in ZIP or CAB. To see their contents they must be viewed using a special program such as Winzip or Enzip.

Index